The Censorship
of English Drama 1737-1824

By L. W. Conolly

The Censorship
of English Drama 1737-1824

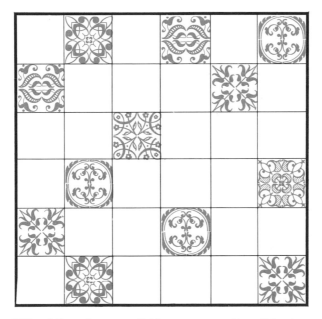

The Huntington Library · San Marino

PUBLISHED WITH THE ASSISTANCE OF
THE UNION PACIFIC RAILROAD FUND

To Barbara

Contents

Acknowledgments

Most of the work for this book was done at the University College of Swansea where I received advice and encouragement from Professor C. J. L. Price for which I am most grateful. I am indebted to Professor Price for many kindnesses over a period of several years.

It also gives me much pleasure to acknowledge the help of Miss Jean F. Preston, Curator of Manuscripts at the Henry E. Huntington Library. Miss Preston and the staff of the Library, particularly Miss Mary Isabel Fry, make the Huntington an unusually pleasant and efficient research library. I am also indebted to Mrs. Betty Leigh Merrell of the Huntington for her most careful editing of my manuscript. My colleague, Dr. Ronald Ayling, read part of the book in typescript and made many useful suggestions for which I thank him. Professor George Winchester Stone, Jr. of New York University also very kindly made a number of constructive criticisms of the typescript. My wife, Barbara, was skillful at detecting errors and ambiguities in my work and she has my warmest gratitude for her help and interest. I must also thank Mrs. Linda Stoddart for her expert typing of my manuscript.

I am most grateful to Mr. Douglas De H. Larpent and Francis Beaufort-Palmer, descendants of John Larpent, for helping me with my inquiries about their ancestor.

While working on this book I have received generous financial support from the Canada Council; I also gratefully acknowledge the award of a University of Alberta research grant. Many libraries have provided valuable help and I am happy to record in particular my thanks to the Folger Shakespeare Library, Washington, D.C., the Huntington Library, and the Carl H. Pforzheimer Library for permission to quote from their manuscripts. Transcripts of Crown-copyright records in the Public Record Office appear by permission of the Controller of H.M. Stationery Office, and a letter in the Staffordshire Record Office is quoted by permission of Rt. Hon. the Earl of Dartmouth. My thanks are also due to the British Library, and to the staffs of the Enthoven Collection in the Victoria and Albert Museum and of the Theatre Collection in the Harvard Library for their many courtesies.

A Note on the Text

In quoting manuscript material I have retained original spelling and, for the most part, punctuation. Very occasionally, for the sake of clarity of meaning, I have silently normalized some punctuation.

I have used the following abbreviations:

B.D.	*Biographia Dramatica; or, A Companion to the Playhouse*, compiled by David Erskine Baker, Isaac Reed, and Stephen Jones. 3 volumes. London, 1812.
C.G.	Covent Garden Theatre.
D.L.	Drury Lane Theatre.
DNB	*Dictionary of National Biography.*
Genest	[John Genest], *Some Account of the English Stage From the Restoration in 1660 to 1830.* 10 volumes. Bath, 1832.
LA	Larpent Manuscript Play.
The London Stage	*The London Stage 1660-1800*, compiled by William Van Lennep, Emmet L. Avery, Arthur H. Scouten, George Winchester Stone, Jr., and Charles Beecher Hogan. 5 parts, 11 volumes. Carbondale, Illinois, 1960-68.
L.T.H.	Little Theatre in the Haymarket.
Nicoll	Allardyce Nicoll, *A History of English Drama 1660-1900.* 6 volumes. Cambridge, 1965-67.
P.R.O.	Public Record Office, London.

The Censorship
of English Drama 1737-1824

a lot is mine . condemned to spend
for a worthless husband, whom I
keep when I ~~have~~ caught .
y ohirs . I cannot help loving the
od for nothing fellow .   _Exit_

yet, sir, strong as appearances a
~~by all that's holy,~~ you see me h
street, involuntary victim.

with him, for the credit of the country.

L O A D E R.

~~Fire him, a snub-nos'd son of a bitch.~~ Le-
vant me, but he got enough last night to pur-

Licence refused

ineffectual.

Condt Fortunately the times are favourable —

To be
omitted = The general Confusion of the Town, which

threatens to attack my Castle, may cover the

Had you but some disguise ——

Mrs. Smith , Sir . Do you m
Mr. S. ~~Damn~~ Hang snuff !
Oh! ~~Damn~~ Hang snuff, Sir . A man that damns snuff, is not

Taylors part

ter Taylor or

The

Iron Mask

Island of St. Marguerite .

Introduction

It was political fears which persuaded the original introduction of the censorship and it has very largely been political fears which have sustained it ever since.[1]

The [Stage Licensing] act ... was intended more to repress moral licentiousness than to prevent political entertainments in the play-house ....[2]

Peculiarly enough, not many plays seem to have suffered, because of political allusion, at the hands of the censor. ... the few dramas stopped by the Lord Chamberlain's command would seem to have been mainly satirical in the personal way. ... In view of the many occurrences of the Lord Chamberlain's veto both in the fifty years which preceded and in the fifty years which followed this period, the lack of an active censorship from 1750 to 1800 is almost inexplicable.[3]

... the power of censoring plays was *often* [my italics] exerted to prohibit their performances ....[4]

These few quotations, all to do with the Stage Licensing Act of 1737, its origin, purpose, and implementation, serve to illustrate some of the confusion and misunderstanding which have surrounded discussions of the theory and practice of the censorship of English drama under the 1737 act. This book is an attempt to describe in detail, for the first time, the nature, extent, and practice of theatrical censorship in England for almost a hundred years after the act was passed, and to assess the significance of the censorship to the theater and society of that period.

The 1737 act did not, of course, create or introduce censorship of English drama. In one way or another the drama had been subjected to censorship for over two hundred years before the act was passed.[5] But the 1737 legislation was a development of considerable

1

importance in the history of stage censorship. Hitherto operated with scarcely any statutory authority, the censorship now became a systematic procedure, fully backed by an act of Parliament. A small but permanent bureaucracy for the licensing of plays was established and remained in force until abolished by the Theatres Act of 1968.[6]

My main concern in this book is with the censorship effected by the Lord Chamberlain and his appointed Examiner of Plays, as regulated by the 1737 legislation. It is as well to remember, however, that the Lord Chamberlain's censorship was but one of the several kinds of interference and control which, in various ways, determined what the footman, or tradesman, or lawyer, in a Georgian theater audience could see and hear. Before the manuscript of a new play ever reached the Examiner, several people might have meddled with it. Managers, for example, altered texts a good deal and in so doing saved the censor a considerable amount of work. Were it not for cautious theater managers the history of theatrical censorship would take much longer to write than it does now. A manager might alter or reject a play for various reasons: it might simply be a bad play; it might be too expensive to stage, even if it had some merit; it might not be suitable for the actors in the company at that time. But it might also be altered or rejected, and in the eighteenth and nineteenth centuries it frequently was, because the manager found it offensive or dangerous in some way or because he judged the Examiner or the audience would. Thus John Beard turned down a comedy submitted to Covent Garden by Dr. Shebbeare in 1767 partly because of the "many sarcasms throughout the piece on trade and nobility,"[7] and an opera called *Helvetic Liberty* was refused by one of the theaters (probably Covent Garden) in 1792 on political grounds. Scores of overtly political plays, many of them scurrilous libel, were never sent to the theaters because it was obvious to their authors (who usually preferred to remain anonymous) that they would be promptly rejected.[8]

Another kind of control was exercised by the actors. Richard Cumberland felt it necessary to warn the actors in one of his *Observer* papers against declining to act "characters of an unamiable sort," for

it is a narrow notion to suppose that there can be any adhesion either of vice or virtue to the real character; or that revenge, cruelty, perfidiousness, or cowardice, can be transported into a man's nature, because he professionally represents these evil qualities.[9]

Like some nineteenth-century compositors who refused to set type because of the immorality of the subject matter,[10] players sometimes refused to speak lines they found offensive. James Lynch records an occasion in 1740 when no actress could be found who was prepared to sing the song "Swains I Scorn Who're Nice and Fair" in John Dalton's alteration of *Comus*,[11] and Mrs. Jordan refused to speak the epilogue to Miss Cuthbertson's opera, *Anna*, on 25 February 1793 because it was a political attack on the opposition.[12]

Even when a text had survived the scrutiny of manager, actors, and the Examiner, it could still be ruthlessly altered by the audience. Common in eighteenth- and nineteenth-century theater history are accounts of audiences demanding the omission or revision of speeches deemed objectionable on moral, political, religious, or personal grounds. Some instances of this are recorded in other parts of this book.[13]

But none of these instances of control or interference—by manager, actor, audience—powerful though they often were (amounting, indeed, to a form of censorship in themselves), was initiated by an act of Parliament. The following chapters are an examination of the official censorship as it was operated under the Licensing Act between 1737 and 1824, the year of the death of England's longest-serving Examiner of Plays, John Larpent. Some attention has already been paid to this period in the two general histories of dramatic censorship which are at present the standard works on the subject, although both are frequently inaccurate and superficial, and their authors' intolerance of anyone who refuses to see all lords chamberlain and examiners of plays as fools and bigots throws some doubt on their ability to write objectively on the subject.[14] In serious histories, biographies, and criticisms devoted to the eighteenth- and early nineteenth-century theater one usually finds the censorship referred to only in passing, if at all, and detailed study is limited to a few articles, mainly by American scholars, on particular plays which were censored or suppressed.

The sources available for a detailed study of theatrical censorship between 1737 and 1824 are not plentiful and the information is scattered.

Easily the most fruitful source is the Larpent Collection of manuscript plays in the Huntington Library, San Marino, California. The brief history of the collection, which serves as a good early illustration of British lethargy and impecuniosity in the preservation of important literary documents, has been told in detail twice—by Dougald MacMillan in the introduction to his invaluable *Catalogue* of the plays,[15] and, more recently and with some additions, by T. C. Skeat in a preface to the British Library's *Catalogue* of plays submitted to the Lord Chamberlain between 1824 and 1851.[16] Although he had no authority to do so, John Larpent, Examiner of Plays from 1778 until his death on 18 January 1824, assumed ownership of all the plays which had been sent for licensing since the 1737 act had come into force. By the time of his death the total number of manuscripts amounted to over two-and-a-half thousand. Larpent's widow, Anna Margaretta, kept the manuscripts and eventually sold them to John Payne Collier and his friend Thomas Amyot for £180. On 23 September 1853 the collection was offered to the British Museum by Collier (Amyot had died in 1850) for the same price, but because of the shortage of funds and "the extreme difficulty in assessing the value of this vast collection in the absence of any kind of list of the plays it contained,"[17] the offer was declined. Shortly afterwards, the earl of Ellesmere bought the collection for his library at Bridgewater House where it remained until purchased, with nearly everything else in the library, by the American collector Henry E. Huntington, in 1917.

On the face of it, the existence of the Larpent Collection should make the study of dramatic censorship between 1737 and 1824 a relatively straightforward task. One need only, it would seem, go through the manuscripts in search of the Examiner's deletions to reach an accurate assessment of both the extent and the nature of the censorship. This would be true first if the collection were complete, and secondly if the Examiner's marks were easily identifiable. But in fact a number of plays have at some time been removed from the collection[18] so that one has to look elsewhere for evidence of censorship or suppression in some cases, and, what makes things much more complicated, it is often tantalizingly difficult to be sure that deleted passages, or speeches marked for omission, in the manuscripts are in fact ones the Examiner objected to. Some of the compilers of *The*

4

London Stage have tended to assume that the Examiner was responsible for most of these deletions and omissions, but I doubt that this
was so.[19] He could by no means always expect to receive scripts free
from other people's alterations. The author would take it for granted
that changes would be made in the text he first sent to the manager.
These would often be made during rehearsals and sometimes, if time
was short and the first night close at hand, no new text would be
written out for the Examiner's benefit. Thus he would frequently be
sent a text containing new speeches hastily scribbled in and discarded
ones untidily scratched out by the author, manager, or even
prompter. To these changes the Examiner would sometimes add his
own, and the problem of deciding who was responsible for which
deletion or alteration is not always possible to solve.

We are not, however, completely without reliable clues. Edward
Capell (Deputy Examiner, 1749-81), for example, often took the
trouble of using red ink to indicate the passages he wanted removed;
John Larpent liked to write "Out" in bold letters in the margin opposite speeches he objected to;[20] both men sometimes sent notes to the
manager specifying required alterations, some of which are preserved
with the Larpent manuscripts; managers sometimes replied; a terse
"Forbid" tells the fate of more than one play, and Larpent's account
books (Huntington MS 19926) also sometimes reveal when a play
was denied a license. But in cases where there are no definite indica-
tions of the Examiner's instructions and where we are unable to say
with confidence that someone other than the Examiner had interfered with the text, we have only the content of the deleted passage
to guide us. Now if we compare passages which we know to have
been censored with passages we only suspect were censored, our
suspicions of censorship, if not confirmed, can often be strengthened.
But in the absence of proof opinions are bound to differ. (A useful
clue sometimes is that, in general, censored passages were included in
the printed text of the play, other deleted passages were not. This is a
clue, not a rule.) No one has given more careful attention to the Larpent plays than Dougald MacMillan, and in his *Catalogue* he points
to those instances where he believes the Examiner was probably
responsible, either wholly or in part, for deletions or omissions in the
manuscripts. Sometimes it is possible to agree with him, at others it is
not. When Collier was owner of the collection he made shorthand

notes[21] on many of the plays, drawing attention to interesting features about the deletions and alterations. More than once he states that the Examiner was responsible for them. Again, it is sometimes impossible to accept this.[22] On the other hand, there are instances where neither MacMillan nor Collier thinks the Examiner interfered with the text, but, on the basis of what was prohibited in other plays of about the same time, it seems to me that censorship had almost certainly taken place. To give two examples, both from the era of the French Revolution: in the licensing manuscript of John O'Keeffe's comic opera, *The Czar* (LA 860), produced at Covent Garden on 8 March 1790, about half the text is deleted or altered in some way. It is impossible to be certain about why all the changes were made or who made them. But I think it very likely that Larpent was behind some of them, including the deletion of two verses of a justice's song:

> I am a jolly trading Justice
> And when a cause is pendant
> A Bribe ne'er fails
> To kick the Scales
> For Plaintiff or Defendant . . .

> A Girl when brought before me
> I make the Jade remember
> 'Tis snivel and cry
> For Bridewell and I
> Commit her to my Chamber. . . .

And in the manuscript of Henry Siddons' *The Sicilian Romance* (LA 1027), produced at Covent Garden on 28 May 1794, it is probable that Larpent was the man who deleted speeches like the following:

If those are our only recomendations, I am afraid we shall sleep in very damp Lodgings. Charity's an unfashionable virtue that never pops its head among the great; and for religion they never name it but to laugh at it.

Such criticisms of England's aristocracy and legal officers were nothing short of seditious in the Examiner's eyes at this time of European turmoil.

Other scholars who have had occasion to study some of the Larpent manuscripts have also attributed various deletions to the Examiner where MacMillan attributes them to no one in particular and where no conclusive evidence to support any attribution is available. In 1965 the Augustan Reprint Society reproduced the licensing manuscript (LA 96) of Charles Macklin's *The Covent Garden Theatre; or, Pasquin Turn'd Drawcansir* (1752).[23] In her introduction (p. iv), Jean B. Kern refers to "the numerous Licenser's marks on the manuscript," and says "It is not surprizing that the Licenser objected to such passages as the description of Miss Giggle's 'nudities,' but his frequent objections to topical and personal references took all the bite out of Macklin's satire." Miss Kern is probably correct in her interpretation of the marks in the manuscript, for the indelicate conversation we find there, the reference to "filthy Lawyers" and the demands that the government reform social ills (in this case, gambling) were not elements the Examiner normally overlooked; but we cannot be certain that the manager or prompter had not already acted as unofficial censor in this case before the manuscript reached the Examiner. Peter Thomson is probably also right when he suggests that some speeches marked for omission in Thomas Holcroft's *The Rival Queens; or, Drury Lane and Covent Garden* (LA 1039) were in fact censored by Larpent (the telltale "out" is there), but he quite properly admits a degree of doubt.[24]

Given the uncertainty of determining responsibility for many of the deletions and alterations we find in the Larpent manuscripts, there seem to be two alternative approaches to assessing the extent and nature of the censorship to which they were subjected. One is to accept as cases of censorship all those marked and deleted passages which, by their content and by their similarity to known censored passages, could well have been cut by the Examiner, even though conclusive evidence of this is lacking; the other is to accept only those cases where reasonably conclusive evidence of censorship, either in or with the manuscript, or from an external source (author's memoirs, preface to the printed play, newspaper reports etc.) is available. The former approach is likely to produce an exaggerated account of the extent of the censorship, the latter perhaps an underestimation, but in order to avoid making claims or basing judgments about censorship

7

Queen C.G. Far from it! I look and admire!

Queen D. Do not my fret works & frieze, my Columns & Corridors, my Architraves and mouldings, my wonders within & without, astonish?

Queen C.G. Grand. Town.

Queen D. What Building can boast so extensive & noble a view!

O'Flan. Faith, I mounted up myself; and there I had as fine a broad prospect of- of- of- of Chimnies. as heart coud wish! All smoke and smother!

Queen D. Apollo himself presides over one.

O'Flan. Right! There I found him with his little Irish Jew's-harp at his back. He presides over you sure enough, for he treads you under his feet. Poor fellow! he is always at his post! Exposed to all weathers, without so much as a shirt to his back. He is what you would call now a true Sans Culottes. Not a morsel of woolen Drapery about him.

Queen D. I can sink forests and fields, Towns & Churches; nay, whole cities with a thought. Ohl

Queen C.G. So can I.

O'Flan. By my soul, those Forests & Fields, and Cities you talk of are as natural as life; what, tho' they are all built of Canvas.

on suspect evidence I have generally adopted the second approach throughout this study.

Another important source for the study of dramatic censorship in this period is the collection of diaries and a journal (all in Huntington MS 31201) written by Mrs. Anna Margaretta Larpent and acquired by the Huntington Library in 1968. The diaries cover the years 1790-1830 (with some gaps in the sequence) and from them we can learn something of Larpent's family background and daily life, his visits to the theater, his approach to his job as Examiner of Plays, and the way he dealt with particular manuscripts sent to him for licensing. Mrs. Larpent often acted as Larpent's adviser and, on occasions, even took on the responsibility of reading and licensing a new play herself. The diaries show that she was, in fact, practically a Deputy Examiner, and so her own views on plays that she read or saw are not without interest. In this respect the records she kept of her life before she married Larpent (in 1782) are revealing. The actual diaries for these years are lost, but we do have her "Methodized Journal" which she compiled from her diaries after her marriage so that Larpent might know something of the life she led before they were acquainted. The journal covers, somewhat sketchily, the years 1773-83 and in it we can trace the development of Mrs. Larpent's views on life, literature, and drama, views which were to have some influence on the Lord Chamberlain's Examiner of Plays. The journal and the diaries naturally tell us more about Mrs. Larpent than about Larpent himself, but they are still easily the most informative source that has yet been found about the man who for nearly fifty years had a very important say in what appeared on the British stage.[25]

Other manuscript material I have found useful for this study is distributed among various libraries, principally the British Library, the Public Record Office, and the Folger Shakespeare Library. Contemporary printed material is thinly spread among the newspapers (including many volumes of cuttings in the British Library), periodicals, diaries, memoirs, theatrical dictionaries and histories, and the prefaces to plays.

Many people in Georgian England had a little to say about the censorship; no one had a great deal to say. But by gathering together all the scattered information it is possible to piece together a more complete picture of the early decades of statutory censorship of English drama than has hitherto been attempted, and at the same time to increase our knowledge of a neglected area of English theater history.

My discussion of the censorship of drama is based firmly on the conviction that literary censorship of any kind is usually indefensible, and that the precensorship unique to the drama is an especially pernicious kind of censorship. Nonetheless, I have tried to avoid playing the game of making the censor look silly—fun though that sometimes is[26]—and I have from time to time defended his actions. I have also been persuaded to recognize that practically all levels of opinion in the eighteenth and early nineteenth centuries accepted the censorship of dramatic literature as an essential control of a powerful social and political force. (One reason we do not censor plays today is that we no longer accept that drama is as important or as influential as it was once believed to be.) It is clear too that the theater and society in general derived some benefits from the censorship. The theater was certainly a more peaceful place than it would have been without the censorship; violence and disruption resulting from political plays were kept to a minimum in a period when a single line could often spark off political feuding in an audience. The censorship also served as the only practicable means of defense against the hordes of unscrupulous personal satirists who thrived in the English theater of the eighteenth and nineteenth centuries.

Yet these were benefits to society, not to dramatic literature; the censorship did nothing to further the development of English drama, but plenty to hinder it. In explaining the dearth of great playwrights in a period of immense achievement in the novel and poetry one has to consider other factors besides the censorship: the discouraging effect of a monopoly whose supporters did their best to limit the performance of legitimate drama in London to Drury Lane and Covent Garden theaters and so placed dramatists at the mercy of a handful of partial and profit-minded administrators; the failure of the copyright laws to protect plays from piracy; the bad taste of spectacle-oriented audiences.[27] Talented playwrights had faced and overcome such difficulties in the past; but the new burden of a censorship which systematically stifled—only rarely with any justification—expressions of opinion on a wide spectrum of ideas and issues had its desired effect. Writers who had anything important to say did not, could not, turn to the theater.

The novelist, said Mrs. Inchbald (and she might have included the poet, too), "lives in a land of liberty, whilst the Dramatic Writer exists but under a despotic government."[28] As Mrs. Inchbald knew, there was more than one despot in that government—manager, actor, audience, critic, censor. What follows in this book is some account of how playwrights (including Mrs. Inchbald) lived under such government between 1737 and 1824, and particularly how they got along with the most consistent and unbending despot of them all, the censor.

1

The Licensing of Plays: Theory and Practice

THE SYSTEM

The Stage Licensing Act of 1737 (10 George II c. 28) was a hasty
and imperfect piece of legislation, which was hurried through Parliament by a worried and harrassed administration anxious to suppress
once and for all Henry Fielding's political satires at the Little
Theatre in the Haymarket.[1] For some fifteen years after the act came
into force a succession of wily actors and managers—James Lacy,
Charlotte Charke, Tony Aston, Henry Giffard, Charles Macklin,
Theophilus Cibber, Samuel Foote—found ways of performing
legitimate drama in one way or another outside the confines of Covent Garden and Drury Lane, the only two theaters in London legally permitted to put on plays after the act.[2] The activities of these people and their struggles to keep the minor theaters open in the middle
years of the eighteenth century have already been well documented
and there is no need to describe them here.[3] The control of theaters
was one important aspect of the Licensing Act; the other was the
control of the plays acted in them. There were fewer loopholes in this
part of the legislation, but the arbitrary nature of the system devised
for the licensing of plays made some degree of injustice in its operation inevitable. Moreover, the failure of those responsible for the act
to put very much thought into the details of the censorship clauses
(III and IV) meant that to make the system work at all efficiently the
Lord Chamberlain had to extend his powers beyond those allowed
him in the act, and the theaters, to avoid disruption of the normal
way of organizing their repertories, had to ignore some requirements
laid down in the act. Consequently, there were irregularities committed both by the Lord Chamberlain's office and the theaters. Fortunately, both sides were prepared to overlook the strict letter of the
law. If this silent compromise had not been achieved further legisla-

13

tion would certainly have been necessary, and the theaters would undoubtedly have been the losers by it.

Clauses III and IV of the Licensing Act laid down a few straightforward requirements to be followed by the presenters of plays, and specified the powers of the Lord Chamberlain with regard to such plays and their presenters. Since these two clauses were the origin of a censorship which lasted for two hundred and thirty years it is well to be quite clear what they said. Clause III stipulated that from 24 June 1737

no person shall for hire, gain, or reward, act, perform, represent, or cause to be acted, performed, or represented, any new interlude, tragedy, comedy, opera, play, farce, or other entertainment of the stage, or any part or parts therein; or any new act, scene, or other part added to any old interlude, tragedy, comedy, opera, play, farce, or other entertainment of the stage, or any new prologue, or epilogue, unless a true copy thereof be sent to the lord chamberlain of the King's household for the time being fourteen days at least before the acting, representing, or performing thereof, together with an account of the playhouse or other place where the same shall be, and the time when the same is intended to be first acted, represented, or performed, signed by the master or manager, or one of the masters or managers of such playhouse, or place, or company of actors therein.

Clause IV introduced the censorship:

. . . it shall and may be lawful to and for the said lord chamberlain for the time being, from time to time, and when, and as often as he shall think fit, to prohibit the acting, performing, or representing, any interlude, tragedy, comedy, opera, play, farce, or other entertainment of the stage, or any act, scene, or part thereof, or any prologue, or epilogue . . . .

The same clause described the punishment to be imposed on those who disregarded clause III or the Lord Chamberlain's censorship:

. . . every person so offending shall for every such offence forfeit the sum of fifty pounds, and every grant, licence, and authority (in case there be any such) by or under which the said master or masters or manager or managers set up, formed, or continued such playhouse, or such company of actors, shall cease, determine, and become absolutely void to all intents and purposes whatsoever.[4]

Thus all that was required of the manager of a properly licensed theater who wanted to present a new play, be it a farce or an opera,[5]

14

or an old play with new material added, was that he should send a true copy of the text to the Lord Chamberlain at least fourteen days before the planned first night, with a signed note indicating the place and date of performance. If, on reading the play, the Lord Chamberlain wished to prohibit the acting of all or part of it he would, presumably, communicate his commands to the manager who would lose £50 and his theater license if he did not obey them.

Lord Chesterfield, in his famous speech against the Licensing Act in the House of Lords in June 1737,[6] was the first to voice reasoned criticisms of a system of precensorship which gave one man such absolute control over the drama and which permitted no right of appeal against that man's decisions. The Lord Chamberlain could suppress a play for any reason he thought fit and he was not required to give any explanation of his decision to anyone. Nor could there be any appeal against his decision. These criticisms were repeated many times over the years, but, unanswerable though they were, they had no impact on successive British governments and it finally took a Private Member's Bill to abolish the precensorship of drama in Britain in 1968. Nevertheless, iniquitous though it was to allow the Lord Chamberlain such powers, they were granted to him by an act of Parliament brought into being by normal constitutional means. What has, however, been largely overlooked in subsequent discussions of the censorship of drama is the way in which the Lord Chamberlain (the duke of Grafton in 1737) created his own methods of operating the censorship quite independently of the act which made him censor. This came about largely because of the shortsightedness of the men who wrote and passed the act.

It ought to have been recognized and anticipated, for example, that neither the duke of Grafton nor the lords chamberlain who would succeed him would have the time or even the interest to read carefully through all new plays and additions to old ones intended for production in Britain. Either he would require help or he would assign someone to do the job for him. Grafton took the latter course and so the offices of Examiner and Deputy Examiner of Plays were created early in 1738. Although the Licensing Act made no provision for such offices the Lord Chamberlain was doubtless within his rights to make what appointments he pleased within his own department. The act did not stipulate that the Lord Chamberlain himself must read plays submitted to him, and there was some precedent for an Examiner in the office of the master of revels. It also made good sense from an administrative point of view to have a permanent Examiner. Lords chamberlain tended to come and go with ministerial changes, and for the sake of continuity and objectivity it was wise to have a censor who was independent of political parties and cliques.

Examiners were paid by the Lord Chamberlain's department, but in order to boost their salaries they were from the very beginning allowed to collect a fee for reading plays sent to them. This was quite illegal and remained so until the 1843 Theatres Act gave the Lord Chamberlain the power to specify what fees his Examiners should receive from the theaters. (There was, it is true, a precedent for claiming such fees. The master of revels, since the reign of Elizabeth, had demanded payment from the theaters when plays were sent to him from time to time, but it is doubtful if he ever had any legal authority to do so.) The fee was charged regardless of whether permission to act the play was granted or refused. The normal charge was two guineas, but sometimes the Examiner would be satisfied with less for a short piece such as an epilogue. No consistent scale of charges seems to have been used before 1843, however. The following entries from "An Alphabetical Catalogue with Notes of Theatrical Representations &ca Submitted For Licensing From The Year 1737, to the Year 1787 inclusive," compiled by John Larpent and his wife, show some typical receipts of licensing fees:[7]

> 1737 1 Tragedy. 2 Comedies. A Masque. & an opera. 5 in all £10.10s.

> 1739 3 Tragedies. 2 Dramatic pieces. 2 Farces. 7 in all £14.14s.

> 1740 A Comedy. Two Dramatic pieces. 2 farces & a Masque—in all 6—£11.11s.

> 1753 A Tragedy. A Comedy. A Farce. An Italian Opera. 4 pieces in all. £9.9s.

> 1757 A Comedy. 3 farces. 3 Operas. In all 7 pieces. £14.14s.

> 1758 2 Tragedies. 6 farces. An Italian Opera. In all 9 pieces £10.10s.

16

The account books of the theaters, which often include entries for the payment of the Examiner, reveal similar inconsistencies in the fee rates. The accounts also show that the Examiner was not always promptly paid by the theaters. M. P. Andrews' interlude, *The Election,* for example, was produced at Drury Lane on 19 October 1774, but Edward Capell, the Deputy Examiner, did not receive his fee until 27 December.[8] It was generally accepted that the theater, not the author, was responsible for paying the fee, although when Frederick Reynolds' new tragedy, *Werter,* opened at the Bath theater in 1785 the manager expected Reynolds to pay the Examiner's fee. Reynolds refused.[9]

In Peake's *Memoirs of the Colman Family* there is an interesting recollection of George Colman the Younger by S. J. Arnold. Arnold once had a long conversation with Colman about Colman's job as Examiner of Plays. One of the points Arnold raised was the very legality of the office. Another was the legality of the Lord Chamberlain's custom of issuing licenses for plays approved for acting by the Examiner.[10] It is common to see the Examiner of Plays described as the "Licenser." He did in fact issue licenses, signed by the Lord Chamberlain, for plays which had passed his censorship. When this practice began is unknown.[11] It may have been immediately or very soon after the Licensing Act was passed, but the earliest surviving license I know of is that for the anonymous comedy, *The Greek Slave; or, The School for Cowards,* acted at Drury Lane on 22 March 1791. The license is now in the Enthoven Collection in the Victoria and Albert Museum. It is handwritten and, on the verso, addressed to J. P. Kemble, dated 17 March 1791:

March 1791.
It having been reported to me, by the Examiner of all Theatrical Entertainments, that a Manuscript entitled *The Greek Slave,* being a Comedy in five Acts, does not contain in it any thing immoral, or otherwise improper for the Stage, I the Lord Chamberlain of His Majesty's Household, in Consideration of the same, do, by virtue of my Office, & in pursuance of the Act of Parliament in that Case provided, allow the said Manuscript to be acted at your Theatre, according to the Copy thereof delivered to me, & signed by Yourself, without any Variation whatsoever, unless such Variation be likewise approved of by me in due form.

Salisbury[12]

But in the Licensing Act there is no mention of any necessity or requirement for issuing licenses. Nor did any subsequent legislation regarding the censorship of plays stipulate such a requirement. When a manager sent a new play to the Lord Chamberlain with his note indicating his intention to produce it he normally, though not invariably, asked for the Lord Chamberlain's "permission" or "approbation," not his license. The license appears to have emerged in the years following the Licensing Act, perhaps with the approval of the theater managers, and possibly even at their suggestion. It was obviously more convenient for them to have documentary evidence of the Lord Chamberlain's permission to produce a play rather than relying on a verbal message or an informal letter. But according to the law it was never necessary for a theater to possess a license to stage a new play. As Arnold pointed out to Colman,

His Lordship's licence . . . is passive, not active. If the Act of Parliament is complied with, and a copy of the drama be sent fourteen days at least before its representation on the stage for his perusal, *should no prohibition be received*, the manager is justified, according to my reading of the act, to produce the piece, without further licence or hesitation.[13]

Arnold was right in his reading of the Licensing Act, but neither the theaters nor the Lord Chamberlain's office took his view. No matter if the Examiner kept a manuscript for more than fourteen days without issuing a license or a prohibition order, the play would not normally be produced. Thus the Examiner and the Lord Chamberlain gained important delaying powers not permitted by the Licensing Act, and occasionally used them.[14]

The Examiner assumed other liberties to which he was not entitled under the act. When a new play was submitted for licensing the Examiner invariably kept the manuscript after it had been licensed or had been refused a license. The act was silent on the question of what should happen to the manuscript, but the Examiner clearly had no right to consider it his own or his office's property. The greatest liberty in this respect was, of course, that taken by John Larpent and his wife in assuming ownership of all the manuscripts submitted for licensing from 1737 to 1824. The managers seem not to have minded being deprived of scripts in this way. An application note written by Charles Fleetwood from Drury Lane in 1738 is perhaps indicative of his own and other managers' acceptance of the custom. Fleetwood expresses his intention of producing James Miller's *The Coffee-House* as soon as the Lord Chamberlain is pleased "to license it." But Fleetwood had originally written "to return it," "return" being deleted and "license" replacing it (LA 3). In fact, once an Examiner had received a manuscript he rarely let it out of his grasp. If he needed to order the omission of some passages he would sometimes return the manuscript to the theater with the omissions marked, but always on the understanding that he would get it back. Frederick Reynolds' *The Crusade*, for example, was returned by Larpent to Covent Garden with a passage marked for omission after it had been submitted for licensing in April 1790, but a covering note indicated that he wanted it back without delay.

It is understandable that the Lord Chamberlain and his Examiners should want to keep the manuscripts of plays for reference purposes, and the Licensing Act perhaps ought to have provided them with the clear authority to do so. If it had, Edward Capell would have been saved the difficulty of explaining to an irascible Charles Macklin in 1770 why he would not return the manuscript of *The Man of the World*. "My Copy being detained," says Macklin, "I asked the Deputy why? or by what right he deprived me of my Copy? For some time he would not assign any reason. I told him, that I should resort to the Laws of my Country for redress; upon which he replied, *that I should but expose myself*, and *that they kept the Copy by the usage of the Office*."[15] Capell must have wished he could have given a better answer that that, but it was the only one he could truthfully supply. Not until 1912 was the Lord Chamberlain's office legally entitled to keep manuscripts of plays submitted for licensing.[16]

One clear irregularity in the operation of the Licensing Act arose when decisions about censorship or suppression were taken neither by the Lord Chamberlain nor his Examiner. Outsiders with some special interest in a particular play might take an active part, invited or uninvited, in its fate. On one extraordinary occasion, General

19

Gunning (of the famous Gunning family) was given the privilege of censoring a play in which there were impolite references to his daughter.[17] On another, an early play of Mrs. Inchbald's may well have suffered the indignity of being refused a license had it not been for the intervention of her friend Sir Charles Bunbury.[18] Outside pressure was not infrequently brought to bear on the Lord Chamberlain and his Examiner, although it was not always effective. Even someone as influential as the earl of Bute could not succeed in having Macklin's farce, *Love à la Mode*, suppressed in 1759. Bute objected to the play because it satirized the Scots, but his demands were resisted.

It is true that the Lord Chamberlain and his officers took certain liberties in the exercise of their duties in regard to the censorship of plays. But it can also be shown that the theaters, on their side, often acted in direct contravention of the Licensing Act.

The theaters, as we have seen, were obliged by the act to send new plays to the Lord Chamberlain "fourteen days at least before the acting, representing, or performing thereof." In the months immediately following the passing of the act this rule was fairly strictly adhered to. Often the Examiner would receive a new piece a good deal more than two weeks in advance of the date on which it was to be acted. But in a very few years managers became less careful, and the time interval between a new play being sent for licensing and its being acted frequently dropped to a few days. A week or less became common. One of the worst offenders was Richard Brinsley Sheridan. It was not unknown for him to send a manuscript for licensing only the day before the advertised date of performance. *The Critic*, for example, was sent on 29 October 1779 and was produced at Drury Lane the very next day (LA 494). And Mrs. Larpent records in her diary that her husband read the manuscript of Sheridan's *The Glorious First of June* on the very day it was performed (2 July 1794), it having been sent by J. P. Kemble only the day before (LA 1032).

One reason for this (apart from simple oversight or indifference) was that the manager would rarely have a final script ready for the Examiner's perusal two weeks before he hoped it would be acted, even supposing that he fixed on a particular date for the first night that much in advance, which is doubtful. By the time he could submit a script, the play would have been rehearsed and would probably be ready for production within the next few days. If so, no manager would want to wait the statutory fourteen days before putting on the play. (Nonetheless, he ought to have been able by then to have specified in his license application a date for the first night; the Licensing Act obliged him to do this, but he rarely did so.) The Examiner, however, was invariably cooperative and never insisted on his fourteen days. The most convenient procedure from the manager's point of view was for him to send the script for licensing as soon as it was ready and hope that the Examiner would quickly approve it in time for an early production. This usually happened, but if the manager had actually advertised the first night's performance before the text had been approved, he might get into difficulties if the Examiner needed longer than usual to read the text, or if the Lord Chamberlain had to be consulted.

The Examiner also proved over the years to be very tolerant toward those managers who allowed unexamined material to be spoken on their stages. No new play was ever produced (in the patent theaters, at least) without having been sent to the Examiner. But it was not uncommon for parts of plays to be performed without official approval. When a new play was acted, it frequently had to be altered or revised to meet objections voiced by the audience on the opening night. This would sometimes involve adding new speeches and changing others. Was this new material sent to the Examiner as it should have been? Almost certainly not, if only because of shortage of time. There is evidence to show beyond much doubt that irregularities of this kind went on. I have already mentioned that Sheridan's *The Glorious First of June* was sent for licensing at rather a late date. According to the biographer of John Bannister, even then the text was not complete. "It was so hastily prepared," he says, "that a portion of it had been performed whilst another was not yet written."[20] We can be sure that the passages written during the performance were not scrutinized by the Examiner. Sheridan was also involved in the performance of some unlicensed lines at Drury Lane on the evening of 8 April 1797. This was the final appearance of Elizabeth Farren (she acted Lady Teazle in *The School for Scandal*), and although no farewell address had been planned, it was found that the audience expected one. Consequently one was written after

21

the play had begun, Sheridan composing the last six lines during the second act. (Richard Wroughton did the first four.) The address, like an ordinary prologue or epilogue, should have been licensed, but unless Larpent was at Drury Lane (and Mrs. Larpent's diary records no visit to the theater for that evening) it obviously was not. An habitual offender against the Licensing Act, Sheridan was also one of those accused by a correspondent in the *Morning Post* on 15 February 1779 of allowing the actors to speak some unauthorized lines in *The Camp* reflecting on the recent acquittal of Admiral Keppel by a court martial.

Larpent, as a fairly regular theatergoer, must have been aware that minor irregularities of this sort were taking place, but so long as he (and others who held his office) was not deprived of his licensing fee too often, and so long as none of the unlicensed speeches proved to be unduly offensive, he did not pay very much attention.

The same is true of successive Examiners' attitudes toward the common practice in the eighteenth and early nineteenth-century theater of ad-libbing. Between 1737 and 1968 ad-libbing in the British theater was illegal, for it was not scripted and hence could not be officially examined. Actors, however, frequently indulged in the practice as a means of exercising their wit, and they could often endear themselves to an audience by producing an extempore remark alluding to recent events or well-known personalities. The part of Bayes in the duke of Buckingham's *The Rehearsal* was frequently used by actors to display their literary as well as histrionic talents, Garrick making especially good use of it for both mimicry and ad-libbing.[22] Samuel Foote probably ad-libbed his way through most of the parts he played[23] and Tate Wilkinson recollects an occasion when he appeared as himself in Foote's *Tea* without any script at all and spoke "just what I could select to please myself . . . ."[24] This happened in Dublin where the Licensing Act did not apply, but there must have been similar occurrences in England. Playwrights, as one would expect, did not encourage actors to meddle with a text they had carefully prepared. Macklin objected to the practice of ad-libbing[25] and one of Arthur Murphy's rules for actors was that "no Player shall come on, imperfect in his Part, or take the Liberty to insert his own Jokes and Witticisms, in the Productions of those Geniuses, for whom he should have the proper Respect due to the

22

Superiority of their Parts."[26] But examiners were less touchy than playwrights in this matter and if the actors took care not to upset anyone with their interpolations officialdom was not likely to intervene.

Intervention was inevitable, though, when the Lord Chamberlain's veto on a play was openly disregarded. Tate Wilkinson found this out in 1759 when he acted scenes from Foote's play, *The Author*, in London after it had been suppressed; although in the provinces, where the Lord Chamberlain's authority was difficult to enforce, *The Author* was acted many times.[27] Indeed, it was difficult for the censors to be sure that any of their directives were followed by the theaters. Obviously it was not feasible for the Examiner or his deputy to be present at every performance of every play, but an official of some sort might have been expected to attend at least the opening night of each new play. Thomas Odell, Deputy Examiner from 1738 to 1749, was, it seems, quite conscientious about this. Thomas Cooke, the playwright, often saw this "thin pale man looking over the prompter's book at the stage-door almost during the performance of a whole play . . . to see if any words were spoke on the stage which were not in the book."[28] But George Colman felt he had no responsibility whatever on this score[29] and there is nothing in the Larpent diaries to suggest that Larpent ever took the trouble to check that his instructions were carried out. It would appear that Examiners of Plays usually considered their job done once a license was issued or refused. It is hardly surprising then to learn of occasional instances in the early nineteenth century of the Examiner's censorship being disregarded.[30]

There was never any doubt that plays acted at theaters in the provinces were just as much subject to the censorship as plays acted in London, and the Larpent manuscripts show that many plays were submitted for licensing from the provinces, occasionally to be denied. But there was some uncertainty about the position of the minor theaters[31] which proliferated in London in the early years of the nineteenth century. On 14 February 1818 Henry Harris wrote to John Larpent to explain how it had come about that Henry Milman's tragedy, *Fazio*, had not been submitted for licensing before its performance at Covent Garden on 5 February.[32] Harris explained that the play had already been acted at Bath six weeks previously and

23

also many times at the Surrey and Olympic theaters (both minors). He therefore assumed that *Fazio* had already been licensed for performance. But apparently neither the provincial nor minor theaters had bothered to apply for a license. Now the Bath theater, like the other provincial theaters, did not normally try to evade the regular licensing prodedure, but it is fairly certain that many plays were acted at the minors without official approval. Some minor theater managers, like Samuel James Arnold at the Lyceum, were conscientious about sending plays to be licensed, but the Surrey theater, as has been recently pointed out,[33] seems to have completely ignored the licensing system. And so when T. B. Mash, an official in the Lord Chamberlain's office, wrote to various minor theater managers on 9 February 1824 to tell them that George Colman was the new Examiner of Plays he reminded them that "all Entertainments of the Stage are to be forwarded to that Gentleman for the Licence of the Lord Chamberlain at least 14 days before they are intended to be performed. . . ."[34]

Generally, however, there was little friction between the Lord Chamberlain's office and the theaters over the licensing of plays. Toleration prevailed, and neither side found it necessary to insist that the strict letter of the law be obeyed. In this way a workable system of theater censorship evolved out of the imperfect legislation of the 1737 Licensing Act.

THE CENSORS

It is easy to get into the habit of talking about lords chamberlain and examiners of plays as if they were nameless, faceless officials who remained in anonymous obscurity as all good censors should. This is partly because the first really controversial Examiner was George Colman, and he did not take over until 1824. (He was also one of the most fanatical and bigoted Examiners ever.) Lords chamberlain, by the very nature of the job they had, tended to avoid publicity and controversy, and although those who held office between 1737 and 1824 were sometimes interesting and influential political figures, they did not often come into the public eye by virtue of their responsibilities as censors of plays. Those occasions when some of them did are described in the following chapters, but since they all played their

24

part in maintaining the smooth running of the censorship system—if only by not interfering in it—each one deserves some mention here.

The Lord Chamberlain at the time of the Licensing Act, and hence the man responsible for the initial moves in creating a workable system of censorship, was Charles Fitzroy, duke of Grafton (1683-1757).[35] He was appointed Lord Chamberlain in 1724 and retained the post until his death on 6 May 1757. Apart from an unsuccessful period as lord lieutenant of Ireland, he held no important political positions. It was Grafton who suppressed Gay's *Polly* in 1728 and he must have been involved in the campaign against the anti-Walpole dramatists in the five years following the Licensing Act, although no information on the precise part he played has been found.

Grafton was succeeded by William Cavendish, duke of Devonshire (1720-64). Unlike Grafton, Devonshire was a popular and successful lord lieutenant of Ireland and an important politician. He became first lord of the treasury in November 1756 in Newcastle's place so that Pitt could become secretary of state and manage the war against the French. But the new ministry lacked support from the king and the Commons, and Devonshire resigned in May 1757. He was then made Lord Chamberlain. Devonshire was, as far as it is possible to tell, a popular Lord Chamberlain with the theaters. When he was lord lieutenant in Ireland (1755-56) he allowed Henry Brooke's *Jack the Giant Queller* to be performed at the Smock-Alley theater after it had been suppressed in 1749 on account of its political satire.[36] Perhaps it was partly this display of tolerance that prompted Benjamin Victor to praise Devonshire for his "Humanity and Benevolence."[37] In England, Devonshire's period of office as Lord Chamberlain was enlivened mainly by Samuel Foote. Devonshire suppressed *The Author*, but resisted strong pressure to do the same to *The Minor*. He was dismissed from office late in 1762 because he refused to attend negotiations for the Peace of Paris.

It was apparently thought by some that the earl of Bute would succeed the duke of Devonshire as Lord Chamberlain,[38] but on 22 November 1762 George Spencer, duke of Marlborough (1739-1817) was appointed. He held the office only until April 1763 when he was made lord privy seal in the Grenville ministry. Marlborough's brief period of office was marred by the foolish banning of William Shirley's tragedy, *Electra,* a decision which was, however, upheld by his successor, Granville Leveson-Gower, Earl Gower (1721-1803). Before being appointed Lord Chamberlain on 22 April 1763 he had been lord lieutenant of Staffordshire, master of the horse, and keeper of the great wardrobe. When Rockingham came to power in July 1765 Gower resigned his lord chamberlainship, but he continued to take an active part in politics. In March 1783 he was in fact offered the post of prime minister, but he declined it.

William Henry Cavendish Bentinck, duke of Portland (1738-1809), twice prime minister, was made Lord Chamberlain by Rockingham on 10 July 1765. He left the office in November 1766 after the fall of Rockingham. But when Rockingham returned to power in April 1782 he was appointed lord lieutenant of Ireland. Twelve months later he became prime minister, but only until December 1783 when he resigned because of the rejection by the House of Lords of Fox's India Bill. After a long political career he was again made prime minister in 1807. As Lord Chamberlain he was involved in no controversy to do with the censorship of plays, but he should be remembered as the man who was instrumental in obtaining a patent for Samuel Foote to operate regularly the Little Theatre in the Haymarket during the summer months.

Francis Seymour Conway, marquis of Hertford (1718-94), cousin of Horace Walpole, was probably more involved in the job of censoring plays than any other Lord Chamberlain who held office between 1737 and 1824. He had two separate periods of office, the first from 29 November 1766 to 10 April 1782, the second from 9 April 1783[39] to 26 December 1783. Like some of his predecessors, he had been lord lieutenant of Ireland for a brief period and also, earlier, a lord of the bedchamber and a member of the Privy Council. His long period as Lord Chamberlain indicates that he was not very active in politics, at least not openly, although Hertford's letters to George III show that he was not entirely without interest or influence in political matters.[40] He seems to have possessed qualities which would have been considered sound qualifications for a censor. William Cole once wrote of his "great virtue and strict morality,"[41] and Walpole even thought him to be "a little of the prude."[42] Chesterfield considered him to be "the honestest and most religious man in the world," and "very much a gentleman in his behaviour to everybody."[43] Hertford was in office when Macklin's wrath was aroused by the suppression of *The Man of the World*, but the play which probably caused him most trouble was Foote's *The Trip to Calais*, suppressed in 1775. Hertford, to his credit, concerned himself also with the less publicized plays that were sent for licensing. This is shown by the letters he wrote from time to time to Horace Walpole, seeking advice on various plays he had read in manuscript.[44] The letters reveal Hertford to have been cautious, but not unnecessarily restrictive,[45] and certainly not intolerant in his attitudes toward plays. When Macklin wrote to Hertford on 4 December 1779 asking him to lift the ban which had been imposed on *The Man of the World* nine years earlier, the playwright was very complimentary to the Lord Chamberlain:

Your Administration, as Lord Chamberlain of his Majesty's Household, is felt & acknowledged by all who have any Interest in the Theatres to be so mild & beneficient as to excite in them a sincere Respect for your Lordship.

Hertford is "lenient" and "always disposed to favour & encourage every dramatic Effort to the full Extent of his official Power . . . ."[46] Macklin was begging a favor, so his words are perhaps sweeter than they might normally have been. Nonetheless, on the evidence that we have, which is not abundant, there appears to be some truth in them.

George Montagu, duke of Manchester (1737-88), was appointed Lord Chamberlain by Rockingham on 10 April 1782,[47] but he held office only until 9 April 1783 when he resigned to become ambassador to France. Hertford then returned to office until James Cecil, marquis of Salisbury (1748-1835), succeeded him on 26 December 1783.[48] He was Lord Chamberlain until May 1804 and thus had to administer control of the drama during the difficult period of the French Revolution and its aftermath when a number of plays were suppressed in London for political reasons. However, by the time Salisbury took office, John Larpent had been Examiner of Plays for five years and it was he, not Salisbury, who seems to have taken most of the responsibility for the censorship.

George Legge, earl of Dartmouth (1775-1810), came to office (14 May 1804) during a period not only of European political turmoil—often reflected in the drama—but also of increasing moral restric-

tiveness in England. Dartmouth was himself active in this movement, holding as he did the influential position of president of the
Society for the Suppression of Vice. As such he had to deal with some
cranky complaints, like that from an anonymous "stranger" who
wrote to him on 17 August 1803 urging him to use his influence to
suppress some recent publications, including two essays in the
November 1802 issue of the *Gentleman's Magazine,* "The one, concerning The Natural History of the Elephant—The other, An
Anatomical Description of a Male Rhinoceros." "Surely, my Lord,"
wrote the stranger, "such Discussions need not be obtruded upon the
minds of the numerous Youth, & Females, into whose hands the
Miscellany in question must very frequently fall."[49] Dartmouth's
response to this is not, unfortunately, preserved, but he did resist (in
his capacity as Lord Chamberlain) an equally cranky complaint
about Madame Catalani's appearing in men's clothes in *The Feasts
of Isis* in 1808. The complainant considered this to be a gross viola-
tion of "an express command of the Almighty," citing Deuteronomy
XXII. v ("The woman shall not wear that which pertaineth unto a
man, neither shall a man put on a woman's garment: for all that do
so are abomination unto the LORD thy God"). He also wondered
why "Egyptian abominations" were being allowed into a Christian
country and wanted to know what the Lord Chamberlain and the
bishop of London (who had originally received the complaint) were
doing about it. Nothing, said Dartmouth in a letter to the bishop. "If
Mad^me Catalini [*sic*] . . . chooses to decorate herself in male attire, I
do not see how the Lord Chamberlain can interfere to prevent it,
without at the same time taking steps to abolish the practice of either
sex . . . assuming the dress of the other and upon the national
theatres, a practice so inveterate, that I much doubt whether the
power of the Lord Chamberlain would be of avail to prevent it."[50]
This pragmatic attitude towards matters theatrical is also noticeable
in Dartmouth's relationship with the minor theaters, whose inevitable rise he did little to forestall despite their threat to the patent
theaters.[51]

Dartmouth died in November 1810, still in office, and then,
strangely, there was no Lord Chamberlain until Francis Ingram
Seymour, marquis of Hertford (1743-1822) was appointed on 7
March 1812. During that time the Lord Chamberlain's deputy
seems to have taken over the responsibility for licensing plays. The

signature of John Thynne, vice-chamberlain, is on the license for the comic opera *Le Tre Sultane*, performed at the King's Theatre, Haymarket, on 22 January 1811 (Enthoven Collection, Victoria and Albert Museum).

Hertford, whose father had served as Lord Chamberlain in the previous century, was involved, as Lord Chamberlain, in the wrangles between the minor and patent theaters;[52] and the tight censorship of political comment exercised over the drama while he was in office may be a reflection of Hertford's own conservative political viewpoint. That he disapproved of radical politics entering literature is shown by the care he took in choosing a poet laureate to succeed Henry Pye in 1813. "Some of our poets," he wrote to the earl of Liverpool, "have I know given much into democratical Politicks, which makes it particularly necessary to be careful in the choice of Mr Pyes successor."[53]

Hertford was Lord Chamberlain until 11 December 1821, when he was succeeded by James Graham, duke of Montrose (1755-1836). Like his predecessor, Montrose could not avoid the minor *versus* patents controversy, but he seems to have left his Examiner to look after the censorship. Montrose was still in office when John Larpent died in 1824.

It is important to know as much as possible about the men who held the office of Examiner (or Deputy Examiner) of Plays because it was the Examiner who first read the manuscript of a new play when it came for licensing and it was usually he who made the first and often final decision about it. He was almost without exception responsible for the censoring (as opposed to the suppressing) of plays, and when he recommended to the Lord Chamberlain that a license be refused altogether his advice was normally accepted unquestioningly.

The first man to hold the office of Examiner of Plays was William Chetwynd. He was appointed by the duke of Grafton on 10 March 1738. There is a copy of the document authorizing the appointment in the Public Record Office:

Whereas by Virtue, and in Consequence, of an Act of Parliament, made in the Tenth Year of the Reign of His Majesty King George the Second, for yᵉ better Regulating of the Stage; I am impower'd to constitute, and appoint, an Officer to examine all Plays, Tragedies, Comedies, Operas, Farces, interludes or other Entertainments of the Stage, of what Denomination soever; I do hereby constitute, and appoint, William Chetwynd, Esqʳ, to the said Office of Examiner of all, and every, the above recited Plays, Tragedies, Comedies, Operas, Farces, Interludes or other Entertainments of the Stage, of what Denomination soever; to have, hold, exercise and enjoy the Same, together with all Salarys, Fees, and other Emoluments to the Said Office, that may Arise, or in any wise legally Appertain. Given under my hand and Seal this 10ᵗʰ of March 1737/8 in the Eleventh Year of his Majesty's Reign.

Grafton.⁵⁴

Chetwynd's salary as Examiner is not stated, but a manuscript note in the British Library indicates that it was £400 a year.⁵⁵

There has been some confusion about the identity of Chetwynd. Dougald MacMillan, both in his article on *The Man of the World* and in his introduction to the *Catalogue of the Larpent Plays in the Huntington Library*, mistakes him for William Richard Chetwynd, Viscount Chetwynd of Bearhaven, undersecretary of state and master of the mint, who died on 3 April 1770.⁵⁶ But the William Chetwynd who was Examiner of Plays came from a different family from the Viscount Chetwynd and did not die until 6 October 1778. There is a note to this effect in the manuscript copy of *The School for Scandal* sent for licensing before its performance at Drury Lane on 8 May 1777. The manuscript is now in the Yale University Library and was described in *Theatre Notebook* by William Van Lennep in 1951.⁵⁷ The note about Chetwynd was written by Sir George Chetwynd, grandson of the Examiner of Plays:

This is the identical copy of 'The School for Scandal' which was transmitted by Mr. Sheridan to my grandfather, William Chetwynd Esq., the then 'Examiner of all Entertainments of the Stage' under the Lord Chamberlain, previously to it's being performed. After my Grandfather's death on 6th October, 1778, this, with numerous other M.S. Plays was found at his House in Old Burlington Street . . . .

The year of Chetwynd's death is also given as 1778 by Samuel Pegge in his "Brief Memoirs of Edward Capell."⁵⁸

William Chetwynd was the son of Walter Chetwynd of Brocton, Staffordshire, and Mary, daughter of William Sneyd of Keele. In

1738 he married Martha Hesketh, a widow, daughter of James St. Amand of St. Paul's, Covent Garden. They had two sons, James, who died in 1774, and George, who served for many years as clerk to the Privy Council. George was knighted in 1787 and created baronet on 1 May 1795. Sir George's eldest son, also named George, succeeded him as second baronet on 24 March 1824, and it was he who wrote the note quoted above.[59]

MacMillan's assertion that Chetwynd never took an active part in the censoring of plays, that "He had from the beginning, generally if not exclusively, discharged his office by deputy,"[60] seems largely, but not wholly, true. There is no evidence in the Larpent manuscripts to show that Chetwynd was ever actively engaged in reading or censoring them, and after Edward Capell's appointment as Deputy Examiner in 1749 the corrections that appear in the manuscripts are unmistakably in Capell's hand. This is not to say that Chetwynd had nothing whatever to do with the business for which he was paid £400 a year. Sir George Chetwynd's note indicates that some of the scripts sent for licensing were seen and perhaps read by Chetwynd. And a letter from Garrick to Capell, 3 December 1760, in which Garrick says he intends to request licenses for two new plays from Chetwynd, also shows that the Examiner was involved in the licensing procedure, as does Capell's note to him about Garrick's letter.[61]

Thomas Odell, appointed Chetwynd's deputy on the same day (10 March 1738) that Chetwynd was made Examiner,[62] was about as well qualified as anyone could be to do his job. He is said, for example, to have written political satires on Walpole's behalf during his early years in London (he arrived there from Buckinghamshire about 1714), an experience which must have proved useful in detecting the anti-Walpole satire in the new plays written while he was Deputy Examiner. Odell also had experience of the theater. In October 1729 he opened the theater in Ayliffe Street, Goodman's Fields, and ran it until the management was taken over by one of his company, Henry Giffard, in 1731. While managing the theater Odell also had an opportunity of acquainting himself with his future employer, the duke of Grafton, when, on 28 April 1730, the Lord Chamberlain ordered him to close his theater because of complaints from the lord mayor and aldermen of the city.[63] (Performances continued after a short hiatus.) Odell was also a playwright. His first play, *The Chimaera*, a comedy, was acted at the theater in Lincoln's Inn Fields on 19 January 1721 (published, anonymously, 1721), to be followed by a ballad-opera, *The Patron; or, The Statesman's Opera*, and a farce, *The Smugglers*, both acted at the Little Theatre in the Haymarket on 7 May 1729 and both published in 1729. Nicoll describes *The Patron* as "Fairly coarse . . . in its coarseness recalling Restoration licence," and close in spirit to *The Beggar's Opera*,[64] which again indicates that Odell was not likely to be hampered by moral or political naïveté in the exercise of his duties as censor. Odell's fourth and final play was another comedy, *The Prodigal; or, Recruits for the Queen of Hungary*, acted at the Little Theatre on 11 October 1744 and published in the same year (an alteration of Shadwell's *The Woman-Captain*). Odell is, I believe, unique in being the only Examiner or Deputy Examiner of Plays to have had a play licensed and produced during his term of office. There is no Larpent manuscript of *The Prodigal* and it would be interesting to know if it went through the usual licensing procedure. Perhaps Odell saved himself the two guineas fee by approving the play himself—or did Chetwynd insist on reading it?

Odell died on 24 May 1749 (*DNB*). For the eleven years during which he and Chetwynd were the censors the period of greatest activity for them was 1738-41 when Walpole's critics were trying to use the drama to bring about his downfall. Thereafter, the censorship goes through a period of over fifteen years of inactivity, largely owing to the fact that after Walpole's resignation the theater and politics stayed well apart. The inactivity was ended by the appearance of Samuel Foote as one of the most persistent and unprincipled personal satirists of his time. Odell, then, after the suppression of the anti-Walpole plays, had a quiet time as Deputy Examiner, unlike the unfortunate Edward Capell.

Grafton decided to appoint Capell as Odell's successor on 23 May 1749 when, presumably, Odell's death was imminent,[65] but the appointment was not made official until November. In the meantime, Henry Fielding, who apparently did not know that Capell had already been chosen, made unsuccessful efforts to have Edward Moore, the playwright, appointed, as is shown by his letter of 29 August 1749 to George Lyttleton.

Capell is remembered as a Shakespearean editor, but he also made his mark as Deputy Examiner of Plays. Both as editor and censor he brought to bear on his work a thoroughness and meticulousness that were not always appreciated by his contemporaries.

A copy of the royal warrant for Capell's appointment is in the Public Record Office. It shows that "in Consideration of the Knowledge, Diligence and good Conduct" required of him Capell was to receive two hundred pounds a year.[67] He was also a groom of the privy chamber,[68] for which (in 1769, at least) he was paid seventy-three pounds a year.[69] Financially, then, Capell was well situated and neither post he held under the Lord Chamberlain occupied very much of his time. He was thus free to devote himself to Shakespeare.[70] His edition of Shakespeare (1768-70) is dedicated to the third duke of Grafton, grandson of the Lord Chamberlain, whose patronage Capell freely acknowledges.

Capell's qualifications for the job of Deputy Examiner were limited to his interest in Shakespeare, which might be taken to indicate an interest in drama generally, and his friendship with Garrick (which cooled somewhat in later years). In addition, he could read French and Italian, the Italian being useful in examining Italian operas submitted for licensing.[71]

There can be no doubt that Capell brought a considerable enthusiasm to his work. His easily identifiable, small, neat handwriting appears in a number of Larpent manuscripts, mostly on account of his conviction that political allusion, however innocent, had no place in the drama. Thus we find several instances of petty interference by Capell in new plays, apart from more serious instances like the suppression of *The Man of the World*. And almost certainly it is to Capell that we can ascribe the dubious distinction of wanting to suppress *The School for Scandal*, an opinion in which the then Lord Chamberlain, Lord Hertford, did not concur.[72] In fact, Hertford seems to have found Capell an overzealous censor, and it may have been this which led him to pass over Capell when Chetwynd died and a new Examiner had to be appointed. Capell expected to get the job, partly, no doubt, because of his experience, and partly because Hertford married the second duke of Grafton's daughter and so "usually favoured the appointees" of the late Lord Chamberlain.[73]

But John Larpent was appointed in Chetwynd's place, although according to Pegge he "never solicited . . . for the post, and was surprised at the offer of it, voluntarily made by his Lordship."[74]

Biographia Dramatica (3: 16) describes Capell as a "scrupulous petty placeman" and "our guardian eunuch of the stage." Harsh words, but they are not entirely undeserved. Capell was usually polite and helpful in his dealings with the theaters and even sometimes took the trouble of suggesting alternative readings to those he censored. But he seems to have lacked any sense of proportion in his approach to censorship (and perhaps to his work on Shakespeare as well), an inability to distinguish between the important and the insignificant. In editing Shakespeare he was, consequently, often pedantic; in censoring plays any political allusion, direct or indirect, real or imaginary, a few lines or a whole play, became a danger to the well-being of the state.

Capell died on 24 February 1781,[75] and it has generally been assumed that from then on John Larpent continued without a Deputy Examiner. But according to Pegge, a James Trail succeeded Capell both as groom of the privy chamber and Deputy Examiner of Plays. Little is known of Trail, but he served as consul general at Tunis in the 1760s[76] and later became undersecretary to the lord lieutenant of Ireland.[77] The Larpent diaries also show that he was a friend and frequent visitor to the Larpents and that he eventually married, on 22 January 1798, Larpent's sister-in-law, Clara. Trail served only a short period as Deputy Examiner. Burke's Civil List Act of 1782 abolished various positions which were financed out of the civil list. The act did not specify the office of Deputy Examiner of Plays for abolition, but the general necessity for economizing, in which the Lord Chamberlain was deeply involved, seems to have led to Trail's dismissal. Unlike Chetwynd, Larpent was an active and conscientious Examiner and he certainly had no need for a deputy. There is no evidence that Trail was involved in the examination or censorship of plays during his brief tenure of office.

On 20 November 1778, John Larpent was appointed Examiner of Plays in the place of William Chetwynd.[78] Larpent was born on 14 November 1741, the second son of John Larpent, who spent forty-three years in the Foreign Office, twenty-five of them as chief clerk. He also had special responsibility for the affairs of Sir Horace

34

Mann.[79] The younger Larpent apparently joined the Foreign Office himself when he left Westminster School and he served as secretary to the duke of Bedford at the negotiations for the Peace of Paris in 1763. He later went to Ireland as secretary to the lord lieutenant, Lord Hertford (1765). By 1769 Larpent was a waiter in ordinary in the Lord Chamberlain's department,[80] and in the Public Record Office there is a copy of a document authorizing payment of £7.10.0 as a quarter's allowance in 1772 to "John Larpent Esq. One of His Majesty's Gentlemen Ushers Quarter Waiters."[81] He was later promoted to a groom of the privy chamber,[82] in which position he presumably enjoyed the same salary as Capell, that is, £73 p. a.

On 14 August 1773 Larpent married Frances Western. By her Larpent had two sons, one of them, Francis Seymour, becoming a distinguished civil servant.[83] Frances died on 9 November 1777, and on 25 April 1782 Larpent married Anna Margaretta Porter, whose father, Sir James Porter, a distinguished diplomat, had been ambassador at Constantinople. Her maternal grandfather was a German aristocrat, baron de Hochepied, and in 1819 the two sons of Larpent's second marriage added Hochepied to the family name. The elder son, John James, became the third baron in 1828 and the other son, George Gerard, served as M.P. for Nottingham and was created baronet in 1841.[84]

Apart from these few basic facts we have known little about Larpent and his family. The Larpent manuscript plays and the letters and notes written by Larpent that were kept with them are indispensable for any study of Larpent's work as Examiner, but the Larpent diaries now enable us to fill in some details about Larpent the man and the kind of daily life he led as Examiner of Plays.

It is not possible to say why Lord Hertford chose John Larpent to be Examiner of Plays in 1778. One would assume that Larpent had shown at some time at least a passing interest in the theater and drama. On the other hand, Hertford may have picked Larpent simply because he was an efficient and dutiful member of his department. But even if Larpent had never read a play or been inside a theater until he became Examiner, it is likely that his marriage to Miss Porter would have stimulated in him a more than professional involvement in the theater. Anna Margaretta was too puritanical and, in any case, socially ineligible, to be an actress, but she was a keen and constant theatergoer before her marriage, and plays, old and new, constituted a good percentage of the books she read. It is only natural to assume that some of this enthusiasm rubbed off onto her husband.

Mrs. Larpent began keeping a daily record of her life when she was fifteen years old. Every evening she wrote down "what persons, I had seen, books read, Sentiments heard &c in the day." For her "Methodized Journal" she reviewed her yearly diaries and "methodized" her entries; that is, she organized them under various headings, such as books she had read, sermons heard, places of entertainment visited, people met, and so on. Her journal begins in 1773. There are full accounts of each year up to and including 1781. Only very brief summaries are given of 1782, 1783, and 1786. The one-volume journal is signed and dated 2 October 1787, but the bulk of it seems to have been copied out in 1784.

The woman Larpent married was a sober, religious person, with a pronounced puritanism in her character. She would frequently spend an evening at Ranelagh, or at a ball or card party, but she rarely seems to have enjoyed herself. Mixing with society was a duty rather than a pleasure. On 28 May 1773 she was at Ranelagh, and her observation on the evening was,

I should have been as agreeably & I am sure more comfortably entertained at home . . . than I was in all that hurly burly. But so it is! one must conform to the world. A young person must sometimes mix in the pastimes stiled diversions, or she is looked upon as ridiculous, particular!

A ball at the French Ambassador's the previous month (2 April) is dismissed thus: "It is right to see the most talked of & admired fashionable Amusements that one may be convinced of their emptiness." Affectation and vanity of all kinds Miss Porter could not tolerate. On one occasion (8 February 1773) she met William Gardener, "a famous Irishman," who sported "20 curls on each side of his head," and she reflected "how horrid it is when Men particularly care for their dress, & take pains about it—Whenever I see a Man's dress *outrée* & as if much time, & great pains had been spent on it, I conclude the person is better ornamented than the mind." In fact, as a young lady, Anna Margaretta had something of an aversion to men. She warned herself constantly about their wickedness and eventually convinced herself that she had no inclination for them at all. One March evening in 1779 she attended a ball where she was not once asked to dance, "but I own (not from vanity, but the consciousness of doing right) that I was pleased to find that I was not mortified or vext at this neglect, which some time ago I should have been—Of all the really Elegant men there, there was not one I even wished for a bow from. I am surely very odd." Odd by some standards perhaps she was, but it was an oddness born of a lack of patience with ostentation and pretentiousness in social gatherings, and a preference for quieter, more intellectual ways of passing her time. Conversation with interesting people entertained her more than the grandest ball. Fortunately, her social position gave her many opportunities to meet quite eminent men and women of her time. In 1776 she met General Paoli and "Dr Johnson *ye great*," and the following year Sir John Fielding, and in 1778 Paoli again, "very often," and at a ball on 5 May 1778 (one of the few she found agreeable) Miss Porter found herself dancing a cotillion with William Pitt, who was "looking fair & rather vacant, being awkwardly tall and dancing ill—perhaps ye latter indicated *good*." It also seems possible that Miss Porter was acquainted with Thomas Malthus, and she was a close friend of the duke and duchess of Queensberry. In addition to meeting and talking with interesting people, Anna Margaretta found great pleasure and instruction in listening to sermons. Each year in her journal has a list of all the sermons she heard and the names of the preachers who delivered them, and her church attendances were well supplemented by a wide range of religious books.

Miss Porter expresses few political opinions in her journal, but she was neither ignorant nor naïve in political matters. She records holding conversations on the American situation and on Admiral Keppel's acquittal in 1779. The American troubles revealed to her a "sad view of human nature," and as regards Admiral Keppel, she regrets that "a brave commander should be made the tool of an opposition." She takes a dim but realistic view of party politics: "The total confusion of right & wrong prevalent in all parties shows how nearly this Empire is verging to its ruin . . . what do the parties that divide this state aim at? to push one another out of posts & places."

Between 1774 and her marriage to Larpent in April 1782, Anna

Margaretta read or reread some seventy plays. Most of them were French or English classics, but some were by contemporary playwrights (Cumberland, Colman, Garrick, Hannah More), and from the very beginning the journal records visits to the theater to see new and recent plays. Often little more is recorded than the fact of the visit, but at times Anna Margaretta gives free expression to her views. These reveal that she not only had a general interest in the theater, but also definite convictions as to what was good and bad, proper and improper in plays. When she became wife of the Examiner of Plays these convictions were to take on a new significance. Sentiment, melancholy, affection, virtue; these were the ingredients Anna Margaretta (like most young women of her station in life) appreciated most in a play. Her reaction to William Mason's *Caractacus*, which she saw on 7 February 1777, was excessively complimentary, but it shows the kinds of things which appealed to her:

I was charmed at the representation of my favorite poem—Every character is nobly drawn! Every incident glows with such a gentle sweet melancholy, so naturally wrought that my Soul melted into every pleasing sensation. The language charming! divine harmony, beams in every line. Such a love of virtue! such examples of piety, resignation, & fortitude! raise the soul to an extatic heighth—Sweet Evelinda how my heart throbbed for her!

Similarly, Thomas Hull's alteration of James Thomson's *Edward and Eleonora* (banned by one of her future husband's predecessors), which she saw at Covent Garden on 1 May 1775, was a "most affecting tale . . . fraught with virtuous sentiments." More interesting in the present context, however, are Anna Margaretta's dislikes. Again, they are fairly predictable. *The Beggar's Opera* is "too shocking . . . such vice laid open!" Farquhar's *The Inconstant* is "a low, indelicate, immoral thing;" O'Hara's burlesque, *The Golden Pippin* (even after Capell had censored it), is "disagreeably vulgar;" and Gay's *Polly* contains "much immorality" and is "better not to be acted, than acted." Indelicacy or immorality of any kind were eschewed by Anna Margaretta. "It is right to abhor, to hate indecent improper language & to discourage it," she wrote on 15 September 1773, and she was wary of reading novels because "they are too seducing, too trivial, too dangerous."

The woman to whom Larpent was attracted was perhaps a little dull, but she had an inquiring mind and was capable of holding and expressing opinions, albeit mostly conventional ones, on politics, religion, literature, and the drama. Her advice to Larpent on matters of taste and propriety in drama would have coincided with that of many theatergoers of the last quarter of the eighteenth century. She would, therefore, have been an important link between her husband (who does not seem to have taken a great deal of interest in the theater for its own sake) and London's audiences. An altogether useful sort of wife for an Examiner of Plays to have.

At the end of her journal, Anna Margaretta gives a brief description of the man she chose to marry. She perceived a "fair honorable character," and thought he enjoyed a "moderate, quiet, decent Situation of life." She was impressed by his "virtuous Moral character" and, in particular, the tenderness with which he had treated his first wife, the respect he held for her memory, and the "very great interest" shown for their surviving son. This latter point was of some consequence to Anna Margaretta, for, her own parents being dead, she was responsible for the upbringing of her younger sister and she hoped that "the Man who felt so much for his Motherless Son, w^d feel for my orphan Child." In all, she married Larpent "in perfect Confidence" and in April 1782 moved to live with him in Upper Grosvenor Street. In August, however, they moved to Hounslow, perhaps because Larpent (having married?) was "turned out of his employments" (as groom of the privy chamber?), and there was a consequent "diminution of Income." There was also, however, "an addition of Comfort, less confinement, [and] less worldly work," which Mrs. Larpent seems to have appreciated.

The Larpent manuscript diaries proper begin in 1790. By then the Larpents had taken a house in Newman Street and also owned a farm near Ashtead (close to Epsom, at that time about four hours' journey from London) where they spent many summer months and holidays. They were, despite Larpent's earlier loss of employments, a fairly wealthy family. Mrs. Larpent had doubtless contributed a sizeable dowry to her husband and probably had an independent income too. Larpent had his £400 a year as Examiner, his fees,[85] and he was also secretary to Lord Hertford, a post he had perhaps retained since they were in Ireland. The Larpents lived well. They had several domestic staff and on 23 April 1790 they entertained as many as seventy people in Newman Street. However, certain un-specified business interests of Larpent's caused a good deal of worry over a long period of time. In January 1796, for example, Larpent suffered "much anxiety about his paym^{ts} & various other cares," and Mrs. Larpent's time was "much taken up in rouzing his Spirits as he had a sad fit of nervous depression & many things to vex him." The financial difficulties continued: on 12 August 1796 Larpent "rec^d an unpleasant letter about money matters"; ten days later "M^r L's business not very pleasant"; in January 1797 "the circumstances of the times" were having an adverse effect on Larpent's financial situa-tion; and on 25 April 1797 Mrs. Larpent confesses that "The times have often embarrassed us" (although a year later when they were forced to reduce their domestic staff they were still able to keep a footman, coachman, and three maids). Relief came on 14 January 1799 when Larpent's brother-in-law, a Mr. Belson, died, and Lar-pent was given his position as clerk in the Privy Seal Office.[86] The improved circumstances enabled the family to take a new house in Charlotte Street, Bedford Square, where they moved in February/March 1799.

During the time of the financial difficulties, the Larpents led a relatively quiet social life. Friends were visited and received (especial-ly the Bowdler family)[87] and theaters were attended, but many eve-nings were spent at home with Larpent reading aloud to his wife, sister-in-law, and children. His interests were wide ranging—politics, travel, sermons, history, literature, and drama, as well as the regular newspapers and periodicals, made up his reading matter. Musical evenings were not uncommon and Larpent sang and played the violoncello. There was also much talk, often political. A frequent topic of conversation was, not unnaturally, the French Revolution. What Larpent thought about the initial stages of the Revolution is not apparent from his wife's diaries, but by 1792 he seems to have been out of sympathy with its leaders. On 12 September of that year Mrs. Larpent records that the "not to be parallelled cruelties" of the French "occupy all our thoughts and conversation," and the family "met to Breakfast to terrify each other with ye french news of the papers." Larpent was certainly sympathetic to some of the victims of the Revolution. On 21 September 1792, Mrs. Larpent's diary has the following entry:

Rose soon after 7. Rouzed by a Waggon full of french Priests—Seen from our Garden [in Ashtead], on the road—Mr Larpent went to them to the Alehouse where they stopt. There were 32. They came from the Duchy of Maine in Normandy, after suffering various persecutions, they landed at Shoreham, found their way to Horsham—There a Subscription was raised, & 7 guineas given to a waggoner, to carry them to London—M^r L offered them victuals, it was a fast day, they declined any—he gave them money, & a direction to Mr Wilmot who is of the Committee for their relief.

As secretary to Lord Hertford, Larpent was also involved from time to time in political pursuits in the borough of Orford, Suffolk. Hertford had acquired control of the borough in 1766 and the parliamentary seat was held by a member of the Seymour-Conway family until 1832.[88]

In June 1804, Larpent took his family to live in Putney; later (March 1811) they moved to East Sheen, Mortlake. At about this time Larpent began to suffer periodically from a painful affliction in his legs which, together with his increasing age, cut down on his social life. Visits to the theater became rare, but from time to time Larpent still had to travel into London to deal with his duties at the Privy Seal Office. The business of licensing plays, however, was dealt with at home. The manuscripts were kept there, rather than in the Lord Chamberlain's office, and Mrs. Larpent occasionally spent some time helping her husband to sort and arrange the burgeoning collection. The interest shown by Mrs. Larpent in undertaking this job typified her attitude toward her husband's work as Examiner. She had better things to read than most of the new plays that came for licensing, but when she was not taken up with Burke ("not a calm searcher of truth, but an able supporter of opinion"), Richardson or Scott (or her sermons) she would sometimes spend an evening reading and discussing a manuscript with Larpent. Indeed, her participation in the licensing of plays was often more active than her husband's, particularly when he was ill. She was almost certainly responsible for licensing most of the Italian operas, and on other occasions she seems to have read and approved new plays on Larpent's behalf. The title page of *The Virgin of the Sun* (LA 1868) is marked "Approved AML," and there were perhaps many other plays which were given official approval not by the Examiner, but by the Examiner's wife. Other informalities of this kind took place. Anna Margaretta's sister, Clara, sometimes gave a helping hand with the new plays. On 31 October 1792 she "red loud a new Farce called Hartford Bridge or yᵉ Skirts of yᵉ Camp" (LA 960), and on 10 April 1795 she did the same for *Love and Money* (LA 1066), "a stupid farce from Norwich." Even George, the Larpents' younger son, joined in. It was he who first read Joseph Holman's tragedy, *The Red-Cross Knights* (on 7 August 1799), a revised version of *The Robbers* which Larpent had previously refused to license. George was twelve years old at the time.[89]

It was never intended that plays submitted to the Examiner for licensing should be used for his family's private entertainment, but it is doubtful if anything was ever censored, let alone suppressed, by anyone other than Larpent. The impression one gets of him from his wife's comments is of a conscientious rather than a negligent Examiner. To take one example: on 8 December 1792 Larpent read the manuscript of Richard Cumberland's new piece, *Richard the Second*. Mrs. Larpent comments that "it appears Extremely unfit for representation at a time when yᵉ Country is full of Alarm, being the Story of Wat Tyler the killing of the Tax Gatherer & very ill Judged." Larpent agreed and decided to refuse it a license. He need then have done no more than communicate his decision to Thomas Harris, the Covent Garden manager who wanted to produce *Richard the Second*. Instead, on 11 December, Larpent left Ashtead to go to London to settle some business and to see Cumberland about his play. On the following day, as Mrs. Larpent puts it, "Mr Larpent had Mr Cumberland abt his play—A true Authors Agony. A curious *tete à tete*." What words were spoken when Examiner and playwright met we do not know; angry ones, perhaps. But the point is that Larpent had done considerably more than he need have done in personally explaining to Cumberland why *Richard the Second* could not be licensed. Three months later, a revised version of *Richard the Second*, called *The Armorer*, was licensed and it appeared at Covent Garden on 4 April 1793. *The Armorer* achieved only one benefit night for its author, but had Larpent been less considerate than he was, Cumberland would have been left with even less for his efforts.[90]

Indeed, despite the fact that the censorship inevitably caused difficulties and disappointments for authors and managers, Larpent seems to have possessed the tact and personality to keep on good terms with most of them. Naturally, and rightly, there were outbursts of anger from some playwrights against his authority, but even those whose plays were censored could speak kindly of him. Thomas Moore, who protested about the censorship of his opera *M.P.; or, The Blue Stocking* (1811), still took the opportunity of using the preface to thank the Examiner publicly for "the politeness and forbearance with which he attended to my remonstrances . . . ." And the Edinburgh theater administrator, W.H. Murray, in a more private communication, expressed his "heartfelt thanks for the many acts of kindness with which you honoured my late Father and myself."[91]

One can see from the later Larpent diaries that Larpent remained relatively tolerant and level headed in his attitude towards the plays he read, in contrast to his wife, who became increasingly censorious as she grew older. Many plays which he licensed were to her contemptible trash, or coarse, or disgusting, and some of the older

43

English playwrights, especially Beaumont and Fletcher and Congreve, she found unreadable; she tried *The Old Bachelor* on 20 January 1810 and felt "as if with people who frequent Brothels—the Morals are execrable." There was nothing especially unusual about an opinion like this in 1810 and Larpent was under severe pressure from many quarters to be more exacting in the cause of morality and virtue. One reviewer of James Kenney's comedy *The World!* found "above fifty blots" which he thought should have been expunged (phrases like, for example, "Heav'n knows" and "what damned effrontery").[92] Another writer urged the Examiner of Plays to an "increase of energy to purify the Stage from incidents, expressions, and allusions, offensive to modesty, and injurious to the principles of moral rectitude." There followed a stern reminder that "Whoever possesses a power of accomplishing a change of such moment to the interests of morality and virtue, cannot but be responsible for the use and for the neglect of it."[93] But fortunately Larpent retained a sense of proportion that some of his critics, and perhaps even his wife, lacked.[94]

The first play suppressed by George Colman when he became Examiner of Plays after Larpent's death was Sir Martin Arthur Shee's *Alasco*, which dealt with the partition of Poland. In the preface to the published play, Shee had this to say about Colman's predecessor:

> The office of Licenser of Plays had been, for many years, administered by its late possessor, with great good sense and discretion. Its powers, at all times obnoxious to a free people, were neither arrogantly displayed, nor vexatiously exercised. No complaints were excited by their severity, and no evils resulted from their relaxation. All, in short, was harmony and peace.[95]

Larpent, Shee continues, was a "respectable functionary," and the energies of the Examiner's office had been "long dormant." Shee's son had the same view of Larpent, the reluctant censor, whose "mild and benignant sway was unmarked by any severe or arbitrary exercise of his formidable authority . . . ."[96] But as Fowell and Palmer have pointed out,[97] Sir Martin and his son were in need of a foil to "emphasise the villainies" of Colman, and we have a right to doubt their impartiality.

It is difficult to establish a rounded picture of John Larpent even with the help of his wife's diaries, for though she wrote many volumes she really says very little about her "M͏ͬ L." But we know more than enough about his personal and professional life to recognize that Fowell and Palmer's description of him as "the lean and holy Censor" who "mercilessly castrated" the wit and fancy of playwrights is, as Mrs. Larpent said of *Pizarro*, more sound than sense.[98] Fowell and Palmer share the popular misconception that Larpent was a Methodist and that he allowed a Methodist distaste for the theater to influence his work as censor. It was Theodore Hook who first accused Larpent of Methodism in the preface to *Killing No Murder* (1809), parts of which were censored because they satirized the Methodists. Larpent thought the accusation libelous and wrote and told the Lord Chamberlain so (Larpent diary, 18 July 1809). There was nothing extreme about Larpent's religion; the old man (he was eighty-three) who died quietly at his home on 18 January 1824 was undistinguished by any kind of eccentricity. As a man he appears to have been of a quiet and kindly disposition, thoughtful and well read, and devoted to his family. As a censor he was, as later chapters of this book show, sometimes petty and overzealous. Most censors are. There have been more liberal censors than John Larpent, there have been more stringent censors; but few have matched the care and conscientiousness with which this moderate and retiring man conducted his unenviable job.[99]

The Censorship of Political Drama, 1737-1745

The purpose of the Stage Licensing Act of 1737 was political. By insisting that all new plays pass through the hands of the censor before their performance, Robert Walpole and his supporters hoped to put an end to the theatrical attacks on members and policies of his administration.[1] This much is commonplace. It is also generally recognized that for the two hundred and thirty-one years during which the censorship operated, political drama in Britain was kept under more or less firm control. But the question of how far the 1737 act fulfilled Walpole's immediate expectations is still of interest, for it raises matters important not only to the political and theatrical history of the last years of Walpole's ministry, but also to the whole development of political drama after the Licensing Act.

There are three quite distinct phases in the relationship between government and the theater between 1737 and the Jacobite rebellion of 1745, the event which induced a long period of almost complete political inertia in the theater. The first phase concerns the failure of the new legislation to control personal and political attacks on Walpole (1737-39); the second, the establishment of firm censorship (1739-42); and the third, following Walpole's resignation, the theater's withdrawal from party political affairs (1742-45).

CONTINUED CRITICISM OF WALPOLE, 1737-39

After the Licensing Act Fielding, we know, quickly ceased to be a theatrical thorn in Walpole's side, but there were others, less gifted, who were equally determined to harass the prime minister into resignation if they could. Despite the Licensing Act personal attacks on Walpole, pointed accusations of government corruption, and

47

rebuttals of major government policies were still to be heard on the London stage, particularly at Drury Lane, for nearly two years after the act came into force on 24 June 1737. One can hardly attribute this continued freedom to Walpole's benevolence. He wanted to bring the theater to heel, but it took him longer to do than he had hoped. Why was it that a new piece of legislation, constructed to stem the strong flow of political satire of the 1720s and 30s, at first seemed more like ill-fitting lockgates than the solid dam it was supposed to be?

First, some examples of antigovernment drama in the months following the Licensing Act. Such plays did not necessarily have to be new ones custom-made to attack Walpole. One of the shortcomings of the Licensing Act, from the government point of view, was that it required only that any *new* "interlude, tragedy, comedy, opera, play . . ." be submitted for licensing. Old ones (i.e. those written before the act was operative) could be performed without any reference to the Lord Chamberlain, and often it was not difficult for an audience to construe characters and speeches in an old play to apply to contemporary political events and personalities. Hence when Shakespeare's *Richard II* was revived at Covent Garden on 6 February 1738 (the first eighteenth-century performance of Shakespeare's original text) the play was soon given a political bias by the audience. Thomas Davies describes how one scene in particular was interpreted. Immediately after Richard leaves the stage to depart for Ireland (II.i) there is a discussion between Northumberland, Willoughby, and Ross in which the audience "applied almost every line that was spoken to the occurrences of the time, and to the measures and character of the ministry." When Northumberland, for example, said, "The king is not himself, but basely led / By flatterers," "the noise from the clapping of hands and clattering of sticks was loud and boisterous," and Ross's line, "The earl of Wiltshire hath the state in farm," "was immediately applied to Walpole, with the loudest shouts and huzzas I ever heard." But even louder cheers had greeted Northumberland's speech on the king's financial expenditure:

> War hath not wasted it; for warr'd he hath not . . .
> More hath he spent in peace than they [his ancestors] in war.[2]

48

The power held by Walpole over the king and the nation, and the failure of the king and the prime minister to respond to the popular demand for war with Spain were the causes of the audience's excitement on this occasion. Eighteen months later Walpole's peace policy was still intact and Fleetwood, manager of Drury Lane, seems to have deliberately chosen George Sewell's old tragedy, *Sir Walter Raleigh*, to allow the audience to show its opposition to the peace. The earl of Egmont was at the performance of 25 September 1739 and recorded the occasion in his diary:

I went with my wife to the play entitled 'Sir Walter Raleigh,' revived by the comedians on occasion of the now differences with Spain. They choose one to represent Count Gundemar, who in all things is like Mr. Giraldini, the Spanish minister at our Court lately recalled, and whenever any severe things were said which bore a resemblance to our ministry's transactions, or our backwardness to resent the insults of Spain, the audience clapped all over the house, to show they took the hint, and their aversion to the measures taken.[3]

So even if all political allusions in the new plays had been rigorously suppressed by the Examiner, political drama would not have been completely stifled. But for reasons suggested below a strict precensorship was not in fact enforced until the early months of 1739. The best example of a new and largely uncensored antigovernment play is James Thomson's tragedy, *Agamemnon*, which, although clearly intended as an attack on Walpole, was licensed for performance with only a few lines of the prologue suppressed.

Agamemnon was received in the Lord Chamberlain's office on 14 January 1738 (LA 4). The Examiner, William Chetwynd, or his deputy, Thomas Odell, would have found nothing very unusual in Thomson's treatment of the Agamemnon of Aeschylus, but whoever took the responsibility of licensing the play ought to have recognized that behind its classical respectability lay obvious and daring political allusion. Through the character of Egisthus Thomson aimed directly at Walpole, stressing both men's dishonourable pacifism and corrupt politics. There could be no mistaking whom Thomson had in mind when he has Agamemnon speak of

> those dust-licking, reptile, close,
> Insinuating, speckled, smooth Court-Serpents,

> That make it so unsafe, chiefly for Kings,
> To walk this weedy World.
>
> (II.v)

And we know that the audience did not miss the point of this, again from Agamemnon:

> But the most fruitful Source
> Of every Evil—O that I, in Thunder,
> Could sound it o'er the listning Earth to Kings!—
> Is Delegating Power to wicked Hands.
>
> (III.ii)

The speech, says Davies, was "greatly applauded."[4]

These speeches were passed over by the Examiner. The only lines to arouse his displeasure were the last six of the prologue, written by Thomson's friend, David Mallet. The prologue explains that the moral of the play is "Vice, in its first Approach, with care to shun," and concludes:

> *As such our fair Attempt, we hope to see*
> *Our Judges,—here at least,—from Influence free;*
> *One Place,—unbias'd yet by Party-Rage,—*
> *Where only Honour votes,—the British Stage.*
> *We ask for Justice, for Indulgence sue:*
> *Our last best Licence must proceed from you.*

The lines were "not allow'd by the Licenser to be spoken"[5] and are accordingly enclosed in inverted commas in most eighteenth-century editions of the play. Perhaps in the last line of the prologue the Examiner saw an allusion to the Licensing Act; and presumably he interpreted the other lines as offensive to government.[6] If he missed the party content of the play then doubtless the irony (intentional or not) of Mallet's description of a theater "unbias'd by Party-Rage" was lost on him. At any rate, in censoring the prologue and licensing the play he struck at the shadow and ignored the substance.

The censorship of part of his prologue to *Agamemnon* did not deter Mallet from adding his weight to the theatrical assault on the prime minister. His tragedy, *Mustapha*, was produced at Drury Lane (with a prologue, uncensored, by Thomson) on 13 February

1739. Its success (fourteen performances in its first season) was largely owing to its political content. The tragedy "was said to glance at the king and Sir Robert Walpole, in the characters of Solyman the Magnificent and Rustan his visier," and on the opening night "were assembled all the chiefs in opposition to the court; and many speeches were applied by the audience to the supposed grievances of the times, and to persons and characters."[7] The political implications are apparent from the first scene of *Mustapha*. Rustan, Emperor Solyman's chief political adviser, "supports / Th' imperial throne of earth's most potent Prince!" and the empress, who holds a "powerful mediation with the Sultan," considers Mustapha, their son, to be her "deadly foe." Moreover, Rustan admits that

> Whate'er I hold,
> Or grasp in distant hope, is hers [the empress'] alone.
> And, as my fairest fortunes, all my aims
> With hers are blended intimate and deep.
>
> (I.i)

The influence of Walpole and the queen over George II, the Prince of Wales' estrangement from his parents, and Walpole's closeness to Queen Caroline are all alluded to here. The empress and Rustan conspire to turn the Sultan against Mustapha and the prince is finally executed, but not before he gets in some solid opposition propaganda. For Mustapha,

> *the Caspian,*
> When terrible with tempest, is less fatal
> To the frail bark that plows it, than a court
> To innocence and worth,
>
> (II.i)

and Rustan he describes as "meanly cunning, cooly cruel, / Grown old in arts of treachery and ruin" (II. i). The audience delighted in such political contumely as once again Walpole smarted under the lash of the theatrical whip.[8]

At first it is difficult to understand how such political satire could continue to flourish in the face of legislation designed specifically to prevent it. A number of factors, some of them already mentioned in passing, have to be taken into account in explaining this.

Of great importance is the fact that Walpole, by 1738, was a very unpopular prime minister who was conducting a foreign policy deplored by large and influential sections of the population, particularly the trading interests. Ever since the Treaty of Utrecht in 1713 there had been conflict between British and Spanish merchants regarding trade in the Spanish West Indies. Throughout most of the 1730s the anti-Spanish feeling in the country ran high, but Walpole resisted the call for war, mainly because he feared retaliation from the powerful French.[9] Added to his unpopular pacifist policy was his reputation for holding on to power by a combination of flattery and bribery. Theater audiences, sharing the general mood of discontent, and eager to hear Walpole and his policies abused in the theater, could hardly be expected suddenly to adopt a nonpolitical attitude merely by virtue of the passing of the Licensing Act. Hence, as we have seen, they sought contemporary political comment even in old revived plays, including Shakespeare's. No censorship could have prevented this. Nothing short of closing the theaters altogether could have done so.

Another important factor promoting the anti-Walpole drama was the stand taken by Frederick, Prince of Wales. His public quarrels with his parents and his open dislike of Walpole had made him the natural leader of the opposition politicians and, mainly through the offices of the prince's personal secretary, George Lyttleton, literary figures who were likely to be useful propagandists were encouraged to seek his patronage. Such patronage was especially important to the dramatists. The coming of the Licensing Act had meant that a play judged offensive to government could be suppressed before its author had earned a penny from it. In such cases he had to rely on sales of the published text for his profits. These could be substantial, but a pension from the prince was a welcome form of security. Thus, the two most prominent opposition playwrights, Thomson and Mallet, each received an annual pension and also secured well-paid posts because of their association with the prince, Thomson as surveyor general of the Leeward Islands in 1744 (£300 p. a.) and Mallet as undersecretary to the prince himself in 1742 (£200 p. a.).[10]

But the prince's involvement in theatrical affairs went further than supplying pensions to playwrights. He took a close interest in the repertory of the patent theatres, particularly Drury Lane, and his specific orders were sometimes communicated to the managers. Thus round about the end of 1738 and the beginning of 1739 Fleetwood at Drury Lane found that he had four opposition tragedies on his hands,[11] and he was in a quandary as to the order in which they should appear. The prince made the decision for him. *Mustapha* was his choice.[12] In addition, of course, the prince frequently used his privilege of commanding performances, not only of the new opposition plays like *Mustapha* and *Agamemnon*, but also of well-established political plays like *Cato* and *The Beggar's Opera*. Nor was the prince unwilling to display his approval of opposition plays when he attended the theater. This had been his practice before the Licensing Act was passed and he continued it after 1737. Robert Dodsley's farce, *The King and the Miller of Mansfield*, was known as a satire on the court and when the prince attended a performance at Drury Lane on 5 February 1737 he was "much pleased and gave public approbation of it."[13] Fielding's *Eurydice Hiss'd*, an attack on Walpole and the Excise Bill, was similarly greeted.[14] Without backing of this sort from the prince, it is difficult to imagine that the theater could have been quite so openly hostile to Walpole as it was at this time.

But, of course, the Prince of Wales was not alone in wanting to perpetuate the political function of the theater. The opposition press, particularly the *Craftsman*, was eager to sustain the notion that drama could and should be involved in politics,[15] and in the 1730s and early 1740s there were willing playwrights enough (Thomson, Mallet, William Paterson, Henry Brooke, Aaron Hill, John Kelly) to keep this opposition hope alive—even if, like Thomson and Mallet, few of the playwrights had any pretentions to understand political argument.[16] Nor should the attitude of the theater managers towards political drama be overlooked. In the second half of the eighteenth century it was a well-established policy of most managers to keep party politics out of the theater. But both theater royal managers at the time of the Licensing Act—John Rich at Covent Garden and Charles Fleetwood at Drury Lane—evidently felt differently. Fleetwood, as we have seen, staged at least three opposition plays before 1740 and accepted others; Rich put on *Richard II* soon after the Licensing Act came into force and was prepared to produce other opposition pieces (Thomson's *Edward and Eleonora*, for example).

Like the opposition playwrights, however, commercial rather than political principle guided their policy, for it was clear that profit was to be made from political drama. No one knew that better than Rich, first director of *The Beggar's Opera*, although it was Fleetwood, as manager of the senior theater royal, who was usually given first refusal of the new opposition tragedies.

Such were the forces against which the Licensing Act was expected to stand—widespread and traditional hostility to Walpole and his policies, royal patronage of opposition playwrights, audience and managerial encouragement of political satire. Faced by these forces it is not altogether surprising that the new and untried legislation should at first fail to control criticism of government in the theater. So far as old plays were concerned, the censors' hands were tied, but their inexperience and uncertainty were shown by their failure to suppress blatant political satire in the new tragedies. The total banning of four plays between March 1739 and the end of Walpole's ministry shows, however, that once they had had time to assess the situation the censors acted decisively. From the moment that Henry Brooke's *Gustavus Vasa* secured its place in the history of drama as the first play to be refused a license under the Licensing Act, systematic and effective political censorship of new plays had arrived. Insofar as it refers to the period up to this moment, John Loftis' statement that there is no evidence to show that Walpole "attempted to stop the expression in drama of disagreement with his major policies"[17] is true; thereafter the man and his policies were well protected by the censors.

CRITICISM SILENCED, 1739-42

It was perhaps unfortunate for Henry Brooke that at the time his tragedy, *Gustavus Vasa*, was sent to the Examiner for licensing on 24 February 1739[18] the applause for Mallet's *Mustapha* was still regularly ringing out at Drury Lane at Walpole's expense. Almost certainly this caused a more careful scrutiny of the new play. By 17 March Brooke was complaining in the *Daily Post* that his play had neither been granted nor denied a license, but in later newspaper notices he says he received "a message from the *Lord Chamberlain* absolutely forbidding the Acting of his Play" on 16 March.[19]

In describing his reaction to the suppression of *Gustavus Vasa* in the printed text of the play (1739), Brooke set the tone for many future apologies for suppressed plays, a tone of innocence and bewilderment. Had anyone, he says, "among Hundreds who have perused the Manuscript, observed but a single Line that might inadvertently tend to Sedition or Immorality, I wou'd now be the last to publish it." He claims to have published the play to show the public he is not guilty of writing anything "of pernicious Influence in the Commonwealth." "*Patriotism*, or the *Love of Country*, is the great and single *Moral* which I had in view thro' this Play." Defenses of this sort become commonplace in such cases as the century progresses.

But for all his pains, Brooke surely failed to convince anyone that he was as politically naïve as he tried to appear. *Gustavus Vasa* concerns the efforts of Swedish patriots, led by their king, Gustavus, to rid their country of the invading Danes, led by Cristiern. The theme is, as Brooke says, the noble one of liberty and patriotism, the struggle against oppression. But, like *Agamemnon* and *Mustapha*, the political implications behind the historical façade are easily apparent. Consider, for example, the opening of the prologue:

> *BRITONS!* this night presents a state distress'd,
> Tho' brave yet vanquish'd, and, tho' great, oppress'd.
> Vice (rav'ning vulture) on her vitals prey'd,
> Her peers, her prelates, fell corruption sway'd:
> Their rights, for power, th' ambitious, weakly, sold,
> The wealthy, poorly, for superfluous gold;
> Hence wasting ills, hence sev'ring factions rose,
> And ope'd large entrance to invading foes:
> Truth, Justice, Honour, fled th' infected shore,
> For Freedom, sacred Freedom—was no more.[20]

It would have needed no great political acumen to see how accurately some of these words (to the opposition's way of thinking) applied to Britain under Walpole. The whole play is aimed at irresponsible and inhumane use of power, cruel and unlimited exploitation and domination of the ordinary citizen. Walpole himself appears unmistakably as Trollio, Cristiern's chief minister, scheming, vicious, and corrupt, while Gustavus, the savior of his country, could easily be equated with the Prince of Wales.

Few of its eighteenth-century readers could have doubted that *Gustavus Vasa* was written to attack and embarrass Walpole and his administration. But there was no unanimity on whether or not it should therefore have been suppressed. Sir John Hawkins was one man who, unconvinced by Brooke's disingenuous claims about his play, approved its prohibition,[21] as did (not surprisingly) the government newspaper, the *Daily Gazetteer*.[22] Charles Dibdin, who saw in Brooke's plays "a turbulent spirit of liberty," thought that this might "serve party purposes, but ought not to pervade theatrical productions," and so had no objection to the suppression.[23] Disagreement came from Johnson in his ironically titled *Complete Vindication of the Licensers of the Stage from the Malicious and Scandalous Aspersions of Mr. Brooke* (1739) and also from the many subscribers to the published play. The *Gentleman's Magazine* also launched a short campaign (in verse) against the suppression in its issues of March and May 1739. But generally the opportunity presented by the suppression of *Gustavus Vasa* for a serious and detailed debate on the principles of the Licensing Act was, unfortunately, passed by. Like other features of the whole affair, this precedent was, by and large, followed in future cases of suppression.

I have mentioned that some of the circumstances of the suppression of *Gustavus Vasa* established a pattern for future occasions of this sort. One final and important contribution made by Brooke to this pattern was that he immediately published his play, not only to defend himself in a preface, but also to give his supporters and the public generally the opportunity of making up the financial loss the author had incurred because of the suppression.[24] Some bought the play specifically to help the author, others, no doubt, simply yielded to the lure of forbidden fruit. A five-shilling subscription edition of *Gustavus Vasa* was issued at the end of April or the beginning of May 1739.[25] The subscribers included Lord Chesterfield (ten guineas), Dr. Johnson, Swift (ten books), and the earl of Marchmont (a prominent opponent of Walpole's 1733 Excise Bill, four books).[26] We can be sure that these gentlemen were acting largely from political motives in subscribing to *Gustavus Vasa*; others had less precise and less serious motives. Thomas Edwards wrote to Lewis Crusius on 8 June 1739 about the suppression of *Gustavus Vasa* and *Edward and Eleonora*: "Such a prohibition alone, as the people are now inclined, is enough to raise their curiosity and pique them into a subscription . . . ."[27] The history of censorship provides numerous instances attesting to the universal truth of this statement. Whatever the motives of the subscribers to *Gustavus Vasa*, Brooke prospered. A trade edition at one shilling and sixpence followed the subscription edition, and Brooke eventually earned between £800 and £1000 from his play.[28]

The second play to be suppressed under the Licensing Act was James Thomson's tragedy, *Edward and Eleonora*. John Rich sent it from Covent Garden to the Examiner's office on 23 February 1739, one day before *Gustavus Vasa* arrived there. Like Brooke's play, *Edward and Eleonora* was subjected to a long scrutiny and the decision to suppress it was not made until 26 March.[29]

Unlike Brooke, Thomson, when he published *Edward and Eleonora* (1739), did not include a preface claiming innocence of the "immoral or seditious" intentions that the *Daily Post*, for example (in its issue of 29 March 1739), assumed to be in the play. The printed text contains only a brief note about the suppression. But Thomson's subdued acceptance of the ban is understandable. His political associations with the opposition and the Prince of Wales were widely known, especially after the production of *Agamemnon*, and the dedication of *Edward and Eleonora* (and *Agamemnon*) to the Princess of Wales emphasized his loyalties.[30] Moreover, the political implications of *Edward and Eleonora* were barely disguised by Thomson; to have denied their existence would have been absurd. The play is set in Palestine. Edward, son of Henry III, is fighting a holy war against the Mohammedans, but is worried about domestic problems in England. Gloster, his chief adviser, urges him to return home to combat the evil and corruption which is engulfing the country. Edward is on the point of doing so when he is stabbed with a poisoned knife by an emissary from the enemy. The resulting efforts of his wife, Eleonora, to save him, and the effect of the incident on the war dominate the rest of the play. The corruption in English government and the eventual death of Henry become of secondary importance. Nonetheless, it is in the description and analysis of this corruption that we find the political allusions which caused the banning of the play.

We are fortunate in having the licensing copy of *Edward and Eleonora* to help us decide precisely what persuaded the Examiner to suppress it. It is doubtful, however, if the deletions in the manuscript tell the whole story. Only two speeches are in fact marked for omission. Both are in Act IV. The first is at the beginning of scene ii, when Archbishop Theald reads of King Henry's death:

> Awful HEAVEN!
> Great Ruler of the various Hearts of Man!
> Since thou hast rais'd me to conduct thy Church,
> Without the base Cabal too often practis'd . . . .

In the manuscript the last two lines are marked with a pencil cross in the margin, the reference to corruption in church government presumably being the cause. Then in scene viii seven lines are similarly marked. Edward, on hearing of the death of his father, is bitter about the way the king was misled and deluded by evil ministers:

> Is there a Curse on Human Kind so fell,
> So pestilent, at once, to Prince and People,
> As the base servile Vermin of a Court,
> Corrupt, corrupting Ministers and Favourites?
> How oft have such eat up the Widow's Morsel,
> The Peasant's Toil, the Merchant's far-sought Gain,
> And wanton'd in the Ruin of a Nation!

Walpole, of course, is the obvious target again, but there is more, much more, in the play which reflects on the political condition of the country under Walpole than was identified by the Examiner in the manuscript.

A hitherto unnoticed article in the *Gentleman's and London Magazine* (Dublin) for June 1762[31] claimed that Thomson deliberately inserted three long speeches, after he had finished the play, "in order to induce the Licenser to prohibit its representation: hoping thereby to render the new Stage-Act, and the Ministry that had procured it, more unpopular." There is no way of knowing whether this extraordinary, though not improbable, charge is true, but there can be no doubt that the speeches (some ninety lines) quoted in support of it were meant to apply to George II, Walpole, and the Prince of Wales (as Edward). The first is from I.i where Gloster advises Edward against continuing the war so that he may return to England which is "Exhausted, sunk; drain'd by ten thousand Arts / Of ministerial Rapine, endless Taxes;" where "evil Counsellors . . . Are gather'd round the Throne" and the king is trapped in the snares of "low corrupt insinuating Traitors." The second passage comes from II.ii where Gloster again urges Edward to save a nation "Robb'd of our antient Spirit, sunk in Baseness, / At home corrupted, and despis'd abroad," and the third passage is Edward's speech on the death of his father in IV.viii, including the seven censored lines quoted above.

By opposition standards these criticisms of the Walpole administration were necessary, accurate, and not especially abusive, but they undoubtedly caused the suppression of *Edward and Eleonora*, which was not performed until 18 March 1775, nearly thirty years after Thomson's death, when Thomas Hull adapted it for Covent Garden. And even then Hull chose to omit what he describes in a preface to the 1775 edition as the "exceptionable passages"— meaning those which the *Gentleman's and London Magazine* claimed Thomson wrote to provoke the suppression. Walpole was immune from criticism even in his grave.

The third play to be refused a license was William Paterson's tragedy *Arminius*. The license application was made by Fleetwood on 15 December 1739 (LA 17), but there is some uncertainty about when the decision to refuse it was made. According to a note on the manuscript the play was "forbid the 19th Jan.ry 1739/40." But the advertisement for the published play in the *Daily Post* of 11 January 1740 indicates that the Lord Chamberlain's prohibition order arrived at the theater on 4 January. The latter date would seem more probable, considering that the manuscript had by then been in the Examiner's hands for nearly three weeks.

The suppression of *Arminius* has produced a story almost as interesting as that concerning Thomson's alleged chicanery with *Edward and Eleonora*. *Biographia Dramatica* (2: 37) gives the standard version:

This play was intended for representation at Drury Lane; but the author, being unluckily acquainted with Mr. Thomson, used to write out fair copies of his friend's pieces for the stage or the press. It happened that the copy of *Edward and Eleonora*, which had been refused a license, was read by the *censor* from one in Mr. Paterson's hand-writing; and this circumstance alone occasioned the present performance sharing the like fate.

Patrick Murdoch gives the story a more histrionic bent:

no sooner had the *censor* cast his eyes on the hand-writing in which he had seen *Edward* and *Eleonora*, than he cried out, Away with it! and the author's profits were reduced to what his bookseller could afford for a tragedy in distress.[32]

This story has gained quite wide acceptance. Of modern writers on this period, Nicoll, Scouten, and Findlater do not question its validity. Loftis, however, finds the story "implausible," and McKillop, after comparing the Larpent manuscripts of *Arminius* and *Edward and Eleonora*, thinks it "unlikely that the two hands should be confused."[33] My own examination of the two manuscripts leads me to the same conclusion as McKillop, although as graphologists we differ. McKillop thinks that "The first three acts of *Arminius* are in one hand, the last two in another; the second hand is somewhat similar to that in which *Edward and Eleonora* is copied . . . ." To my eye, the handwriting of the *Arminius* manuscript does not change until after the first six speeches of the fourth act. Up to that point it is very different from the handwriting of the *Edward and Eleonora* manuscript (which is the same throughout). For the rest of the fourth act of *Arminius* the handwriting is still not very similar to that of *Edward and Eleonora*. The fifth act is in the original hand. The possibility of the Examiner's having taken the handwriting of the *Arminius* manuscript to be the same as that of the *Edward and Eleonora* manuscript is, I think, extremely remote. And if he had done so it would be difficult to explain why it took so long (from 15 December to at least 4 January) for the prohibition order to be made. The handwriting story was doubtless prompted by the healthy desire to make the censors look foolish, but in this case the folly perhaps lies elsewhere.

Having rejected the usual account of the suppression of *Arminius*, we have to look for an alternative—something no one has yet done.[34] But it is not hard to find. When Arthur Murphy published his *Arminius* in 1798 he quoted Tacitus on his hero:

Arminius was the Great Hero of Germany. TACITUS tells us, That "he fought with alternate vicissitudes of fortune: a man of warlike genius; and, beyond all question, the deliverer of Germany. He had not, like the Kings and Generals of a former day, the infancy of Rome to cope with; he had to struggle with a great and flourishing Empire: he attacked the Romans in the meridian of their glory; he stood at bay for a number of years with equivocal success, sometimes victorious, often defeated, but in the issue of the war, STILL UNCONQUERED."

In Paterson's play, Arminius' fight against Caesar is made more difficult by the apathy of some of his own people. Segestes, his rival, for example, has made peace with Rome. Arminius himself is captured by the enemy, but, after escaping, he leads his small army into a decisive battle against the Romans and defeats them, thus rescuing his country from foreign domination. According to Scouten, "Paterson's innocuous tragedy did not contain any political or satirical matter for contemporary application,"[35] but in fact the political element in *Arminius* is as intense as in any of the other opposition plays of this period. Consider the political situation at the end of 1739. Pressure on Walpole to declare war against Spain had finally forced him reluctantly to abandon his peace policy (in October). But the ensuing war was conducted with neither enthusiasm nor efficiency. Walpole's advisers (principally the duke of Newcastle) were but mediocre and Britain's early engagements with the Spaniards went badly. The war that had been declared "amidst the rejoicings of the mob, the ringing of bells, and the prince of Wales toasting the multitude from a city tavern,"[36] was not producing the glorious victories expected from the country's armies and navy. What was needed was a more vigorous, more determined, and more belligerent leadership from the hesitant and reluctant ministry. *Arminius*, in preaching the justice and glory of honorable war, was a forceful reminder of this, and as such potentially very embarrassing to the administration. But in addition to supporting and encouraging war Paterson also directly attacks Walpole. No audience in 1740 would have failed to equate Segestes, an abject lackey of a foreign power, devoid of patriotism and courage, with Robert Walpole. Arminius, complains Segestes,

> loads me with Reproaches for the Peace
> I have concluded—says I have betray'd
> The Freedom of my Country, yielded up
> The Glory of the *Germans*, and become
> A tame submissive Slave.
>
> (I.i)

Substitute "Britons" for "Germans" and we have Walpole to the opposition tee. And Arminius? Clearly the Prince of Wales, "His noble Worth and Valour, the Regard / He bears to Freedom and the publick Welfare, / All plead in his behalf" (I.i). Like Edward, he is destined to be his country's savior:

> 'Tis you, my Lord,—may the kind Gods protect you!
> 'Tis your victorious Arm that yet must save her!
> In you she hopes; on you she turns her Eyes;
> You from impending Slavery must redeem her;
> And make these Tyrants of the Earth to feel
> The Force of Freedom and insulted Virtue.
>
> (III.vi)

Arminius was obviously in the same category as *Gustavus Vasa* and *Edward and Eleonora*. It was not Paterson's handwriting, but his politics which damned *Arminius*.

John Kelly's play, *The Levee*, is very different from the other prohibited opposition plays of this period. A short farce, an attempt to make Walpole look silly as well as wicked, it must have come as a welcome relief to Fleetwood from the heavy tragedies that had been demanding his attention. There is no Larpent manuscript of *The Levee*, nor do we know any of the license-application details. It is from the title page of the first edition (1741) that we learn that the play was "Offer'd to, and accepted for Representation by the Master of the Old-House in *Drury-Lane*, but by the INSPECTOR of FARCES denied a Licence." No explanation of the suppression is offered, but there is no difficulty in finding the reason. The very first speech of the play alerts us to a political application. Gulph, porter to Lord Shuffle, offers this opinion: "WELL, the Slavery of being a great Man's Porter, is next to that of being a great Man: Nay, were it not for the Profits, either of these Posts wou'd be insupportable." Lord Shuffle, the "great Man," is, of course, Walpole and the political satire throughout *The Levee* is directed principally against his abuses of the prime minister's powers of patronage. A penniless but honest and intelligent young man, Brightwell, plans to attend Lord Shuffle's levee where he has reason to believe he might be granted some preferment. Cutwell, one of Brightwell's creditors, having more experience of political dealings ("Statesmen always write the Obligations they receive and the Promises they make on sand") is less optimistic. After a lengthy conversation in Act I Cutwell concludes that Brightwell is far too honest and uncorrupted to be of any use whatever to Lord Shuffle:

> And pray what Pretensions can you have to Merit? You, who make a conscience of lying; boggle at betraying a Friend; are averse to Bribery; want Humility to truckle to a Favourite of the Livery; despise a Cast-off Mistress, for a Help-Mate, and kick at pimping. Nay, with what Face can you attend a great Man's Levee thus disqualified?

At the levee itself, Lord Shuffle is seen to be totally indifferent to the hopes of those expecting favors, forgetful of the promises he has made on this account, arrogant in manner, and careless of forgotten promises. *The Levee* is an effective attack both on Walpole personally and on the system of political patronage which was open to so much abuse. And so it was suppressed.[37]

THE THEATER'S WITHDRAWAL FROM POLITICS, 1742-45

Robert Walpole resigned as prime minister in February 1742. By then the censorship had long since taken a firm enough grip on the drama to prevent the acting of new opposition plays.[38] Moreover, the new political circumstances after February 1742 took much of the impetus out of political satire. When Walpole fell, few radical changes were made in the administration, but one important one was the return of Lord Carteret as secretary of state. He took over the conduct of the country's foreign policy and stimulated a vigorous war effort. This answered one of the most persistent demands of the opposition. The changes in personalities and policies after February

63

1742 thus removed the two grievances most commonly expressed in opposition plays—Walpole himself and subservience to foreign powers.

After 1742 it was not found necessary to suppress a play for political reasons for another twenty years, and the English theater was not to be so politically involved as it was between 1737 and 1742 until the outbreak of the French Revolution when political censorship of the drama again became very active. By the time of Walpole's death in 1745 as calm a political atmosphere existed in the theater as at any time in the eighteenth century. Indeed, the changed political circumstances meant that plays which would have been considered as inspired by party politics before 1742 could, after this date, be viewed by everyone as wholesome patriotism. The best example of this is probably the masque, *Alfred*, written jointly by the leading opposition playwrights, Thomson and Mallet. This was first produced privately at the country home of the Prince of Wales in Cliveden, Buckinghamshire, on 1 August 1740. The masque portrays the struggles of King Alfred against the Danes who have invaded England. Familiar opposition sentiments appear:

> That prince who sees his country laid in ruins,
> His subjects perishing beneath the sword
> Of foreign rage; who sees and cannot save them,
> Is but supreme in misery!
>
> (I. ii)

The spirit of Queen Elizabeth rises to inspire Alfred:

> She . . . shall rouse *Britannia*'s naval soul,
> Shall greatly ravish, from insulting *Spain*,
> The world-commanding scepter of the deep.
>
> (II. iii)

This, in 1740, was good opposition incitement to pursue the war with greater determination and to look to the Prince of Wales as Britain's hope for the future. The ode, "Rule Britannia," in *Alfred*, now considered to be the apogee of patriotic exhortation, was in fact written as a piece of party political propaganda. After the private performance the prince was eager for *Alfred* to be produced publicly. Fleetwood accepted it and it reached the Examiner's office where it was, surprisingly, licensed (LA 27). But it was not actually put on at Drury Lane until 20 March 1745. By then its sentiments did not clash nearly so strongly with government policies and its production seems not to have caused any political stir.

By the time the 1745-46 theatrical season opened in London, politically controversial drama was simply not being acted, nor did anyone expect that it would be acted. The landing of Charles Edward, the Young Pretender, in Scotland in the summer of 1745 guaranteed that there would be no immediate revival of government criticism in the drama. The theaters, in response to the mood of the public, became staunch government mouthpieces. They remained so, with isolated exceptions, for the rest of the century. The flurry of serious party political drama written and acted in the period immediately following the Licensing Act, and the efforts of opposition groups to fan the flames of political drama, resulted from unique circumstances: unpopular government, cooperative theater managers and playwrights, enthusiastic audiences, powerful patronage, and uncertain censorship. From time to time during the rest of the century, some of these circumstances arose again. But the forces needed to promote strong opposition drama were never again united in the total way they were for a few years after 1737. When there were efforts made to use the drama as a means either of expressing views unacceptable to government or of criticizing individual ministers, a more wary and efficient censorship proved easily adequate in dealing with them.

The Censorship of Political Drama, 1745-1789

War, civil or foreign, has generally inclined English drama toward patriotism and chauvinism. The eighteenth century was no exception. The 1745 Jacobite rebellion, for example, prompted the writing of new plays[1] and the revival of old ones[2] to fortify the London theatergoers' conviction that the revolution of 1688 had produced a just and permanent political and religious settlement in Britain which ought not to be changed. Benjamin Victor wrote to Garrick on 10 October 1745:

The stage (at both houses) is the most *pious*, as as [sic] well as most *loyal*, in the three kingdoms. Twenty men appear at the end of every play, and one stepping forward from the rest, with uplifted hands and eyes, begin singing, to an old anthem tune, the following words—

> 'O Lord our God arise,
> Confound the enemies
> Of George our King;
> Send him victorious,
> Happy and glorious,
> Long to reign over us,
> God save the King.'[3]

The Seven Years' War and the almost perpetual hostile relations with France during the second half of the eighteenth century produced further displays of loyalty and patriotism, often appealing to audiences' crude prejudices against the traditional enemy. War, or the prospect of war, was the signal for a veritable deluge of patriotic plays, masques, ballads, songs, prologues, epilogues, and pantomimes.[4] It would be pointless to list them all. They range from full-length tragedies like Glover's *Boadicia* (Drury Lane, 1 December

67

1753) and Brown's *Athelstan* (Drury Lane, 27 February 1756) to jingoistic songs like "To Arms, to Arms" and "Britons Strike Home." Even Shakespeare's *Henry V*, frequently revived in the mid-century, was reduced to the same level of appeal, containing as it did "the Memorable battle of Agincourt, with the total overthrow of the French army" (a point invariably stressed in the playbills). Entertainments of a general patriotic tone, or ones written to celebrate specific victories of Britain or her allies, were common. The defeat of the French fleet off Cape Finisterre on 25 October 1747 produced an appropriate song and chorus at Drury Lane on 16 November 1747, and the Prussian victory at Rosbach ten years later was celebrated in a pantomime, *Harlequin's Frolic*, at the Little Theatre on 26 December 1757. Not surprisingly, the less cheering aspects of Britain's foreign policies—the serious ministerial disagreements about strategy during the Seven Years' War, especially between Pitt and Newcastle; abortive and damaging naval expeditions led by Byng, Hawke, and others; the widespread dissatisfaction with the terms of the Peace of Paris—were passed by in favor of maintaining a spirit of aggression against the enemy.

In other words, when the country was threatened by an external power or by insurrection, party politics took a back seat. As regards the theater, the period under discussion is quite normal in this respect. But where the post-1745 drama differs from that of earlier periods is in its relative isolation even from political disputes which did not directly affect the country's security. London's theatergoers constituted a politically sensitive and informed group of people, and the years 1745-89 were full of political controversy—the ministerial squabbles of the 60s, the Wilkes troubles, Junius, Irish problems, demands for social reform, and so on. Yet the acted drama scarcely took cognizance of these matters; it had parted company from politics.

There is no single consideration to explain why political comment so rarely entered the repertory of the mid- and late-eighteenth-century theater. Clearly the rapid decline of political satire after 1737 points to the Lord Chamberlain's censorship as an important factor. And so it was. The extent of the Lord Chamberlain's direct intervention in the drama's handling of political themes is discussed in detail below, but it is important to recognize that the barrier his office erected was not a single, isolated one. It was strengthened by others, less formidable perhaps than the official one, but by no means of negligible effect in denying the drama a significant political function. If the censorship was an effective external check on political drama, there were other checks from within the theater itself.

Thomson died in 1748; Brooke avoided political controversy after 1750; Mallet became a friend of government. Only Charles Macklin and, later, Thomas Holcroft, openly brought political satire into their plays during the second half of the eighteenth century. Most playwrights now left politics well alone. Often this must have been simply a matter of practical necessity; because of managerial and government censorship, political plays could not easily reach the stage. But with some playwrights there was a clear case of principle involved. Cibber's defense of political censorship in his *Apology* is well known.[5] Charles Dibdin was another who thought that "Licentiousness and its concommitant, sedition," should be kept "within their proper bounds" by an official censorship,[6] and Benjamin Victor and Joseph Cradock were two other playwrights who wanted politics kept out of drama.[7]

It is clear, too, that managers had grown wary of accepting anything that might prove politically controversial. They staged few such plays and, in addition, we know the opinion of managers like Sheridan, Wilkinson, and Foote on the subject of politics and the theater. Wilkinson states quite categorically in his *Memoirs* that political matter "certainly has not any connection or business within the walls of a theatre . . . ."[8] Foote refused, in July 1761, to include in his company's performance of Bentley's comedy, *The Wishes; or, Harlequin's Mouth Opened*, a prologue flattering Bute,[9] and Sheridan was as emphatic as Wilkinson when he wrote to Whitbread on the subject in 1815: "Keep politics out of the Theatre."[10] This was a view that Sheridan had long held. In a Commons debate on 3 December 1795 he said that a theater was "no fit place for politics" and he would not think much of "the principles or taste of the man who should wish to introduce them into stage representation."[11] The reasons behind the managerial veto on political drama were probably varied, but all managers must have been aware of the "inflammatory effect" (Sheridan's phrase, in his letter to Whitbread) that political or allegedly political plays could have on an audience. There was, for example, the famous 1754 riot

69

at the Smock-Alley theater in Dublin on 2 March during a performance of Miller's *Mahomet,* parts of which were interpreted as allusions to current political problems.[12]

In addition to the internal checks operated by the managers and the playwrights, the audiences also refused to tolerate certain kinds of political drama. Anything of an unpatriotic nature would certainly have met with a hostile reception, but no one was foolish enough either to write or stage such works. Also offensive to the audiences were ministerial propaganda plays. There were in reality hardly any genuine plays of this kind produced, or even written, but more than one play was damned because its author was known to be a favorite of the government. Although it achieved a dozen performances in the winter of 1763, Mallet's tragedy, *Elvira* (Drury Lane, 19 January 1763), was almost certainly denied greater success because of its unwelcome political associations. It was performed at about the time that the Seven Years' War was ended by the Treaty of Paris. The terms accepted by Bute's ministry were widely considered to be less advantageous to Britain than they could have been, and Bute was accused of paying too high a price for peace. In *Elvira*, the Portuguese king, Don Pedro, is a man of peace who shuns unnecessary war:

> . . . wars,
> Of mad ambition or of blind revenge,
> But shame the prince, and curse the land he rules.
>
> (II. iii)

These pacific sentiments, together with the fact that the author was a known friend of Bute, were seized on as evidence that the play was a piece of ministerial propaganda in support of Bute's peace policy, and it was, accordingly, opposed.[13] John Home's tragedy *The Fatal Discovery* (Drury Lane, 1769) and Hugh Kelly's comedy *A Word to the Wise* (Drury Lane, 1770) were also opposed because their authors were linked with the ministry.

But audience reaction to plays or speeches in plays reflecting *unfavorably* on government was a different matter. Since few such plays ever reached the stage it is difficult to be absolutely certain about this, but what evidence there is suggests that audiences still had a keen appetite for political satire. Despite the several factors limiting the audiences' opportunities for enjoying a laugh or jeer at the ministry's expense—and we shall have to add the Lord Chamberlain's censorship to those already described—there remained abroad enough of the spirit of Fielding's plays to set off a few sparks of excitement in the political nullity that was, by and large, the mid-eighteenth-century drama.

Two recent commentators have offered suggestions along these lines, but have not followed them up to any extent. Both George Winchester Stone, Jr. and James Lynch recall the "political and very Whig reaction"[14] still produced by *Cato*, wthout giving actual instances of such a reaction, and Lynch claims that "Frequent passages in new plays seem to allude to contemporary troubles in parliament and the ministry." He offers as an example Southampton's speech from Henry Jones's *The Earl of Essex* (Covent Garden, 21 February 1753),

> How ill had Providence
> Dispos'd the suffering world's opprest affairs,
> Had sacred right's eternal rule been left
> To crafty politicians' partial sway,
>
> (I. i)

but can only say that this "probably reminded the audience of the current factionalism in the cabinet during the ministry of Pelham . . . ."[15]

Perhaps it did, but we should try to be more precise. The evidence is not abundant, but we can improve a little on Stone and Lynch. We know, for example, that when, in December 1762, Miss Brent spoke the lines, "When Princes are oppressive in their Government, Subjects have a Right to assert their Liberty," the audience at Covent Garden, much to the regret of the *St. James's Chronicle*, burst into "very loud Applause." "We are sorry to see the Spirit of Party run so high," wrote the paper's drama critic (7-9 December 1762), and he was probably no happier when, a year later, the Covent Garden audience again demonstrated its political allegiance by taking up a line in that honored focal point of political protest, *The Beggar's Opera*. Soon after the earl of Sandwich had risen in the House of Lords on 15 November 1763 to produce and condemn John Wilkes' *Essay on Woman*, public contempt of his hypocritical behavior, boosted by popular enthusiasm for Wilkes, prompted loud cheers in

71

the theater when Macheath spoke the line, "That *Jemmy Twitcher* should peach me, I own surpriz'd me!" (III. xiv). Henceforth, says Walpole, "the nick-name of *Jemmy Twitcher* stuck by the Earl so as almost to occasion the disuse of his title."[16] Summer audiences at the Little Theatre in the Haymarket were equally ready to laugh at ministers. Sylas Neville records how the audience there on 22 July 1767 applied a line in Nahum Tate's farce, *A Duke and no Duke*, to the unstable ministry of Chatham, which was likely to collapse at any moment. Shuter, in the part of Trappolin, "made yᵉ house laugh" with his speech to Mago, the conjuror, in Act I: ". . . I should be glad to see you at Court. It may be the better for you, for as I take it, we shall have some change of Ministers, and so Farewel."[17] And even after it had been censored, Macklin's *The Man of The World* was still greeted as a political play. The *Morning Herald* reviewer wrote (11 May 1781) that the politics of the play "suited the taste of the audience," although he credited Macklin with being equally severe on opposition and government politicians alike.[18]

Incidents also occurred at Drury Lane in this period which showed that audiences did not cut themselves off from political affairs when they entered the theater. By the late 1760s John Wilkes's popularity had declined, and when Garrick, acting Hastings in *Jane Shore*, came to the passage in Act III where Hastings "laments the horrors of civil dissension, and execrates those sons of sedition who wish to renew the scene of desolation, the spirit with which he delivered himself, no less than the continued thunders of the plaudit it produced, gave offence to some overzealous *Patriots*, who, considering both as an intended reflection on Wilkes, hissed very violently." Wilkes, who was then in prison, wrote to Garrick warning him not to be so enthusiastic in the speech next time.[19] When *The Clandestine Marriage* was first performed at Drury Lane on 20 February 1766, there was, Cradock tells us, a political incident in the theater. When Canton, the Swiss servant, told Lord Ogleby in Act II that the newspapers contained nothing "but Anti-sejanus and Advertisements," several people immediately "jumped up in the pit, and pointing to a side-box, violently exclaimed, 'There he is, turn him out, turn him out, I say.'"[20] The man they were pointing at was the Reverend Dr. James Scott who wrote for the government under the name of "Anti-Sejanus."

The conclusion we should draw from the occurrence of political incidents at the London theaters is not that there was still a flourishing political drama in England between 1745 and 1789, but rather that theater audiences were as politically alive as ever. Audiences clearly did not need (and rarely got) a new political play to rouse them into political demonstrations. These demonstrations could be embarrassing and politically damaging to government, and it was the business of the Examiner of Plays to see that they were kept to a minimum. He could not control incidents which arose out of old plays, but he was supposed to make sure that nothing detrimental to government developed from new ones. In trying to keep politics and drama apart he had the support of most managers and playwrights, and, consequently, it was not often that he found it necessary to intervene. But there were occasions when direct action was required. As regards political plays, the Examiner's job was basically to prevent embarrassment and opposition to the British government from occurring in the theater. It is this motive which lies behind the limited amount of political censoring he was obliged to perform between 1745 and 1789.

The Seven Years' War produced the first known case of political censorship of the period. In 1762 an anonymous farce called *The Bourbon League* was suppressed after Priscilla Rich and John Beard had agreed to produce it at Covent Garden.[21] The suppression perhaps surprised the managers, for the farce contains a good deal of abuse and mockery of Britain's enemies and plenty of praise of British liberty, courage, and royalty. A typical piece of chauvinism, it seems.[22] But in addition to chauvinism, *The Bourbon League* posed, in its farcical way, some questions which the British government might have found it difficult to answer satisfactorily, questions about the presence of foreign spies in England, about inadequate civil defense and about the government's war policies.

Less than a year later a more serious and substantial play, William Shirley's tragedy *Electra*, was denied the Lord Chamberlain's license. Shirley finished writing *Electra* in the spring of 1745.[23] The story of the return of Orestes from exile to depose the unlawful king, Aegisthus, and achieve "a nation's rescue, / A tyrant's over-throw, / A King's revenge" (I. iii) had unmistakable parallels to

73

the Jacobite interpretation of the '45. Aegisthus, a tyrant and usurper, is opposed by the attractive and youthful Orestes (aged about twenty in Shirley's play; Charles was twenty-five at the time of the rebellion) who wins the support of a people sorely dissatisfied with its monarch. Aegisthus is overthrown, the rightful monarch is restored, and the people are contented again. No London theater manager in his senses would have touched such a play in the winter of 1745-46; no London audience would have tolerated it. It did not need much perception on Shirley's part to recognize this and, "from an apprehension that the subject . . . might be considered as invidious and offensive while the nation continued in so unhappy a situation," he wisely put his play to one side. Not until early in 1763 was Shirley able to persuade someone (John Beard at Covent Garden) to stage *Electra*. By this time, nearly seventeen years after the end of the Pretender's rebellion, Shirley must have felt that all political parallels which would have applied in 1745 would go unheeded. But the Lord Chamberlain and his advisers took a more cautious line, for "to the very great surprise of all persons who had ever seen it," *Electra* was refused a license. Shirley, astonished at the decision, protested that there was nothing in the play which could be judged exceptionable, but his "humble representation of truth" made no impression on the Lord Chamberlain, the duke of Marlborough. So Shirley took the usual course in such cases of preparing the play for publication, "in vindication of himself," as he says. Before the play went to press, however, the earl Gower replaced Marlborough as Lord Chamberlain and Shirley thought it worthwhile attempting a second application for a license. Gower proved no less resolute than his predecessor and the application again failed. Not unnaturally, Shirley wanted to know exactly why his play had been suppressed; his inquiry to the Lord Chamberlain received the blunt reply that "the office never assigned reasons for refusing the licence," and, of course, it was under no obligation to do so.

We can only speculate about the reasoning behind the suppression of *Electra* (presumably it was feared that Shirley's tragedy might give life to dormant Jacobite sympathies if it were performed),[24] but it is easier to unravel the motives of the Lord Chamberlain and his Examiner when considering the censorship of plays concerned with more immediate political issues than those raised by Shirley's play—

electoral and parliamentary reform, for example. The Examiner was hypersensitive about anything critical of Parliament or the parliamentary system. Consider, for example, his censorship in 1774 of a brief interlude called *The Election*, by Miles Peter Andrews, himself a member of Parliament in later years. Political disputes and controversies were naturally heightened in election years when radical policies and philosophies could be brought more immediately to public notice. The election of October 1774, although held at a critical juncture in England's relationship with her American colonies, was dominated more by the spread of radical domestic ideas than discussion of foreign policies.[25] The call for parliamentary reform, including the abolition of corrupt electioneering practices and the introduction of shorter parliaments, became a major issue during the election. *The Election*, set to music by François Barthélémon, concerns the reaction of an honest baker to the offer of a large bribe from a parliamentary candidate. At the risk of ruining an advantageous marriage proposal for his daughter, and against the advice of his wife, the baker refuses the bribe and votes for the man he thinks best suited to represent him in Parliament. The piece was sent for licensing on 15 October 1774 (LA 380) and was produced at Drury Lane on 19 October, but only after changes demanded by Edward Capell, the Deputy Examiner, had been made. In the licensing copy Capell carefully marked in red parentheses some verses of a song for omission. For good measure he also drew a diagonal red line through them. In the margin alongside the verses he wrote, "This was not in the Copy you shew'd me, nor should be in this (dele.)." The offending verses appear almost at the end of the interlude. They are sung by Trusty, the successful (and honest) candidate in the election, and originally read

> Thank ye for your Favour
> Each Article I'll sign
> Your Pleasure shall be mine
>
> I thank ye for your Favour
> Parliaments Triennial are better for the Nation
> So 'tis my Inclination
> To Shorten their Duration.

These were replaced by the less controversial

> I thank ye for your favour
> My self I resign
> Your pleasure shall be mine
>
> I thank you for your favour
> Thro' Life I will support the Nation
> Still bound by Inclination
> To this Noble Corporation.

The following January Capell found it necessary to write to Garrick to advise him that some lines in Bate Dudley's comic opera *The Rival Candidates* (Drury Lane, 1 February 1775) were improper, including references to members of Parliament as "powder'd Monkies in short Jackets,"[26] and it was doubtless also Capell who was behind the suppression of a song in J. Hough's musical drama, *Second Thought is Best*, performed at Drury Lane on 30 March 1778. The title page of the printed text (1778) tells us that it includes "the Song rejected by the Lord Chamberlain." The play contains several songs and none are marked as having been omitted from the performance, but it can only have been this, from Act I:

> The nation is in ruin, Sir,
> The nation is in ruin, Sir;
> I rave! I swear! Aghast I stare!
> To see such mischief brewing, Sir.
>
> II.
>
> The constitution is at stake,
> The constitution is at stake,
> The storm is near; I quake for fear!
> The pillars at their centre shake.
>
> III.
>
> For Britain's safety, night and day,
> For Britain's safety, night and day,
> I grieve, I pine, (such sorrow's mine)
> And sometimes fast, and sometimes pray.
>
> IV.
>
> Then let us loud our voices raise,

Then let us loud our voices raise,
And do our best, and leave the rest
To wiser heads, and better days.

The kind of criticism of Parliament and politicians we find in these inconsequential plays by Andrews, Dudley, Hough and others is but slight and Capell's interventions were as silly as they were irrelevant. But with Charles Macklin's *The Man of the World* we encounter much more serious political satire.

The Man of the World was submitted three times for a license before its performance was allowed.[27] On 2 August 1770 Samuel Foote submitted it from his Little Theatre and a license was refused (LA 311); over nine years later, on 4 December 1779, Harris sent a revised version from Covent Garden with the same result (LA 500); finally, in the spring of 1781, another revised version (LA 558) was submitted and a license was granted. The comedy appeared at Covent Garden on 10 May 1781, nearly eleven years after the original license application.

The source of the trouble throughout was the play's central character, the irascible, unscrupulous flatterer of the great, Sir Pertinax Macsycophant (Sir Hector Mackcrafty in the 1770 version). Macklin makes Sir Pertinax the apologist for all that is ill in British political life—insatiable greed for power and influence, corrupt electioneering practices, the lack of principle and integrity in politicians, the subordination of idealism to selfish pragmatism. In all three versions of the play, but especially in the 1770 one, the Scottish M.P.s (and the Scots generally) come under particular attack for their herdlike political unanimity. In addition to the politicians, the lawyers, clergy, and nobility are subjected to Macklin's hard-hitting, often bitter, satire. The satire was softened for the 1779 version, but it still contained a good deal of political comment which was bound to be judged offensive by the Examiner (now John Larpent). We have, for example, Sir Pertinax's son, Egerton, explaining why he will not actively support his father's Parliamentary friends:

Then, Sir, I must frankly tell you, that you work against my Nature,— You would connect me with Men I despise, would make me a devoted Slave to selfish leader's, who have no friendship but in Faction, no Merit but in corruption, nor Interest in any Measure but their own, and to such

Men I cannot submit.—for know, Sir, that the malignant ferment, which the venal Ambition of the times provokes in the heads and hearts of other Men, I detest.[28]

Given the strictness of the censorship at this time, it is not surprising that licenses were refused for the 1770 and 1779 versions of *The Man of the World*. It is surprising, however, that when the third and successful application was made in April or May of 1781 (there is no precise date on the manuscript) there still had not been any sweeping changes to remove politically controversial speeches. Indeed, some speeches which had actually been deleted by Larpent in the 1779 manuscript reappear in almost identical form in 1781 and are not marked for omission. In the 1779 manuscript, for example, Sir Pertinax describes to his son a typical scene at a court levee, with everyone pressing to catch the eye of the Minister and show by their sycophantic demeanours a willingness to obey his every command. The speech begins,

Zounds, Sir, d'ye not see what other's do! Gentle, and Simple!— Temporal, and Spiritual, Lords,—Member's,— Judges,—Generals, and Bishops? aw crooding, bustling, pushing foremost, intull the middle of the Circle; and there . . . .[29]

This was corrected by Larpent to exclude the Lords and the Members from the circle, but in the 1781 manuscript the correction is ignored and the original 1779 speech given. This is true of several other deleted passages in the two manuscripts. Now as MacMillan points out,[30] changes in the successive texts caused by the censorship (milder treatment of the Scots, fewer direct accusations of corruption in government) together with changes in the political situation which made some of the satire less immediate, dulled the cutting edge of *The Man of the World* considerably. But it is still remarkable that Larpent should have allowed some of the political content even of the diluted 1781 text to pass uncensored, especially since he had forbidden some of it less than two years earlier.

Nonetheless, Macklin's and Harris' persistence had been rewarded, and *The Man of the World* was a big success. Less determined men would have succumbed far sooner to the seemingly inevitable.

Finally, it is worth looking at the suppression of a play by John Logan, minister of the Church of Scotland, lecturer, essayist, poet, playwright, and manic depressive. In 1783 he offered to Thomas Harris his tragedy, *Runnamede.* Harris liked it and put it into rehearsal. But the license application was refused.[31]

The subject of Logan's play, as the title indicates, is the confrontation between King John and his subjects at Runnymede in 1215 and the signing of the Magna Carta. The first (1783) and subsequent editions of the play make no mention of its suppression in London, but the reasons for Larpent's veto are fairly obvious. The opening speech of the play certainly would not have pleased him. The archbishop of Canterbury addresses the rebellious barons:

> BARONS of England's realm, high Lords of parliament,
> Hereditary guardians of the kingdom!
> Your country calls you to her last defence.
> Our antient laws, our liberties, our lives
> May in a moment fall. Red o'er our heads
> The ruthless tyrant holds oppression's rod,
> Which, if not warded, by heroic hands,
> Will crush the British liberties for ever.
> Ourselves, our children, our posterity
> Are slaves or free from this decisive hour.
> For now the crisis of our fate is come,
> And England's in the scale.

The archbishop's speech sets the tone for a number of other statements of Britain's problems. The cause of all the trouble is the king, against whose arrogance and indifference to his subjects' complaints the barons are protesting. The doctrine of the limited power of the monarchy is forcibly preached in Act IV where King John confronts the rebels. The barons make their case clear. Britons, they say, have rights "Which never king did give, and never king / Can take away." The rights include "general suffrage," and "these great pillars, freedom of the mind, / Freedom of speech, and freedom of the pen" (Act IV). The king agrees to the demands, his forces join with those of the barons to repel the French army waiting to take advantage of civil war in Britain, and the Magna Carta is signed. All ends peacefully. Such is the political content of *Runnamede.* It takes up no more than a quarter of the play which has as its principal interest a conventional love theme. In fact in *Runnamede* Logan was offering the London theater nothing more than a sentimental love theme garnished with a spirit of liberty and justice such as any true Briton would have been proud to acclaim. Yet the play was banned.

Like others before him, Logan was an innocent victim of circumstance. What he would have called a play of fine patriotic sentiment, fully in accord with the British constitution and the beliefs and wishes of all Britons was, with some justification, deemed offensive and seditious in the prevailing circumstances of 1783. The decade had opened gloomily for His Majesty's ministers. On top of the American troubles had come Irish ones. War had meant unpopular extra taxation. There was a Wilkite revival in the south and a new energetic and organized growth of radicalism in the north. The Gordon rioters threatened to burn London to the ground, and George III himself was under strong verbal attack—"the influence of the Crown has increased, is increasing, and ought to be diminished," are the words we remember now (they were spoken by Dunning on 6 April 1780). North, beset with enormous domestic and foreign difficulties, resigned in the spring of 1782 and the government stability he had engineered since 1770 went with him. In 1783 the problem of the influence of the crown became particularly acute when the king openly encouraged opposition to Fox's India Bill. The issues raised in the political parts of *Runnamede*, then, were far from being dead ones. Reform, insurrection, the power and influence of the crown, even foreign invasion, were all matters of intense public interest. The king was convinced (in 1782) that chaos was threatening the country. He believed, says one modern historian, that "a revolutionary spirit was abroad and would, unless resisted, convulse England as it had New England."[32] In the event, he was wrong, although no one who had witnessed the Gordon riots could have doubted that, given the right encouragement and incentive, Londoners, at least, were prepared to destroy their city and themselves. It was John Logan's misfortune that *Runnamede* seemed to offer this encouragement.

The pettiness and injustice of much of the censorship described in this chapter are obvious, but it has to be admitted that the Examiners were sometimes tolerant of political comment, especially in times of relative political stability. Capell, for example, allowed Barry to speak a prologue at Covent Garden on 28 September 1750 which he might have rejected ten years later:

> When Vice or Folly over-runs a State
> Weak Politicians lay the blame on Fate.
> When Rulers useful subjects cease to prize,
> 'And damn for arts that caus'd themselves to rise:'
> When jealousies and fears possess the throne,
> And kings allow no merit—but their own,
> Can it be strange that men for flight prepare,
> And strive to raise a Colony elsewhere?
> This custom has prevail'd in every Age,
> And has been sometime practis'd on the Stage.[33]

It was also Capell who was the uncooperative Examiner when Bute wanted Macklin's *Love à la Mode* (Drury Lane, 12 December 1759) suppressed. Bute objected to the unfavorable portrayal of the Scotsman, Sir Archy Macsarcasm, and, says Horace Walpole, "tried to have the play prohibited," but to no avail.[34] Larpent seems to have been especially tolerant in the early 1780s. As we have seen, he licensed *The Man of the World* in 1781 and at the beginning of the same season a piece by Frederick Pilon called *The Humours of an Election* (Covent Garden, 19 October 1780) was allowed to make some surprisingly outspoken political points, especially about Scotsmen. A canvasser's advice to one of his helpers, for example, is, "Cry no bribery, no corruption, no hired mob; and if our party meet such opposition, cry, no Scotchmen, and it will do wonders." And this at a time when the king's ear was still commonly supposed to be open to Bute. Then in 1784 Larpent licensed the prologue to Pilon's farce, *Aerostation; or, The Templar's Stratagem* (Covent Garden, 29 October 1784). The prologue was such that it caused one gentleman in the box lobby at the theater to express his "astonishment that the minister should suffer the prologue (which contains several severe strokes on the late taxes) to be spoken!"[35]

However, as the end of the eighteenth century approached, the London stage could boast of little in the way of meaningful political drama. In 1787 Thomas Holcroft was practically alone in finding it "piteous, most piteous, that, not only the learned, but, the political world should treat the stage with neglect; nay, with contempt."[36] The Examiner's life, so far as politics was concerned, was a quiet one. But the events in Paris in the summer of 1789 provided a new political stimulus for the drama and John Larpent's uneventful routine was suddenly disturbed.

4

The Suppression of Political Comment on the Stage During the French Revolution and Napoleonic Wars

By the time of the French Revolution, the English government, through the Lord Chamberlain and his Examiner of Plays, had established firm control over the drama. The English theater took little or no part, therefore, in the intense debates and arguments about the great social and political upheavals that shook France in 1789 and, not long after, the whole of Europe. The censorship of plays which were sympathetic to French republicanism or which were in any way critical of British society or government was frequent and probably had widespread support among the British public, especially after the outbreak of war between France and England in 1793. But there remained a significant radical minority in England which, while free (for the most part) to voice its opinions elsewhere, was denied access to the theater. In England, unlike in France,[1] government leaders never attempted, so far as one can tell, to manipulate the theater for propaganda purposes by instructing theater managers what plays to produce, but there were those who argued, by implication at least, that government should make more effective use of the propaganda value of the theater. John Haggit, for example, author of the anti-republican play *Count de Villeroi* (published 1794, but never acted), recognized that the stage is "most powerfully calculated to influence the public mind," and "this honourable and useful part of its office," he says in his preface, is not being properly realized. The French have gained "an astonishing encrease of popularity to their cause" by judicious use of the theater, and the English ought to follow suit.

And follow suit the English did, without any prodding from the government. The playwrights of the 1790s and early 1800s gave their audiences every opportunity to applaud wildly the patriotic effusions and jibes at the hated *sans culottes* and their political successors. William Hazlitt attributed the paucity of social and political satire in the plays of the 90s to this propagandist character of the theater—"the 'horrors' of the French Revolution were, it seems, to become a Medusa's shield to screen every species of existing vice or folly from the glance even of ridicule, and to render them invulnerable and incorrigible."[2] It was unwise and unprofitable for any playwright to become associated, even remotely, with republicanism, and those who found themselves under such suspicion were usually vociferous in their denials. Mrs. Inchbald, for example, a friend of the French sympathizers William Godwin and Thomas Holcroft, was one playwright who found it necessary to defend her work against charges of republicanism. Her comedy *Every One Has His Fault* was acted at Covent Garden on 29 January 1793. Government newspapers (especially the *True Briton*) took great exception to some parts of the play, particularly to references to the high cost and scarcity of provisions in London, and Mrs. Inchbald felt obliged publicly to defend herself against the charge that the play contained "dangerous or seditious expressions . . . ."[3]

It is Holcroft, however, who provides the most revealing and most distressing example of the fate awaiting the dramatist tainted with republicanism. Holcroft's involvement in reform-minded political societies led to his being tried for high treason; his mildly political plays led to his being accused of republicanism. Of the former charge he was acquitted in court; of the latter he was convicted and condemned time and again by the massed juries of Drury Lane and Covent Garden theaters. Holcroft's attacks on aristocratic pride and arrogance; his ridicule of society's follies and corruptions; his pleas for humanitarian behavior in the world—all of these, while never approaching anything like a revolutionary fervor, or sowing any seeds of civil rebellion (the plays would not have been licensed had that been the case), nonetheless aroused strong and relentless disfavor from the theatrical public. The hostility to his work became so severe that his only hope of achieving an unprejudiced hearing for a new play was to present it anonymously. Holcroft himself describes his difficulties in his "Advertisement" to *Knave or Not?* (1798):

84

THE unrelenting opposition which the productions of the author of the present comedy have experienced for several years is well known. . . . Since the appearance of The Road to Ruin, his comedy of The Deserted Daughter only has escaped; and that, as he imagines, because it was not known on the night of its first performance by whom it was written. Love's Frailties, The Man of Ten Thousand, and Knave or Not? have sustained increasing marks of hostility: so that the efforts made to afford rational amusement to the public, emolument to the author, and improvement to morals, have been rendered feeble and almost ineffectual.

The wonder is that Holcroft continued to write plays at all. But audience opposition did eventually triumph and he left England in despair. On 26 February 1799 he wrote to the Commissioners for the Income Bill:

I have no income; that is, I have neither landed nor personal property, that brings me either rent or interest. My income has always been the produce of my labour; and that produce has been so reduced, by the animosity of party spirit, that I find myself obliged to sell my effects for the payment of my debts, that I may leave the kingdom till party spirit shall subside.[4]

Holcroft died in London, penniless, in 1809.

A good example of how sensitive some people had become to political comment which even remotely seemed to imply republican sympathies can be found in M. G. Lewis's *The Castle Spectre* (Drury Lane, 14 December 1797). Near the beginning of the third act Motley says that we all "spread our nets to catch something or other—and alas! when obtained, it seldom proves worth the trouble of taking. The Coquette fishes for hearts which are worthless; the Courtier, for titles which are absurd . . . ." Lewis gives a note at this point in the 1798 printed text of the play: "On the strength of this single sentence, it was boldly asserted on the morning after the first performance, that the whole Play was written to support the Cause of Equality; and that I said in it, all distinctions of rank ought to be abolished, and thought it extremely wrong for any persons to accept titles!"

The audience, then, successfully directed the playwrights' output in these years away from radically inclined plays toward what Frederick Reynolds called the "trumpery trap-claps" of patriotism.[5] But for those brave few writers prepared to defy the audience dictatorship, there were the other usual obstacles to overcome. Besides the Lord Chamberlain's censorship there was the theater managership. Regardless of his own political leanings, the manager was bound to be wary of accepting politically controversial plays, partly because of the likelihood of a hostile audience reaction and partly because he knew that in the more extreme cases there would be no hope of obtaining the Lord Chamberlain's license. It is difficult to say with any certainty in most cases why a manager rejected a particular play—there could be any of several reasons. But we do know that an opera called *Helvetic Liberty* was turned down by one of the managers in 1792 principally because of its political content. The anonymous author, who calls himself "a Kentish Bowman" on the title page of the printed text tells us of the affair in a postscript to his opera. He submitted it to an unnamed theater, "but in that paradise I found politics to be the forbidden fruit, lest the people's eyes should be opened and they become as gods knowing good and evil: in brief, my Piece was politely returned, with an assurance, that it was too much in favour of the liberties of the people, to obtain the Lord Chamberlain's licence for representation." If the bowman had been as familiar with the theater as he presumably was with the archery range, he would not have been quite so disappointed with the manager's decision. His opera is based on the story of William Tell and depicts him as a popular hero leading a just and successful rebellion against tyrannical government. There is an abundance of revolutionary sentiment and talk of the people's natural rights and liberties. Tell's philosophy of government, for example, is that "To rule, is but a compact 'twixt the people and the crown, the which to violate, or crown, or subject, should find equal punishment;" and he later advocates the extinction of all titles and privilege in society. The rebels' aim is to oppose the evils they have endured for so long "till we have broke the chains of despotism, and given the mortal wound to ruthless tyranny; so we shall renovate our natural rights, and bring the weal felicity." Tell and his followers are, of course, fighting against Austrian tyranny in Switzerland in the fifteenth century, but the allusions to what had happened in France and what might or ought to happen in England were obvious. Whoever the manager was who rejected *Helvetic Liberty*, he was certainly right in his prediction of the Lord Chamberlain's decision.[6]

The story of the Lord Chamberlain's direct interference in the drama of the Revolution and the Napoleonic wars begins in 1789, soon after the fall of the Bastille on 14 July. Throughout the summer of that year the minor theaters (Astley's, the Royal Circus, and Sadler's Wells) successfully exploited the immense public interest in the events in France with a series of spectacular extravaganzas, and Harris at Covent Garden and Kemble at Drury Lane hoped to emulate them when the winter season opened. But their plans were seriously disrupted by the censor.

Kemble came up with John St. John's *The Island of St. Marguerite*, an indifferent opera which would not win its author great literary fame, but was sure to attract attention on account of its topicality. The plot contained obvious allusions to the fall of the Bastille, and by choosing the famous and mysterious "Man in the Iron Mask" as the hero of the play[7] St. John reminded the public of the inhuman treatment some of its prisoners had undergone. The play ran into trouble with the Lord Chamberlain as soon as it was submitted for a license in mid-October 1789, and after some preliminary announcements and surmises in the press an advertisement (dated 30 November 1789) in the published text explained the problem:

The subject, however proper for the Stage, was not free from difficulties. The Author, as appears from his prologue, knows the value of liberty, and, consequently, could not withold his applause from a people struggling for a free constitution: but delicacy required that even the appearance of any thing that might be construed into an insult to a foreign country should be avoided. To steer through those opposite extremes seems to have been the design throughout the piece; and when the pruning hand of authority prescribed certain passages, the Author submitted chearfully, though in all probability more was lost in spirit, than gained in decency, by such corrections.

This explanation of the censorship of *The Island of St. Marguerite*—that some of it might be offensive to France—is partly true, but it does not give the complete story. The survival of two manuscripts of the opera in the Larpent Collection (LA 845 and 848) enables us to see the details of the censorship and so modify the account given to the public in 1789. The more interesting

87

manuscript is LA 845. This was the one originally sent to the Examiner of Plays and it shows the excisions made before a license was granted. (LA 848 is a fair copy of the censored and revised original.) When J. P. Collier read through LA 845 he concluded that *The Island of St. Marguerite* had been censored because of the "free sentiments it inculcates, considered dangerous in 1789."[8] We should regard this explanation of the censorship not as a contradiction but as a complement of the published explanation. Some of the changes required by Larpent do indeed show a fear of "free sentiments," but others can only be explained by accepting that there was a genuine desire not to upset the French. This, for October 1789, is a plausible enough explanation. England and France were still at peace; there were still vestiges of monarchical government in France; and London had a good many self-exiled French aristocrats in its midst who might return to power. The political position in France was still fluid; better not to gloat over her troubles, criticize the old system, or praise the new, until a definite course was clearly discernible. Such, perhaps, was Larpent's reasoning. At any rate, allusions to the fall of the Bastille and to the alleged inhumanity of the place were removed from the original text of the opera. Even the most casual references, such as the Commandant's in act one, scene two to "The general Confusion of the Town, which daily threatens to Attack my Castle" are deleted in the original text. Stronger stuff, like the following speech by the Commandant to Carline in defense of the treatment given "The Mask," also disappeared from the text: "This is Heaven, to what some Wretches Suffer in this Place—This Mask, has all the Luxuries of Life—others depriv'd of Light, and Air & Space to move their Weary Members turn & wreathe in Vain each harrass'd Sinew till convuls'd with Agonies too sharp to bear they gain a Temporary Torpor." Nor was it only the dialogue which was altered at the Examiner's direction. At the end of the manuscript the Commandant is led off to his execution. Two stage directions give explicit instructions for this. The first, immediately prior to the Commandant's final speech, is "Dead March"; the second, at the end of the speech, is "Ext Commandant to Execution, & Mob to Release the Mask & Carline." Both directions are deleted in LA 845 and no reference to an execution remains in LA 848 or the printed text. It would seem that the Commandant of the Island of St. Marguerite was allowed a happier fate on the boards of Drury Lane than his counterpart at the Bastille suffered in the streets of Paris.

The evidence from the deletions in LA 845 bears out the information given by *The Times* (5 and 7 November) and the printed play's "Advertisement" about the censorship of *The Island of St. Marguerite*. But what of Collier's explanation? It could be argued that the opera's allusions to the fall of the Bastille, with the scene of a popular uprising against authority, constitute the "free sentiments" mentioned by Collier. But Collier could have pointed to other deletions in the original text to support his interpretation of the censorship. At one point, for example, the allusions to the fall of the Bastille begin to lose their directness and take on a crusading tone of social and political reform in general. Toward the end of the opera the mob bursts into revolutionary song:

> Generous Hearts Assert your freedom
> > Vindicate the Rights of Men
> To Fame and Glory's Temple lead 'em
> > Never to return again
>
> Huzza! to Justice we appeal
> > And then this Castle's own
> Our peace we'll Stamp with freedoms Seal
> > And Liberty we'll crown
>
> We once was free shall we be Slaves
> > No we'll Sacrifice our Lives
> That Land alone which danger braves
> > Liberty once lost revives.

There is, of course, no doubt about the allusion in the second verse and it was doubtless intended by St. John to carry over into the other two verses. This in itself is probably sufficient to explain why in LA 845 all three verses are deleted and "To be omitted" is written alongside them in the margin. But there could well be, as Collier thought, another reason for the suppression of these verses. They have an obvious rabble-rousing quality which places them in quite a different category to the censored speeches of the Commandant. Given effective delivery—the right degree of controlled enthusiasm and emotion—the fervent appeal to Justice and Liberty could easily submerge the Bastille allusion beneath a wave of radical sentiment. The rhetorical question at the beginning of the third verse, with its emphatic answer providing a splendid opportunity for direct audience reaction, might have been especially provocative.

In LA 848 and the printed text (from which I quote) the following verses are substituted:

SONG. By an Officer.
Neighbours, friends, with bosoms glowing,
    Ever panting to be free,
Generous hearts, with zeal o'erflowing,
    Crown this day with liberty.

Chorus.   Then join the chorus, lads rejoice,
    The day is all our own;
Hark, to the call, tis Freedom's voice,
    And liberty we'll crown.

Thus shall we be great and glorious,
    Tyranny and torture cease;
Thus shall justice be victorious,
    Freedom, harmony, and peace.

Rights of Men and Slavery are gone; but Freedom and Liberty are still there and Tyranny has now entered. Not very much change from LA 845 in fact. If the new version was allowed by the Examiner it is a little surprising, but some subtle and not insignificant changes have been made. The original version was sung entirely by the mob. In the new version the mob sings only the middle verse, and that is perhaps the least effective in its potential emotional impact. Giving an officer the other two verses at once lessens the *rapport* between gallery and stage and gives an air of respectability to the sentiments expressed.

The allusions to events in France in *The Island of St. Marguerite*, although curtailed by censorship, still gave the piece a modest success—albeit negligible compared to that of the minor theater productions. At Covent Garden, however, Thomas Harris' efforts came to absolutely nothing.

"The Bastile business is entirely laid aside at Covent Garden Theatre," reported *The Times* on 17 November 1789. Why? The answer is given by Frederick Reynolds, the author of the new Bastille piece, in his *Life*. He confirms that a play called *The Bastille* (which has not survived) had been in rehearsal at Covent Garden and that it had been ready for production—"But, when the parts were studied, the scenery completed, and the music composed, the Lord Chamberlain refused his license."9 Reynolds was then asked by Harris if the expensive scenery they had prepared for *The Bastille* might not be used in an opera Reynolds was then writing, called *The Crusade*. Reynolds agreed and *The Crusade* was acted on 6 May 1790, but as it happened, only two of the Bastille scenes were actually used. Ironically, even *The Crusade*, a frivolous piece concerning the wars between the Christians and the Saracens, was censored. An exchange of letters between Larpent and the theater shows that a short passage containing the mildest of social and political satire was unacceptable to the Examiner.10

The suppression of the Bastille play was obviously a setback for Harris, but undeterred he immediately made new plans to profit from occurrences in Paris. Again, however, he was prevented by the Lord Chamberlain from carrying them out. The piece in question this time was a revival of Charles Dibdin's pantomime, *The Touchstone; or, Harlequin Traveller*. This had first been performed at Covent Garden on 4 January 1779, and it was Harris' intention to revive it in November 1789 with additions and alterations alluding to what was happening in France. In this way he perhaps hoped to gather some of the profits denied him by the suppression of *The Bastille*. We do not know who did the revisions for Harris but the manuscript text (LA 851, marked "Forbidden") is a gay celebration of recent events in France, with a good deal of colorful Parisian scenery and spectacle, a proportion of quieter reflection on the meaning of the Revolution, and a number of chauvinistic reminders that France was still a long way behind England's achievements. The chauvinism, of course, was quite acceptable to the Examiner, but a procession of the Three Estates, an appeal to England for sympathy, and a lengthy speech on freedom and liberty are all missing from the text eventually licensed (bound with the original in LA 851). When the pantomime appeared at Covent Garden on 30 November 1789 the special feature the notice in the papers drew attention to was "a Grand Spectacle, being a Representation of a Jubilee Procession of the Nobles, Clergy, and People at *Rome* [my italics]." No wonder it

91

mustered only three performances! (30 November; 3, 4 December.) Not only was it poorly presented as a spectacle—"in a very inferior stile to that of Sadler's Wells," said *The Times*—but who was interested in *Rome* in November 1789? With scenes of Paris and allusions to the recent events there Harris could reasonably have hoped for success from *The Touchstone*. But again he was disappointed.

It is also worth mentioning here that the provincial theaters were not exempt from the ban on references to events in Paris in 1789. The epilogue to Ann Yearsley's *Earl Goodwin*, performed in Bath in 1789 and later in Bristol, contained the following lines:

> *Lo! the poor Frenchman, long our nation's jest,*
> *Feels a new passion throbbing in his breast;*
> *From slavish, tyrant, priestly fetters free,*
> *For* VIVE LE ROI, *cries* VIVE LA LIBERTE!
> *And, daring now to* ACT, *as well as* FEEL,
> *Crushes the convent and the dread Bastile!*

A note in the published text (1791) indicates that "These six lines were omitted by command of the Lord Chamberlain." In the manuscript (LA 846) the lines are obliterated and "Out" is written alongside them in the margin.

The censorship of *The Touchstone*, as with *The Island of St. Marguerite* and Covent Garden's stillborn *Bastille*, was probably motivated as much by a diplomatic desire to protect the feelings of French aristocrats as a need to suppress the politically undesirable spectacle of the overthrow of established government. But as the republican position in France strengthened, and as relations between England and France's new régime deteriorated, the Examiner's sensitivity toward French feelings disappeared and his opposition to liberal political opinions hardened. In one sense this was an improvement in the position. In the latter months of 1789 there existed the anomalous position in which three minor theaters, specializing in mass crowd appeal, were free to put on very popular and lucrative shows, while the patent theaters were denied the same opportunities and rewards. It is true to say, in fact, that in 1789 the stages of the patent theaters were the only places in Britain where discussion and comment on the French Revolution were legally prohibited. But as the Revolution developed, comment on it was permitted and plays alluding to French affairs appeared frequently. The comment was, however, of a very limited nature, and all plays which reflected, directly or indirectly, on Britain's relationship with France or other European powers were very carefully scrutinized by the Examiner of Plays. Even such an antirevolutionary play as Edmund Eyre's tragedy *The Maid of Normandy; or, The Death of the Queen of France* could run into trouble. Why this play should have been suppressed as late as 1794 when (following the outbreak of war between England and France early in 1793) antirevolutionary plays were especially appreciated by the British government, is not altogether clear, but it seems to have been because the play was based partly on the suffering and execution of the French queen.[12]

As regards Britain's relationship with other European powers during the Revolutionary and Napoleonic wars, Larpent was exceedingly cautious, sometimes rightly so. For example, in November 1810 John Philip Kemble wanted to produce another play called *Gustavus Vasa* at Covent Garden. This was an alteration of William Dimond's *Hero of the North*, first staged at Drury Lane on 19 February 1803. The new version, probably prepared for production by Kemble himself, was originally to be called *Gustavus of Sweden* and was listed as such in Larpent's account book for 21 November 1810. But Larpent, having consulted the Home Secretary (Larpent diary, 21 November 1810), later insisted on a change of title and on several other alterations, apparently because it was feared that the play as submitted for licensing by Kemble might have an unfortunate influence on Britain's relationships with Sweden, which were delicately poised in 1810. Gustavus IV of Sweden had taken his country into an alliance with England against France, but he was deposed by an army coup in March 1809 and abdicated. His successor, Charles XIII, was friendly to England but he was forced to conclude treaties with England's enemies, Russia in 1809, and France in 1810. "This capitulation," we are told, "involved the entrance of Sweden into the Continental System, and consequently war between her and Great Britain; but the Admiralty privately instructed Vice-Admiral Sir James Saumarez, commander in the Baltic, to avoid hostile action; and the tactful manner in which he carried out this difficult duty rendered possible the resumption of friendly relations in 1811-12."[13] It is understandable that in these sensitive political cir-

93

cumstances the British government would not want to risk offending the new Swedish king by allowing public expressions of sympathy and support for the man his army had deposed. The "gallant" Gustavus arrived in England early in November 1810 (*Morning Chronicle*, 14 November 1810) and Kemble undoubtedly intended *Gustavus of Sweden* to be acted in honor of the ex-king's presence in the country. In the play (LA 1642) Gustavus is described as a "virtuous victim of a tyrant's hate," and his people are said to be "every where in arms; and let their loved Gustavus once more lead them on, will crush their tyrant and redeem his crown!" These and other similar passages were censored by Larpent before he would license the play. In addition, Larpent insisted that whenever Gustavus' name was mentioned "Vasa" should be added to it so that the play turned out to be about the famous Swedish hero of Henry Brooke's suppressed 1738 play rather than the deposed and exiled monarch.[14]

Larpent took care to protect the feelings of other friendly or neutral governments. In 1794 he censored those parts of John O'Keeffe's farce *Jenny's Whim; or, The Roasted Emperor* which poked fun at Morocco (neutral) and Spain (friendly),[15] and several years later he censored, rather needlessly, a play called *The Siege of Sarragossa; or, Spanish Patriots in 1808*. The play was intended to be produced at the Norwich theater and was submitted for a license by the manager, J. C. Hindes, on 18 January 1813 (LA 1756). Bound with the manuscript is a note from Hindes to Larpent, dated 1 February, indicating that the author of the play (probably George Bennett) agreed to the deletion of a passage in the first act where a French general offers protection to Spanish captives during the siege of Saragossa (which took place in 1808-09 during the Peninsular War). A Spaniard replies, with heavy irony,

> do we not behold
> The smiling nations of the continent,
> The rich possessors of that sacred boon
> Which only Frenchmen have the pow'r to grant
> In ease and luxury! with minds serene,
> Blessing the hour France gave protection to them:
> Nay—has not our dear Ferdinand—our King
> Found it in the Gaols of Bayonne French Protection.

Perhaps Larpent would not trust the audience to detect the irony; in any case he probably censored the speech because of the worry, however remote, of giving offense to subjugated allies of Britain.[16]

It was difficult, then, for playwrights to comment openly on any aspect of Britain's involvement in or conduct of the European war. One doubts if many people outside the Lord Chamberlain's office realized the extent to which the drama was restricted in this respect. On one occasion a member of Parliament asked the government if it was true that the Lord Chamberlain had ordered the Drury Lane company not to continue the recitation of a monody to the memory of Sir John Moore, commander of the unsuccessful Spanish campaign in 1808-09. Spencer Perceval, chancellor of the exchequer, replied in the Commons that he could "scarcely believe" this to be the case.[17] But Larpent's account book for February 1809 shows that the monody, written by M. G. Lewis, was indeed refused a license, although it was spoken twice at Drury Lane before the prohibition was enforced.[18]

It was natural enough that while affairs of great magnitude were being settled on the battlefields of Europe, domestic issues in England should receive less attention from government and public alike. Yet there were, of course, social and political problems of considerable importance facing England before the defeat of Napoleon—the slave trade, Parliamentary reform, Catholic emancipation, and a host of lesser but still controversial matters. With the notable exception of the slave trade, the drama hardly ever contributed to the debate on these problems. James Plumptre believed that the stage "had a very considerable part in influencing the public mind with respect to the state of the *Negroes*, and the infamous traffic of the *Slave-trade*,"[19] and a number of plays, including James Cobb's *Paul and Virginia* (Covent Garden, 1800), the pantomime *Furibond; or, Harlequin Negro* (Drury Lane, 1807), George Colman's *The Africans* (Little Theatre, Haymarket, 1808), and Thomas Morton's *The Slave* (Covent Garden, 1816), took a liberal line on slavery, unhindered by authority. But plays which touched on other political and social matters were not treated so leniently, particularly plays like Richard Cumberland's *Richard the Second* and Joseph Holman's *The Robbers*, both of which seemed to offer encouragement to subversive social philosophies.

Cumberland's opera was sent to John Larpent on 8 December

1792 and was refused a license (LA 963). Some three months later, on 16 March 1793, after the author had made substantial alterations, it was submitted again, this time under the new title of *The Armorer*, and was granted a license (LA 976). *The Armorer* appeared at Covent Garden on 4 April and ran for only three nights. The songs and choruses of this production were published in the same year.

So much for the bare facts. The suppression of *Richard the Second* raised Genest to one of his infrequent outbursts of anger against the Examiner. Genest had not seen the manuscript of the play and so had to admit that it was "impossible to say positively that there was nothing exceptionable in it," but he was certain that "no one but a dog in office could suspect Cumberland of writing any thing of a bad political tendency" (7: 103). It is a pity that Genest chose this occasion to get so abusive, for it is perfectly understandable, given the climate of crisis at the end of 1792, with a French war imminent, that Cumberland's opera should have been suppressed.

Richard the Second has nothing to do with Shakespeare's play of that name. It is concerned with the Peasants' Revolt led by Wat Tyler in 1381, a subject bound to arouse heated emotions in England in December 1792. Cumberland's version of the rebellion is generally more reactionary than republican in tone. The part of the plot concerning the rebellion (there is a conventional love theme as a subplot) shows the rebels to be foolish, violent, unprincipled villains with only Tyler himself and a character called Jerry Furnace emerging with any credit. Furnace, a peace-loving blacksmith (the armorer of the revised opera), has joined the rebellion more out of necessity than inclination, having murdered a tax collector who had insulted and threatened to carry off his daughter.[20] With the exception of this tax collector, the king and his supporters are generous and courageous. Richard himself displays impressive courage in facing the rebels at the end of the play and commendable humanity in pardoning Furnace for his crime. What we do *not* get from Cumberland is a sympathetic presentation of the peasants' reasonable demands (such as we get in Southey's unacted *Wat Tyler*) or an account of the treacherous behavior of the Court in revoking promises made to the peasants and executing many of them without trial. But granting that Cumberland's version is hardly favorable to the rebels, objections

96

from the Examiner were still inevitable. *Richard the Second* showed the willful murder of a government tax collector carrying out his lawful duties; it depicted a popular uprising against established government; and it presented a people dissatisfied with their king. In addition, much of the dialogue was bound to smack of treason to patriotic Englishmen with a wary eye on the events in France. One of the rebels' songs is as follows:

> Let us march, let us march, let confusion arise,
> Sound forth our triumphs, and shout to the Skies:
> Our gallant Wat Tyler, and brave Captain Straw
> Set us free from our Taxes & order & Law;
> And when war is awaken'd, destruction's the word,
> And our march shall be trac'd by fire, famine & Sword.

The prudent wife of a would-be rebel tells him to take care over what he says. "Why we pay tax for our heads, don't we? Surely then we may use our tongues at free cost" is the curt reply; the tax collector is told by the local priest that he is good for nothing "but to extort the filthy wages of Mammon, to whom thou art an hireling"; Jack Straw defends the murders he has committed: "I can safely swear I never took off any head, that did not look like an Attorneys." Such dialogue was hardly likely to meet with Larpent's approval, and although Cumberland had no intention of creating sympathy for the political aims and behavior of the rebels, his opera was still refused a license.

After *Richard the Second* had been refused a license there was a long delay before it was rewritten to the Examiner's satisfaction. When *The Armorer* finally appeared at the beginning of April 1793, it was a very different play from its original—and a much inferior play, too. The manuscript text shows more fully than the printed songs and choruses the changes Cumberland was forced to make. The main plot concerning the rebellion is dropped altogether. Wat Tyler is no longer a character in the play, nor is his name ever mentioned. Jerry Furnace is still there, and he still murders. But the victim's rank is reduced from tax collector to procurer; he still wants to abduct the beautiful Rosamund, but it has nothing to do now with evading taxes. His master, the earl of Suffolk, wants to enjoy her company, with or without her consent. Thus the political implica-

97

tions of Jerry's crime are removed, and, in addition, his behavior after the murder changes. In *Richard the Second* he flees from the law to join the rebels; in *The Armorer* he stays to face his trial: "Let come what will, the laws of my Country, & the authority of my King shall neither be evaded, nor opposed by me." *Richard the Second* is a political play; *The Armorer* is not. *The Armorer* relies entirely on its original's subplot, and this was good enough to hold an audience for only three nights.

An altogether more original, powerful, and memorable kind of social comment than that in *Richard the Second* is found in Friedrich Schiller's *Die Räuber* (1781), Joseph Holman's English translation of which was banned from the London stage. English enthusiasm for German dramatic literature at the end of the eighteenth century was considerable; Coleridge, it is well known, was ecstatic about *Die Räuber*.[21] But although the first English translation of Schiller's play appeared in 1792 (by Alexander Tytler), no attempt to stage it appears to have been made until Holman took his version to one of the London theaters, probably as late as 1799. In some prefatory comments to *The Red-Cross Knights* (1799), his later and acted adaptation of *Die Räuber*, Holman gives some information about the suppression of his original translation. But he never published the translation, nor has the manuscript survived. The absence of a text thus makes it difficult to discover precisely what was deemed objectionable in it. Fortunately, however, a letter written by Holman about *The Robbers* (obviously to Larpent) reveals something of the reasons for the suppression. The autograph letter, now in the Folger Shakespeare Library, is dated 29 March [1799] and is worth quoting at length, not only because it helps explain the suppression of *The Robbers*, but also because it provides a good example of the humiliating position playwrights were constantly in vis-à-vis the Examiner:

On examining the Robbers I find the doctrine of predestination will with the omission of a very few lines, be totally excluded.

On the character of Francis which you deem objectionable, I have one observation to offer: that the Author has invariably exhibited him an object of destestation [*sic*]. Unlike Richard 3d Iago and characters of a similar nature, he is drawn without courage, or any one point, that can render him, for an instant, capable of inspiring a sensation but of abhorrence.

98

In the character of the elder Brother Charles de Moor, the Author has sketched a picture of morality to accord with the purest ethics. In him we see every trait of character, which commands admiration, when devoted to a good cause, become a torment to the possessor, when perverted from the proper channel.

Humbly conceiving that no objection will be assigned against the play on the general scale, I hope I may be favoured with so much indulgence, a[nd] to be permitted to remove, or new shape any passages, that may be deemed improper.

The great celebrity of the play makes the permission of presenting it to the public . . . an object of very material consequen[ce] to my interest and being thus circums[tanced?] will I hope procure me your pardon for the liberty I take and the trouble I gi[ve] you. . . .[22]

If the characters of Francis and Charles in Holman's play were anything like those in Tytler's translation of *Die Räuber*—which seems not unlikely since both writers were, after all, translating the same play—then Larpent's reservations about them are under-standable. In *The Robbers* (set in Germany at the beginning of the sixteenth century) Charles, the hero, is fighting in a civil war. As peace is declared he receives a letter from his deceitful brother, Francis, telling him that he (Charles) has been disowned by his father. Charles's despair at the news drives him to a life of robbery and murder—he becomes the leader of a ruthless gang of robbers. However, his love for his father and for his mistress takes him back home. He eventually discovers the treachery of Francis, which in-cludes imprisoning and attempting to starve his father to death, and duly punishes him. But there is to be no happy ending. The father dies, and Charles's guilt for the crimes he has committed is such that he can neither resume his life with his followers nor accept a happy domestic future. So he makes two final decisions: one, after some puzzling amateur psychologizing, is to stab his mistress to death, and the other is to surrender himself to the state to be punished for his many crimes.

Charles is the more important and more interesting of the brothers. Apart from being courageous and patriotic in war, and a devoted and faithful son and lover, he is also something of a rebel and potential reformer. Even before he is deceived by his brother he ex-presses discontent with the general state of society: "What a damn'd

99

inequality in the lot of mankind!—While the gold lies useless in the mouldy coffer of the miser, the leaden hand of poverty checks the daring flight of youth, and chills the fire of enterprise" (Tytler, Act I). The discontent becomes less specific but more passionate when he receives his brother's letter: "Oh! that I could blow the trumpet of rebellion through all nature, and summon heaven, earth, and seas, to war against this savage race!" (Act I). And more: "Ha! where is he that will put a sword in my hand, to extinguish with one mortal blow this viperous race! that will teach me where to strike, that I might destroy the germ of existence!" (Act I). Charles's misanthropy progresses from the reflective to the active when he accepts the leadership of the newly formed band of robbers which proceeds to kill and destroy with a callousness and ruthlessness allowing of no compassion or mercy. In one episode, in order to free a captured colleague, they set fire to a town and eighty-three of its citizens burn to death. The sizzling of the flesh is music to the ears of one of the band:

Ay, the devil burn 'em! a few sick wretches too—women in labour, perhaps, or just at the downlying.—Ha! ha! in passing one of those little barracks, I heard some squalling—I peep'd in, and what do you think it was? a child, a stout little rogue, that lay on the floor beneath a table, and the fire just catching it!—Poor little fellow, said I, you are starving for cold there—and so I chuck'd him into the fire!   (Act II)

In this and other campaigns, Charles gives his support and leadership. But his intelligence and his social conscience take him beyond the goal of personal gain pursued by his men. The parallel to the Robin Hood approach to crime is obvious in the following speech, although Robin was never as ruthless as this:

This ruby I drew from the finger of a minister whom I cut down at the chace, at his prince's feet. He had built his fortune on the miseries of his fellow-creatures, and his elevation was mark'd by the tears of the fatherless and the widow.—This diamond I took from a treasurer-general, who made a traffic of offices of trust, and sold honours, the rewards of merit, to the highest bidder.—This Cornelian I wear in honour of a priest whom I strangled with my own hand, for his most pious and passionate lamentation over the fall of the Inquisition.   (Act II)

If this is the kind of dialogue Larpent met in Holman's play it must have come as something of a shock to him. He had certainly never come across anything quite like it before in his capacity of Examiner of Plays. Such violent misanthropy, such vicious antisocial behavior and such fierce emotion, although not directly linked with the events in France or calls for social or Parliamentary reform at home, must have seemed to him to embody the spirit and mood of the Revolution. At the end of the play, as Charles leaves the robbers, he tells them: "Go, and devote what yet remains of life to mankind's service, to your country's cause. Go serve *that* generous nation which wages war to vindicate the rights of man!" (Act V). There can be no doubt what Larpent would have thought of that!

That the character of Schiller's hero also worried Larpent and the Lord Chamberlain we can infer not only from Holman's letter to Larpent quoted above, but also from Holman's "Advertisement" to *The Red-Cross Knights*, the play which took the place of *The Robbers*. Holman was at first puzzled by the decision to refuse *The Robbers* a license. He was aware, he says, of "an objection which has been made to CHARLES DE MOOR," that "the grandeur of his character renders him more likely to excite imitation than abhorrence," but he initially rejected this criticism as unfounded. Then he gave the matter more thought and soon "found much to justify the licenser's decision." And so he wrote *The Red-Cross Knights*, performed at the Little Theatre in the Haymarket on 21 August 1799. Charles, fighting in a civil war in Germany, becomes Ferdinand, suppressing a rebellion in Spain. Like Charles, Ferdinand is deceived by a false brother (but only a step-brother this time), and there remains a mistress at home. But the bulk of the play, concerning Ferdinand's activities while he believes he is a disinherited son, changes drastically. Ferdinand's distress leads him not into the criminal course taken by Charles, but into a holy war against the Spanish Moors. And the events on Ferdinand's return home are far happier than those experienced and engineered by Charles. The new play, thought Mrs. Larpent after reading the manuscript on 7 August 1799, was "a ludicrous farrago made out of the Robbers" (Larpent MS diary).

In her "Preface to the Plays" in *Poems and Plays* (1799), Mrs. Jane West, novelist, poet, and unsuccessful playwright, sets out in no uncertain terms her complaints against the German drama—"these audacious blasphemies against our Maker, these libels upon all governments, these pasquinades upon the moral virtues, these denunciations of every Christian excellence, these institutes of every vice . . . ." German plays are "demons and monsters of philosophism," and she asks that "our rulers, in their care for the security of the body politic, carefully watch against the introduction of that seed of immorality which generally ripens into anarchy, sedition, and every public ill."[23] Larpent agreed and obliged.

The Examiner must also have detected an element of subversiveness in several plays of this period which strove to criticize England's aristocracy. One such play which he suppressed, quite unjustly, was Lady Eglantine Wallace's mildly satirical comedy, *The Whim*, which she hoped to produce at Margate in the summer of 1795. According to her *DNB* biographer (J. K. Laughton), Lady Wallace, a colorful and controversial figure, left England for Europe in disgust when *The Whim* was banned,[24] and she does not appear to have made any effort to rewrite the play to meet the Examiner's objections. The play is based on the story of the Feast of Saturnalia. Lord Crotchett, a scholarly recluse, longs for a revival of the justice and honesty of Athens and Rome. To express his admiration for the Ancients he decides to give his own Saturnalian Feast. This is his "whim." His servants are made the masters of the household for the day and he obeys all their orders. Given this freedom, the servants allow full rein to their opinions of the aristocracy. Apart from the comedy resulting from the reversal of the characters' normal social roles, the action of the play is provided by efforts to resolve a conventional father-daughter disagreement about a suitable husband for the daughter, Julia. All this amounted to, thought the editors of *Biographia Dramatica*, was "a strange jumble . . . of nonsense and vulgarity" (3: 401), but some of the dialogue of *The Whim* retains a briskness and pointedness which can still hold our attention and the plot and motive of the play are unusual and provocative enough to have deserved as much success as many of the other applauded pieces of the time.

The most substantial discussion and explanation of the suppression of *The Whim* is provided by Lady Wallace herself. One of the few playwrights of her time to get really annoyed about censorship, she prefaced the published text of the play with a lengthy "Address to the

London Sept.r 7th 1795.

The Whim a Comedy, for the
use of the Theatre Royal
    at Margate.

        Tho.s Shaw — Proprietor &
a Manager.

Intended to be perform'd there, with all
convenient speed.

Prohibited from being acted.

Public, upon the Arbitrary and Unjust Aspersion of the Licenser against its Political Sentiments," and the title page indicated that the play was "Offered to be Acted for the Benefit of the Hospital and Poor of the Isle of Thanet, but Refused the Royal Licence." The Address ranges from a defense of her play and her motives in writing it, through a defense of the social utility of the drama, to an attack on the misguided system which allows complete freedom to the press but which enforces the censorship of plays. It is a vigorous yet controlled onslaught on John Larpent and the system he operated. Lady Wallace also quotes the text of a long letter she wrote to the Lord Chamberlain, Lord Salisbury, about the suppression of her play. In the letter she raises the possibility that Larpent might have taken exception to an uncomplimentary allusion in Act II to Lady Jersey, mistress of the Prince of Wales (Genest, 10: 202 attaches much importance to this) and so banned the play; or perhaps, she increduously suggests, some ridicule of "our late faithless allies" (Prussia, Holland, and Spain) prompted the veto. But the deletions in the licensing manuscript support neither of these contentions. As Lady Wallace's later comments in her Address reveal, the most important, perhaps the only, reason for the suppression of *The Whim* was the satirical treatment of England's ruling classes.

Of the thirty-four passages which Larpent marked for omission in *The Whim*, all but a few reflect directly and unfavorably on aristocracy, nobility, and even royalty. The rest express radical political opinions on foreign and domestic issues. The ruling classes are accused by the servants in *The Whim* of licentious behavior, lack of charity, reckless gambling habits, dishonesty, deceit, tyranny, corruption (among judges),[25] and degeneracy. Fag makes several of these accusations in a speech near the beginning of the play:

You may say that—for to be arrogant—false—in debt to tradesmen—to give money only to girls and gaming—to defame friends, without truth or humanity, a great man is above minding . . . .

And Lord Crotchett is in agreement with his servants:

What are their modern balls, masquerades, and assemblies, but nurseries of gamesters, loose women, and wretched husbands!   (Act I)

Most of the criticism consists only of a brief sentence or two and is usually a witty comment (of varying degrees of success) rather than a direct accusation, but Larpent did not allow the wit to divert him. Foil and saber alike are blunted by the Examiner.

Criticism of the ruling classes is inevitably combined in some speeches with general political and social comment. After having enjoyed a taste of authority for a day, Fag reflects on "how apt one is, when in power, to abuse authority, and, amidst indulgences, to forget the hardships we impose, and to look down with contempt on those who are our inferiors—only in their fortunes" (Act III). And the servants' plea for greater charity and humanity in British affairs includes peace with France and a redistribution of the taxation burden so that "every one should be able to pay for bread, even if twice as dear" (Act I).

There is no record of any performance of *The Whim*. Possibly the play might have stimulated local discontent with the aristocracy. But the criticism leveled by Lady Wallace against some of her own social counterparts was fair and necessary and in refusing to license the play Larpent and Salisbury were helping to create the very social atmosphere they were ostensibly trying to curb. For the discouragement and suppression of open discussion of the shortcomings of the ruling classes was likely to give rise to more dissension than unity in the country.

Several factors—Lady Wallace's spirited protest, the involvement of a provincial theater, the possibility of more than one motive behind the censorship—make the suppression of *The Whim* especially interesting, but other plays too, like Richard Cumberland's *The Box-Lobby Challenge* (LA 1009), Thomas Holcroft's *Knave or Not?*, and John O'Keeffe's *She's Eloped!*[26] were censored to protect the aristocracy from criticism. Still other plays of the period, plays containing a wide variety of social and political satire, suffered the same fate. Some speeches in Thomas Morton's comedy *A Cure for the Heartache* (LA 1149) were cut because of criticism of nabobs and suggestions that self-interest governed the behavior of most members of Parliament; Larpent refused to license a musical entertainment by Thomas Dibdin called *The Two Farmers* (LA 1301, not published) because it dealt with the acute problem of the scarcity and high price of corn in the country;[27] James Boaden discovered that he was not allowed to write about the growing social difficulties related to crippled and destitute soldiers returning from war (in *The Maid of Bristol*, LA 1388); and Richard Cumberland—again—ran afoul of the censor when in the fifth act of his comedy *The Sailor's Daughter* (LA 1409) he was critical of the government's failure to deal with the persistent social problem of dueling.

It is by now clear, I hope, that in the period of the French Revolution and the Napoleonic Wars John Larpent was remarkably successful in keeping the English stage clear of the unseemly paraphernalia of republicanism or anything which might have encouraged it, leaving ample space for the chariots and flags of Britannia. He also succeeded in isolating the theater from the vigorous debates about reform, republicanism, and revolution which were being conducted in just about every other place and medium in Great Britain. In an intensely political period the English drama was politically paralyzed. The restrictiveness of Larpent's censorship on the drama had become so severe that by 1811 it was no longer possible for a playwright to suggest in a play what everyone knew to be true—that members of Parliament sometimes used bribery to win votes from their constituents. Thomas Moore dared to say this in *M.P.; or, The Blue Stocking* (LA 1688) and Larpent duly censored it.[28]

AFTER WATERLOO

In August 1815 Larpent denied a license to an anonymous musical entertainment called *The Duke's Coat* (LA 1899), an amusing little piece whose plot hinges on a series of mistaken identities following the Battle of Waterloo. The duke of Wellington is referred to in the play and at one point is gently mimicked. This was enough to prompt Larpent's veto. The author, when he published the play,[29] complained about the suppression: "It has been suggested to me," he wrote, "that the Licenser may think the Battle of Waterloo too grave and tragical a subject for an Interlude: to this supposed objection I answer, that however indecorous it might be to introduce on the Stage the painful details of so recent an event, there surely can be no indecorum in *omitting* all such details, and in representing a little comic anecdote, which is supposed to have taken place after the battle . . ." And well might the author have complained. The pettiness of

Larpent's attitude towards this perfectly harmless and inoffensive play can be matched by many similar examples, but his decision to ban *The Duke's Coat* showed that the Examiner, now an old man, did not feel inclined to relax his grips on the drama even though England itself could at last relax after the final defeat of Napoleon. Not that Larpent was alone in his stance against greater freedom for the drama, especially as far as politics were concerned. Writers for and about the theater continued to express in the early nineteenth century what was by now the traditional view, that politics should never be permitted to intrude into the theater. Alicia Lefanu wrote her comedy, *The Sons of Erin; or, Modern Sentiment* (Lyceum, 11 April 1812) expressly to help improve Anglo-Irish relations, but she made it very clear in an "Advertisement" to the published text (3rd edition, 1812) that "All considerations of a political nature respecting the Irish nation have been carefully avoided, as such are neither agreeable to the Author's habit of thinking as a woman, nor, in her opinion, suitable to this species of composition." Another playwright, Richard Lalor Sheil, echoed these sentiments in the preface to his tragedy *The Apostate* (Covent Garden, 3 May 1817, published 1817) where he speaks of the "illegitmate assistance of political allusion." Managers too, in their traditional role as supporters of the censorship, were still usually only too happy to cooperate with the Examiner. Elliston, for example, went to some pains to water down the political content of Byron's *Marino Faliero* (with its republicanism and allusions to the Cato Street conspiracy) before submitting it for licensing in April 1821, stressing in his application that "we have so curtailed [the play] that I believe not a single objectionable line can be said to exist" (LA 2224).[30] It was at about this time that Leigh Hunt detected a growing division between literature and politics, noting that some readers who "in proportion as they are fond of poetry are averse from politics, or at least, whenever they come to the one, chuse to be abstracted and wrapped up from the other."[31] And only nine years after Larpent's death Bulwer Lytton observed that "the English, instead of finding politics on the stage, find their stage in politics." "To see our modern plays, you would imagine there were no politicians among us . . . ."[32]

The usual view of the relationship between politics and drama in the early nineteenth century has been that expressed, for example, by

E. B. Watson: "Of the nation's political life almost nothing is traceable in the drama."[33] Recent research, however, has shown that this position must be modified somewhat. In addition to political incidents in theaters, such as the audience suppression at Drury Lane on 29 December 1821 of a piece depicting the installation of the unpopular George IV as king of Ireland,[34] one occasionally finds, in the many dramatic periodicals published during the first quarter of the century, references to political comments in the plays themselves—usually complaints. In the *Cornucopia; or, Literary and Dramatic Mirror* for April 1821 we find the following (p. 76):

> IT is much to be regretted, that in these times of political agitation, the theatres are not exempt from the influence of party spirit, and that the managers too readily lend themselves to the gratification of a clamorous and ill-timed expression of feelings, which are totally at variance with the objects of their establishment. . . . We would wish to see this practice entirely exploded, even to the omission of all clap-traps and political sentiments in the pieces . . . .

Which pieces the author does not say, but recent scholarship has shown that the early years of the century witnessed a definite trend toward political and social satire in the plays presented at the minor theaters, saloon theaters, penny gaffs, and even sometimes at the major patent theaters. Pantomime and melodrama both hazarded fitful satirical comment on important issues of the time, despite the restrictions of censorship. David Mayer, in his intensive study of early nineteenth-century pantomime, is well aware of these restrictions and concludes that "rigorous censorship is surely the main reason that pantomine . . . did not produce trenchant and incisive comment on issues of political and religious importance."[35] Still, as Mayer says, pantomime was freer than other dramatic forms, for only the dialogue could normally be inspected by the Examiner and "the nonverbal portions of the harlequinades provided endless opportunities for a tentative and general satire on follies and issues."[36] Mayer notes that controversial political matters like the Corn Laws, the Poor Laws, Parliamentary reform, Luddite riots, Catholic emancipation, and the Peterloo Massacre all received attention in the pantomimes, making them "the only effective means of satire to hold the stage in the first thirty years of the nineteenth century."[37] Melodrama was less pointed in its satire, but Michael Booth has interpreted many melodramas as plays about class distinction and sees other melodramas as plays about industrial unrest in which the writers take a position "strongly sympathetic toward the discontent of the factory worker."[38] When Bulwer Lytton wrote his essay on the English stage quoted above, perhaps he had not seen John Walker's melodrama *The Factory Lad* (Surrey, 15 October 1832) which did deal with substantial political issues like the Poor Law system and its corrupt operation.[39]

These trends toward social and political satire in the early nineteenth-century theater are interesting and deserve further study, but as far as the serious legitimate drama was concerned the censorship, helped by conservative attitudes about politics and drama, retained its firm control, thereby denying the repertory of the patent theaters a currency and vitality which was increasingly exploited by the minors. Of those playwrights who still put their faith in Drury Lane and Covent Garden theaters, only James Sheridan Knowles showed much inclination to challenge accepted doctrines about political drama. Knowles, an active Whig supporter in Scotland in the 1820s, was coeditor of the Glasgow *Free Press*, which took an extraordinarily liberal line on such issues as the abolition of capital punishment, repeal of the Test and Corporation Acts, free trade and parliamentary reform. Knowles is also said to have declined to kneel when presented to William IV, a radical act if ever there was one.[40] And it seems that William's predecessor, George IV, may have known something of Knowles's politics, for it has been claimed that *Virginius* was censored at the king's instigation. Both this play and *Caius Gracchus*, in their uncensored versions, show rather more than the "vaguely democratic devotion to liberalism" noticed by a recent critic.[41] Hence Larpent's attention to both of them.

The tragedy of *Virginius; or, The Liberation of Rome* was originally produced, apparently unlicensed, at Glasgow in the spring of 1820 and was, says Richard Brinsley Knowles, a success, running for fourteen or fifteen nights.[42] After Glasgow *Virginius* went to Covent Garden and was duly submitted for licensing from that theater on 8 May 1820 (LA 2151). The play opened on 17 May and two days later the *Morning Herald* printed a curious little story which said that after *Virginius* "had passed the ordeal of the LORD

CHAMBERLAIN'S Office, the manuscript was demanded for inspection in a high quarter, and returned with some pencil erasures." Whether it really was George IV who was responsible for such erasures, as William Archer and others have stated,[43] is open to speculation, for the licensing manuscript does not contain any erasures at all and indeed shows no evidence whatever of censorship by anyone. The whole story about the royal censorship of *Virginius* may, then, be apocryphal, but it should be pointed out that the printed text of the play (1820) indicates that numerous passages were omitted in the representation, and there is good reason to suppose that George IV would have been personally unhappy with several aspects of the play. With George III dead only a few months, some comments in the play on insanity might not have been appreciated, and the new king was unquestionably sensitive about references to marriage, even casual and innocent ones like those in *Virginius*, in view of his current divorce problems with Queen Caroline.[44] It was also possible to make comparisons between the king, to be crowned in the summer of 1820, and Appius, the tyrant who becomes head of state in *Virginius*. Several short passages on tyranny and the rights of the people were cut from the acting version of the play, which prompted Hazlitt to ask: "Is the name of Liberty to be struck out of the English language, and are we not to hate tyrants even in an old Roman play?"[45]

Another "old Roman play" written by Knowles was *Caius Gracchus*, originally produced in Belfast on 13 February 1815, but not in London until 18 November 1823, in an abbreviated and censored version. The play has to do with the rise of Caius Gracchus as a popular hero who works for the good of the people against corrupt rulers. But the Senate eventually conspires to overthrow him and the people desert him. The play deals, often in an illuminating and convincing way, with political problems of importance: the use of violence for political ends, the fickleness of public opinion, the arrogance of governments and their abuse of power. The *Caius Gracchus* submitted for licensing from Drury Lane (LA 2384) is shorter than the published text (Glasgow, 1823) and lacks some strong political speeches by Caius, but Larpent still hesitated to license it. The playbill for the first night (in the Enthoven Collection of the Victoria and Albert Museum) indicates that the play is being acted "*In*

110

consequence of the Sanction of the Licenser having been at length obtained for its Performance." Some interesting entries in the diary of James Winston, Drury Lane administrator, give some explanation of the licensing delay. On Monday 10 November 1823 Winston received a letter from Larpent "saying the subject and some of the passages of *Caius Gracchus* was improper and the Tragedy could not be performed till he consulted with the Lord Chamberlain, who was in Scotland." Two days later Winston learned that it was Larpent's wife who was objecting to the play, but negotiations with her seem to have been speedy and successful, for on the next day, 13 November, a license was granted for the tragedy, "cutting out some passages."[46] Considering the Larpents' concern about the play, the passages cut out of the manuscript are surprisingly few.

> Why are they [the laws], in the rich man's grasp, a sword,
> And in the hand of the humble man, a reed?
>
> (II. iii)

> Now, show yourselves,
> The men you should be —*if your Liberties*
> *And Rights are dear to you, be faithful to them.*
> *Fear not the Senate* . . . .
>
> (IV. ii, italicized words censored)

Passages like this are deleted in the manuscript of *Caius Gracchus*, but neither the extent nor the nature of the censored material justified the delay in licensing the play or even merited the attention given the censorship in the newspapers.[47] More substantial and serious cases of censorship had too often been passed over in silence.

Of other plays censored for political reasons between Waterloo and Larpent's death the most remarkable is a short, anonymous and unpublished musical piece called *The Hustings* which Samuel Arnold sent for licensing from the Lyceum on 24 June 1818. The manuscript (LA 2031) is marked "Licence refused" and there can be no uncertainty about the reasons. The play is a farcical and disrespectful depiction of an election in which M.P.s, candidates, and electors are all made to look silly and incompetent. Parliament is said to have been "Be-rogued" and new members must be elected to "misrepresent" the borough; the high bailiff of the borough exclaims that people have no need to go to plays "while every Hustings gives them a farce for nothing;" a girl says her lover is "an honest open hearted fellow not at all fit for an M.P." Frequent references are made to controversial issues like the length of parliaments, placemen and pensioners, the liberty of the press, and the Corn Laws. And there is some scathing criticism of the country and government in general: "The Country is in such a state—the Parliament so bad, the Laws so villainous—the trade so unprofitable—the land so uncultivated & the whole Island so miserable . . . ." It is hard to imagine that Arnold ever believed such a play would be licensed. Sentiments similar to those of the author of *The Hustings* are found in a few other plays of this period. In John Faucit's *Justice; or, The Caliph and the Cobler* (Drury Lane, 28 November 1820), for example, a high-ranking politician admits, with commendable frankness, that "I may fill my place though I know I'm not fit for it, and that will be possessing as much wisdom as most men in office—What I can't do I can get others to do for me as long as I can do one thing, take the money." Larpent, commenting that the speech was "perhaps objectionable in the present times but not in common times," marked it for omission (LA 2179). And the kind of social and political criticism J. R. Planché injected into his burletta, *Sherwood Forest; or, The Merry Archers* (Adelphi, 12 March 1821) was also too outspoken for the censor. On bribery: "here is the General absolution that salves our Concience. This shuts the mouth of the most vociferous orator, blinds the Eyes of the Church, deafens the Ears of the Majistrates, obliterate[s] the Judgment of the Law, arrest[s] the [word illegible] of Justice & dries up the fountain of Mercy"; on juries: "Juries almost always follow the directions of the Court"; on the clergy: "it is really a Strange Doctrine that Churchmen should commit with impunity Crimes for which other men suffer without Mercy"; and on society in general: "we find Politicians without Brains—Majistrates without Justice—Noblemen without honor—traders without honesty—philosophers without morality—& Christians without religion" (LA 2217). For over forty years John Larpent had been responsible for suppressing such viewpoints in order to keep English drama as politically innocuous as possible. His record over these years is a depressingly impressive one.

5

The Censorship of Personal Satire

Although no precise rules were set out in the 1737 Licensing Act to guide the Lord Chamberlain and his Examiner of Plays as to what they should and should not allow to appear on the British stage, a policy soon developed of prohibiting satiric attacks on prominent members of society. The policy was, as far as possible, consistently and rigorously applied, and whenever the Examiner came across recognizable evidence of personal satire he would strike it out of a play. But, understandably enough, he was bound to have difficulty in controlling mimicry, an unscripted and often spontaneous form of personal satire which could neither be detected nor censored in the licensing manuscript of a play. Mimicry, depending as it did on the imitation of obvious physical eccentricities, mannerisms, and deformities, could be painful and embarrassing to its subjects,[1] and, not surprisingly, they often tried to suppress it. Those who protested the mimicry might supplicate, threaten,[2] bribe, or seek recourse at law, but in a number of important cases they appealed to the Examiner of Plays for mercy.

In the area of mimicry and personal satire no playwright in the period between the Licensing Act and John Larpent's death caused the office of the Lord Chamberlain more trouble than Samuel Foote.[3] The large majority of his plays were based, to a greater or lesser degree, on the mimicry and satire of persons well known to the public. For the friends and admirers of Foote this represented a noble effort on his part to flay prevailing vice, folly, and corruption; to his enemies it represented a mean and cheap way of making quick money. To Charles Dibdin, for example, Foote was a man "who seemed fondly to fancy that to torture individuals was the only way to delight their fellow creatures . . . who knew no quality of satire but personality, who would sacrifice his best friend for the gratification of tormenting him . . . ."[4] Foote rarely admitted that any of his characters were based on real people, and usually argued that they were merely representative of a particular vice or folly. If anyone chose to see himself in one of the characters it was probably the result of a guilty conscience. When the Lord Chamberlain suppressed two of his plays (*The Author* and *The Trip to Calais*) following complaints of personal satire, Foote denied in both cases that the plays contained such satire. There could have been few, however, who believed him.

Foote's *The Author* is important in the history of stage censorship after 1737 on two counts. It represents the first known instance of a Lord Chamberlain granting a license for performance and later withdrawing it, and it also provides the first known instance of an individual causing a play to be suppressed because he considered himself to be unjustly satirized in it.[5] The individual concerned was a Mr. Apreece, an eccentric Welshman who appears in *The Author* as Cadwallader, and it was to satisfy his wishes that the Lord Chamberlain, the duke of Devonshire, suppressed the play on 18 December 1758. It had first appeared on 5 February 1757 at Drury Lane after Lacy's and Garrick's successful application for a license on 27 January (LA 129). It enjoyed a long run in its first season and was revived several times in the following season. The last performance before the suppression was on 1 February 1758.

In *The Author*, Foote employs the stock situation of a disguised father investigating the true character of his son (he used it again three years later in *The Minor*) who in this case lives in poverty as a hack writer. Cape, the son, hopes to marry Arabella, daughter of the wealthy Mr. and Mrs. Cadwallader. Neither of the Cadwalladers is presented in a very flattering light, but the ignorant, pretentious, and proud Cadwallader receives no mercy from Foote. Cadwallader is not at all happy about his daughter marrying a penniless young man, even if he is a poet (among Cadwallader's many pretentions is a literary one), but when Cape's disguised father reveals himself as a man of "capital Fortune," the reservations are removed, the marriage agreed upon, and everyone is happy.

Apreece was well known in London at this time, although it is uncertain just when Foote first met him. But he became, according to

114

one source,[6] Apreece's "intimate acquaintance" and must quickly have recognized his comic potential. In addition to his pride in his family background and aristocratic connections, Apreece's

peculiarities were of so singular a nature, as to render him a very easy prey to the English Aristophanes. In his person he approached to the larger size, but seemed to be incumbered more by his deportment than his corpulence; with a broad unmeaning stare, and aukward step, he seemed to look and walk absurdity. His voice was loud, his manner of speaking boisterous, and his words were uttered rapidly and indistinctly; his head was constantly moving to his left shoulder, with his mouth open, as if to recall what he had inadvertently spoken.[7]

Foote was well equipped to take full advantage of these oddities and his skill in doing so was rewarded by his audiences: "Loud bursts of laughter from the boxes were so many acknowledgments of the writer's and actor's skill, and the strong resemblance to the original."[8] There is no record of Apreece's having offended Foote in any way which might have led to his being mocked in *The Author*; indeed, if we are to believe an article which appeared in the *Town and Country Magazine*, the character of Cadwallader was in fact created at Apreece's suggestion and with his encouragement and support:

The late Mr. Ap—ce, who was a very singular man, told Foote one day at dinner, that the ministry had quite overlooked him, and that he thought if Foote would bring him upon the stage, he was sure government would certainly take notice of him. Upon this hint Foote wrote the Author, and Ap—ce was so much resolved that his own character should be known in that of Cadwallader, that he lent the mimic a suit of cloaths he had been very conspicuous in at court. Somebody hinted that he did not use his friend well, thus to expose him. "You are quite mistaken, I do it at his own request, in order to make his fortune."[9]

If this was indeed the case—unlikely though it seems—it helps explain why Apreece enjoyed the play so much.[10] He seems to have had no objections to it until he realized that he had become a public laughingstock. Davies tells us that whenever Apreece "went to any public place, to the park, the play-house, to an assembly, or a coffee-house, he was immediately pointed at; the name of Mr. Cadwallader was whispered loud enough to be very distinctly heard; laughs were sometimes half-suppressed, at other times more freely indulged."

When the ridicule got too much to bear, Apreece decided to try to have *The Author* stopped. After an unsuccessful attempt to persuade Garrick to withdraw the play, Apreece approached the duke of Devonshire, probably on the day Foote advertised the first performance of the play in the 1758-59 season for 18 December at Drury Lane. It was to be on Foote's benefit night following *The Merchant of Venice*. Foote had written an additional scene for Wilkinson for the benefit performance,[12] and it was during the rehearsal of this scene that the news of the prohibition arrived at the theater. Wilkinson describes the reaction of those present:

. . . Mr. Foote, as the command came so unexpectedly, even while I was actually rehearsing the new scene, was thrown into a consternation and panic not to be described. . . .

Mr. Foote appeared shocked, pale and dejected, for in the Author he had depended on honours flowing thick upon him, which this hasty killing frost not only nipped but cut the root, so as to prevent its being for that year a tree bearing fruit; nay even Mrs. Clive was melted, who hated him. . . .[13]

According to Wilkinson, Apreece had no difficulty in persuading the Lord Chamberlain of the justice of his case, and the verdict he gave was final: "All appeal, all interest to counterbalance was in vain; he would hear no petitions; that day was the final will and pleasure . . . ."[14]

Not long after the suppression, Wilkinson, in defiance of the ban, acted a scene from the play at Drury Lane. On his benefit night on 14 May 1759, as well as playing Othello and scenes from *The Diversions of the Morning* and *Taste*, he took off Foote and Mrs. Clive as Mr. and Mrs. Cadwallader in *The Author*. The performance "cheered the audience, as they had not seen it for two years,"[15] but it brought trouble for Wilkinson. News of the illegal performance reached the Lord Chamberlain, probably via Apreece, and the following day Wilkinson received a letter from Devonshire, couched, he says, "in severe terms" and reprimanding him for "taking the liberty on Monday night to restore and act a scene from the Author, which had been prohibited . . . ." The play had greatly offended Mr. and Mrs. Apreece and "therefore it was expected no such rude infringement should be again repeated."[16] No further action seems to have been taken, and Wilkinson did not provoke Devonshire into adopting more drastic measures: "high authority had laid its weighty commands, and I was obliged, though much against my will, to submit."[17]

In the provinces, as Sybil Rosenfeld shows,[18] the ban on *The Author* was not enforced, but in London, where the Lord Chamberlain's control was obviously easier to apply, *The Author* was not permitted such freedom. Apart from occasional performances of the prologue or epilogue, it was not seen in London in its entirety after December 1758 until 11 August 1769 when Apreece had been dead for some years.

For Apreece, then, the quickest and easiest means of defense against Foote's ridicule was to seek the help of the Lord Chamberlain, whose decision on this occasion happened to be against the playwright. But when the friends of George Whitefield made a similar appeal to the duke of Devonshire in 1760 his response was somewhat different.

Mary Belden deals in some detail with the controversy aroused by the supposed attack on George Whitefield and the Methodists in Foote's *The Minor*.[19] The controversy led some influential people to make efforts to have the play suppressed by the Lord Chamberlain. The efforts were not entirely successful, but LA 177, a copy of the third edition of *The Minor*, shows that although the play ran at the Little Theatre throughout the summer of 1760 free from any official interference, when it moved to the winter theaters it was played as censored by the Lord Chamberlain's office. Several speeches in the Larpent text are either altered or deleted because of their controversial nature. This censorship was almost certainly the result of the strong criticism leveled against the play during the summer and autumn of 1760.[20]

The countess of Huntingdon, for many years the friend and patroness of George Whitefield, the famous Methodist preacher who appears in *The Minor* as Mr. Squintum,[21] was one influential person who made determined but fruitless efforts to have the play suppressed.[22] More influential than the countess of Huntingdon was Thomas Secker, archbishop of Canterbury (the son of a dissenter and educated at a dissenting academy), but he had no more success than the countess in trying to get *The Minor* banned. A letter from the duke of Devonshire to Garrick about a meeting with the archbishop is dated 25 October 1760:

I HAD a long conversation with his Grace, who would have authorized me to have used his name to stop 'The Minor,' but I got off from it, and concluded with sending a recommendation by Mr. Pelham to the author, to alter those passages that are liable to objection; his Grace would not point them out, so I think very little alteration may do. This to yourself; let me hear what has passed.[23]

A slightly different account of the meeting between the duke and the archbishop is given by Horace Walpole in a letter to George Montagu (24 November 1760). According to Walpole, the archbishop *did* point out the passages he objected to:

Did I tell you that the Archbishop tried to hinder *The Minor* from being played at Drury Lane? For once the Duke of Devonshire was firm, and would only let him correct some passages, and even of those the Duke has restored some. One that the prelate effaced, was, "you snub-nosed son of a bitch." . . . Foote says he will take out a license to preach, Sam. Cant against Tom Cant.[24]

Other opposition to *The Minor* came in the form of numerous pamphlets,[25] one of which, a *Letter to David Garrick, Esq.; Occasioned by the intended Representation of the Minor at the Theatre-Royal in Drury-Lane*, appeared shortly before the opening night (22 November 1760) and demanded that the play be withdrawn.[26] This attack on him personally, together with the widespread antagonism toward the play, perhaps led the cautious Garrick to think of abandoning *The Minor* altogether, but judging by the success it had enjoyed during the summer it seemed certain to be a profitable production at Drury Lane, and he must have known that Rich was planning to stage it at Covent Garden.

Moreover, *The Minor*, in its attack on Methodism, reflected the prevailing mood of the government in 1760, and so received the backing of the Lord Chamberlain. Even so, a minority group was able to exert sufficiently strong pressure, if not to completely win its case, at least to force some concessions.

What these concessions were can be discovered from the Larpent text of *The Minor*. The character to suffer most from the censorship was Mrs. Cole, the old bawd and procuress who claims she has been converted from concerns of the flesh to concerns of the spirit by Mr. Squintum. Unfortunately, she does not find it easy to shake off her old way of life, but she sees no harm in continuing her profitable business at the same time as working as one of Squintum's disciples. By placing the beliefs and sometimes the very words of Whitefield and the Methodists in the mouth of a bawd, Foote is able to make those beliefs sound ridiculous and hypocritical. The only way the censor could rescue the Methodists from this ridicule was to delete all of Mrs. Cole's references to her newly discovered spiritual interests. In her first speech about Squintum, for example, she speaks of the benefits she has derived from following him—"But for him I had been a lost sheep; never known the comfor[t]s of the new birth; no—" —and then goes on to arrange an evening's entertainment in her brothel for Sir George Wealthy and his cronies. To eliminate the ridicule of Whitefield, the censor simply deleted Mrs. Cole's expression of gratitude to Squintum. A few speeches further on (still in Act I), Mrs. Cole regrets the fact that a certain "black-ey'd girl, from Rosemary-Lane" is such a reprobate: "But she'll mend; her time is not come: all shall have their call, as Mr. Squintum says, sooner or later; regeneration is not the work of a day. No, no, no." This speech is deleted in the Larpent text of the play, obviously because the dignity of George Whitefield and his fellow preachers was bound to suffer when their sermons were paraphrased on the stage by the like of Mrs. Cole.[27] Further on in the text, Mrs. Cole refers again to her spiritual adviser: "in my last illness, I was wish'd to Mr. Squintum, who stepp'd in with his saving grace, got me with the new birth, and I became, as you see, regenerate, and another creature." Most of this speech is deleted.[28]

Another character who loses some of his lines is Sir George Wealthy. He is no friend of those who, like the Methodists, condemn carnal pleasures, and he frequently ridicules the sect. In one instance, when one of his servants describes Mrs. Cole's efforts to convert him, Sir George makes fun of ignorant preachers:

Dick.   I believe she has some such design on me; for she offer'd me a book of hymns, a shilling, and a dram, to go along with her.

Sir George. No bad scheme, Dick. Thou hast a fine, sober, psalm-singing countenance; and when thou hast been some time in their trammels, may'st make as able a teacher as the best of 'em.

Dick. Laud, sir, I want learning.

Sir George. Oh, the spirit, the spirit will supply all that Dick, never fear.

(Act I)

The last three speeches in this exchange are marked for omission in the Larpent text. Sir George has another speech partly censored later on in the play. In his penultimate speech of Act I, he succinctly sums up the innocent hypocrisy of Mrs. Cole: "How the jade has jumbled together the carnal and the spiritual; With what ease she reconciles her new birth to her old calling!" The censor left the first half of this intact, but the second half is deleted, probably because of Sir George's irreverent use of the favorite Methodist phrase, "new birth."

The part of the play which suffered most from the censorship was Shift's epilogue. In the Drury Lane production of *The Minor*, as in the Little Theatre one, Foote himself took the part of Shift (in addition to those of Smirk and Mrs. Cole). In the epilogue, Foote savagely mocked George Whitefield, both by mimicking him and by parodying his sermons. The result on the printed page is to make Whitefield a bigoted, mercenary creature; on the stage Foote doubtless made him look utterly ridiculous as well. As Collier noted in his copy of *Biographia Dramatica*,[29] the "chief part" of the epilogue was found objectionable. The following section is boxed in for omission (Shift has just called upon people to give up their work and listen to him):

> With labor, toil, all second means dispense,
> And live a rent-charge upon providence.
> Prick up your ears; a story now I'll tell,
> Which once a widow, and her child befell,
> I knew the mother, and her daughter well;
> Poor, it is true, they were; but never wanted,
> For whatsoe'er they ask'd, was always granted:
> One fatal day, the matron's truth was try'd,
> She wanted meat and drink, and fairly cry'd.
> [Child.] Mother, you cry! [Moth.] Oh, child, I've got no bread.
> [Child.] What matters that? Why providence an't dead!

Further on, Shift parodies Whitefield's attacks on the theater, and although the untidy deletions in the text make it very difficult to tell exactly which lines were objected to, it is probable that the censor wanted the whole section about the theater omitted.

> Let's go see Foote! ah, Foote's a precious limb!
> Old-nick will soon a football make of him!
> For foremost rows in side-boxes you shove,
> Think you to meet with side-boxes above?
> Where giggling girls, and powder'd fops may sit,
> No, you will all be cram'd into the pit,
> And crowd the house for satan's benefit.
> Oh! what you snivel; well, do so no more,
> Drop, to attone, your money at the door,
> And, if I please,—I'll give it to the poor.

Foote's decision to use Whitefield's condemnation of the "giggling girls" and "powder'd fops" of the theater (as well as an attack on himself which may or may not have been fictitious) as the climax of the epilogue was obviously an excellent way of making sure that at the end of the play the audience not only thought Whitefield ridiculous, but also thoroughly disliked him. Foote must have been particularly unhappy that he was not allowed to treat the Drury Lane audience to such an effective finale.

With the exception of the passages censored because of bad language, most of the censorship in *The Minor* seems to have been designed to protect George Whitefield from ridicule rather than the Methodists in general. Some telling blows against Whitefield's followers were left intact, but very few satirical references to Squintum remain in the censored version, and the effectiveness of Foote's mimicry of Whitefield in the epilogue must have been seriously reduced by the heavy censorship. Mrs. Cole's part in the play was not a very substantial one to begin with, and after the censorship the opponents of *The Minor* must have been at least partially satisfied that justice had been done. Certainly, there was rather more than the "very little alteration" Devonshire had spoken of in his letter to Garrick on 25 October.

The censorship of *The Minor* did not have an adverse effect on its popularity. The public were either satisfied that the substitutions they heard for the censored speeches were as good as the originals,[30] or they found other things in the play to amuse them. At any rate, it was one of the most successful of the 1760-61 season.[31] For this good fortune Foote and Garrick were largely indebted to the duke of Devonshire. A more conventional Lord Chamberlain might well have suppressed *The Minor* the minute the archbishop of Canterbury raised objections, not to mention the countess of Huntingdon. The interest Devonshire took in the play and his liberal and fair attitude toward it, were not often matched by other holders of his office. The censorship of *The Minor* attempted to protect the individual, Whitefield, while permitting what many people would have considered justified ridicule of his sect.

Devonshire took action against *The Author* and *The Minor* only after they had been performed many times. In 1775, however, the then Lord Chamberlain, the earl of Hertford, refused to license *The Trip to Calais* at all, and consequently the play, Foote's last original work, was never acted.[32]

The Trip to Calais contained a thinly disguised portrait of the infamous Elizabeth Chudleigh, duchess of Kingston. There is no need here to give the already well-documented details of the duchess' life, a life lived for the most part, in the words of her *DNB* biographer, in "extreme dissipation."[33] It culminated in 1776 in her widely reported trial in Westminster Hall before the House of Lords for bigamy.[34] She was found guilty, whereupon she left the country and spent most of the rest of her life on the Continent. Her case had first come before the Court of King's Bench on 24 May 1775, and it was at this time that news of Foote's new play began to appear in the press. It was obvious from the beginning that the duchess was to be a principal character. The *Town and Country Magazine* carried the following notice:

Notwithstanding Mr. Foote has hitherto performed to very numerous audiences, he does not propose being remiss in producing some new performances, which will speedily make their appearance. The first, we hear, is a comedy, in which some well known characters will be highly pourtrayed; and the ground-work of the piece is to be the *denouement* of a certain *Double Marriage*, that has lately made so much noise in the polite world, and among the lawyers. We are told this piece is to be entitled the *Siege of Calais*.[35]

The duchess was not without her supporters, and several days before Foote submitted his play for licensing the first of scores of items against *The Trip to Calais* appeared in the newspapers. The *Morning Post* on 14 July 1775 claimed to know "from pretty good authority," that "a certain new satirical Comedy has been refused the Chamberlain's licence, on account of the severity with which a certain Duchess is supposed to be treated therein." The next day the paper reported that Foote had said that the censors "are better calculated to judge of a *marrow pudding*, than the merits or demerits of a dramatic production." On 19 July it was again asserted that no license would be available for Foote's play, and on 21 July that "a certain dramatic piece shall not receive the Chamberlain's license, till every passage which is supposed to reflect upon her Grace [the duchess of Kingston], be totally expunged."[36]

All of these reports were somewhat premature, but, as Foote's letter printed in the *Morning Chronicle* on 3 August 1775 shows, not inaccurate.

THE prophetic effusions of the collectors or makers of paragraphs, have for once proved true, Mr. Woodfall: The *Trip to Calais* has been rejected by the Lord Chamberlain; to guess from whence these gentlemen obtained their intelligence (as their advices preceded by many days the delivery of the piece to the Lord Chamberlain) would be a very difficult task: however, you find what was only prophecy is *now* become history. . . .

Shortly after the play was suppressed, the duchess, with Foote's permission, read it in manuscript. Had she hitherto doubted that Foote would have dared to portray her in any detail, those doubts must instantly have been dispelled when she read the play. *The Trip to Calais* is concerned with the efforts of Jenny Minnikin, daughter of a London pinmaker, to avoid marrying the man chosen by her parents. She elopes to Calais with her own choice of lover, and on hearing that they have been followed by her parents, takes refuge in a convent. After failing to persuade Jenny to leave the convent, her parents seek the advice of Lady Kitty Crocodile, who is in deep mourning following the recent death of her husband. Lady Kitty sees Jenny, and her solution to the problem is that Jenny marry her own choice and her father's choice as well. Jenny agrees, becomes maid of honor to Lady Kitty, and, rather perfunctorily, the play ends.

The character based on the duchess of Kingston is Lady Kitty Crocodile. She is first mentioned in Act II where we learn that she has come to France because "She couldn't bear to stay in England after the death of her husband, every thing there put her so much in mind of her loss. Why, if she met by accident with one of his boots, it always set her a-crying; indeed, the poor gentlewoman was a perfect Niobe." She makes her first appearance towards the end of the second act. Cruelty (to her maid of honor) and hypocrisy (over the death of her husband) soon reveal themselves as her principal traits. She is jealous of Miss Lydell, her maid of honor, and makes her life miserable by treating her kindly in public and cruelly in private. To impress her visitors with the deep grief she feels for her late husband, Lady Kitty has a special "Chamber of Tears" for receiving them where she gets "deck'd out in her dismals . . . ." In hypocrisy, says her servant girl, "she would be an over-match for a Methodist." "And as to cruelty," she goes on, "there never was so ingenious, so refined a tormenter: The Fathers of the Inquisition themselves, would be proud to receive instructions from her."

It would have been perfectly obvious to a contemporary audience whom Foote had in mind when he created Lady Kitty. The duchess of Kingston's mourning on the death of her second husband, Evelyn Pierrepoint, in 1773, had been extravagant in the extreme, and it was probably because of her mistress' cruel treatment of her that Miss Penrose, a former maid of honor of the duchess, had given Foote information about her which he used in the play.[37] A reference to Lady Kitty's intimate association with the Pope in Act III would have recalled to the audience a similar intimacy enjoyed by the duchess of Kingston, and Lady Kitty's proposal that Jenny commit bigamy would inevitably have reminded everyone of the duchess' imminent trial.

But Foote, in his usual obstinate way, refused to admit that any personal allusions were intended in *The Trip to Calais.* One report of the affair has it that Foote read the part of Lady Kitty Crocodile to the duchess, whereupon she exclaimed, " 'This is scandalous, Mr. Foote! Why, what a wretch you have made me!' 'You' (replied the humorist) 'this is not designed for your Grace; it is not you!' "[38] He claimed that Lady Kitty did not represent an individual, but a type, and that her character would "suit nine, out of ten, widows of fashion

in the kingdom."[39] This claim formed the basis of his attempt to persuade the Lord Chamberlain to change his mind about suppressing
The Trip to Calais. Soon after Foote received the news of the suppression he claimed in a long letter to Lord Hertford that the
duchess, having read the play, "could not discern . . . a single trait in
the character of Lady Kitty Crocodile, that resembled herself."[40] But
she was hardly likely to give Foote such satisfaction. Even after all
hope of reversing Hertford's decision had gone, and Foote was argu-
ing with the duchess about the proposed publication of the play, he
held firmly to his claim that she was not in any direct way
represented in *The Trip to Calais*. But no one (except perhaps his
friends with the *Morning Chronicle*) could really have believed him.

According to Horace Walpole, Foote was enraged by the suppression,[41] but the playwright was, after all, attempting to make profit
out of someone else's misfortunes and difficulties. The duchess of
Kingston was no angel, but when Foote decided to satirize her in *The
Trip to Calais* she was facing a serious criminal trial. Her case was,
therefore, sub judice, and the appearance of Foote's play at this time
was not likely to create the sort of atmosphere necessary for a fair and
unbiased hearing.[42] In these circumstances the Lord Chamberlain
really had no alternative but to suppress *The Trip to Calais*.

Foote had little reason to feel satisfied about any aspect of his clash
with the duchess. When it also developed into a bitter feud with William Jackson, the duchess' secretary, he must have rued the day he
created Kitty Crocodile. Even after it was clear that *The Trip to
Calais* would not be acted, Jackson, who seems to have enjoyed this
sort of thing, continued to publish vicious personal attacks on Foote
in the *Public Ledger*. Foote responded by satirizing Jackson as Dr.
Viper in *The Capuchin* (Little Theatre, 19 August 1776). Jackson
had by then bribed one of Foote's former coachmen to accuse Foote
of a homosexual assault on him. Foote was acquitted of the trumped-
up charge in the Court of King's Bench on 9 December 1776,[43] but
the sorry affair ruined his health and career. He gave up the Little
Theatre to George Colman, wrote no more plays, and died the following year.

Samuel Foote was a much-censored playwright, but the extent
and nature of the Lord Chamberlain's control of personal satire will
not be appreciated without some discussion of other instances of this

kind of censorship. Even people of no great social status, men like Apreece, for example, were occasionally eligible for the Lord Chamberlain's protection, but usually such protection was reserved for those on somewhat higher rungs of the social ladder.

During the recurrent mental illness of George III *King Lear* was kept off the English stage, partly no doubt because theater managements and audiences considered it bad taste to attract attention to the king's distress, but also because the Lord Chamberlain reminded theaters from time to time not to perform Shakespeare's tragedy. Whitbread wrote to the Lord Chamberlain, Lord Hertford, from Drury Lane on 28 November 1814 to assure him that *King Lear* would not be acted there,[44] but at Covent Garden Kemble wanted to act Lear before his retirement. It was, however, "intimated to the proprietors by the Lord Chamberlain, that it was not the wish of the Government that the play should be performed at the present time [June 1817]."[45]

The king's alleged insanity had had faint repercussions in the theater some years before. William Douglas, fourth duke of Queensberry, was convinced as early as 1788 that George was insane and that recovery was impossible. The Prince of Wales, he believed, should be made regent and granted the full powers of the monarch. Pitt and the government, however, took the line that the king's return to sanity was not beyond hope and that the Prince of Wales should be given only powers limited by Parliament, pending the king's recovery.[46] The duke of Queensberry had been a lord of the bedchamber for twenty-eight years when the crisis arose and his attitude towards George III during his illness seemed to many to be entirely disloyal. His "ratting" made him many enemies and when the king regained his sanity in February/March 1789 the duke was dismissed from the household.

The affair was seized upon by the Liverpool playwright Robert Oliphant for a brief allusion in his comedy, *The Learned Lady; or, Double Reform*, performed in Liverpool in 1789. The Liverpool theater was being managed that summer by James Aickin and J. P. Kemble. On 6 August Kemble sent the manuscript of *The Learned Lady* to James Wrighten in London and asked him to get it licensed. Wrighten sent the manuscript with a brief note to Larpent on 8 August and a week later the Examiner wrote to Kemble:

126

Sir,

A Comedy entitled *The learned Lady, or double Reform*, with your name affixed to it, has been transmitted to me, & as Mr. Wrighten informs me that you wish to have the Licence as speedily as possible on account of its being for a Benefit, I have it to the Ld Cham^n for his Signature & will forward it to Mr. W. as soon as it returns: But I must take Leave to observe that there is a Passage in the 2^d Act in the foll^g Words vizt "It was not Q. in the corner I hope? there has been such an Increase of Rats lately, His Māty's Rat Catchers have been doubled." which I dare say you will agree with me is of so personal a Nature that it ought to be omitted, & I rely upon you therefore to have it expunged, & that you will acquaint me by a Line, with its being so.[47]

The lines objected to by Larpent occur in the following exchange between Folio and Jeremy:

Fol. What was that noise I heard a little while ago[?]

Jer. Only a large rat run across the room & frightened my mistress.

Fol. It was not Q in the corner I hope, there has been such an increase of rats lately, his Majesties Rat catchers have been doubled.

"Q" was, of course, the popular title assigned to the duke of Queensbury. In the manuscript Folio's speech about him is deleted and "too personal" written alongside it in the margin. Some months later *The Times* may have been referring to this incident when it observed that "The Duke of QUEENSBURY has made a particular request to Lord SALISBURY, that, in the next representation of HAMLET, the young Prince's exclamation of 'A Rat,—a rat,— dead for a ducat!' may be omitted,—as containing 'much offence.'"[48]

The scandal surrounding the marriages of George III's son also occasioned some firm censorship. The Prince of Wales secretly married Maria Fitzherbert in December 1785 when he was twenty-three years old. The marriage was invalid because the 1772 Marriage Act forbade the marriage of royal persons under twenty-five without the king's consent, and so the prince was at least legally free to marry, albeit reluctantly, the Princess Caroline of Brunswick in April 1795. But by this time his marriage with Mrs. Fitzherbert had long been common knowledge and this second marriage was considered by many to be bigamous. Consequently any plays dealing

127

with marriage might be seen as reflections on the Prince of Wales and his two wives. *La Perouse*, for example, adapted from Anne Plumptre's translation of Kotzebue's play, was apparently denied a license for this reason. Larpent received the play (LA 1313) from Norwich and an entry in his account book for 7 March 1801 shows that he rejected it. The play concerns the difficulties of Peyrouse who, shipwrecked on a desert island, takes himself a native wife in addition to the one he has at home. After several years his first wife, Adelaide, finds him, and Peyrouse suddenly has two wives on his hands. It would have been easy enough to have seen this as a replica of George's position, with Adelaide being Mrs. Fitzherbert and Malvina, the native wife, being Princess Caroline (even though the prince was no longer living with her).

Even after Caroline's death in 1821 the troubled marriage of the Prince of Wales (now George IV) was not forgotten. The Examiner of Plays still watched carefully for comments on bigamy and divorce, and anything that seemed too close to the king's former marital difficulties was likely to be censored. *Spanish Bonds; or, Wars in Wedlock* (LA 2361), a two-act farce, was quite heavily censored before being acted at the Little Theatre on 2 August 1823. The play contains a character who is suspected of committing bigamy, and the plight of one woman who is deserted by her husband is perhaps not far removed from that of Princess Caroline for much of her married life: "What a lot is mine—condemned to spend my life in seeking for a worthless husband, whom I shall not be able to keep when I have caught—yet in spite of every thing, I cannot help loving the dear, ungrateful, good for nothing fellow." This speech, like many others in the play with suspected royal allusions, is deleted and marked "out" in the manuscript.

There are also several speeches about marriage deleted in the licensing manuscript of another piece acted just a few months before *Spanish Bonds*. The anonymous burletta *Green in France; or, Tom and Jerry's Tour* (LA 2330; Adelphi, 6 January 1823) seems to contain no obvious allusions to George IV's marriages, although some speeches may reflect the public interest which arose in 1822 over the validity of the marriage between the marquis and marchioness of Donegal. According to the *Annual Register* it was the dispute over the legality of this marriage which gave rise to the controversial New

Marriage Act of 1822.[49] This is not the place to discuss early nineteenth-century marriage legislation,[50] but it had become a sensitive social issue and Larpent was clearly out to make sure that members of the royal family and the peerage were not embarrassed by allusions, real or imaginary, to their particular marital circumstances.[51]

We should not be surprised, of course, that members of the peerage were well sheltered by the Lord Chamberlain from scandal or ridicule in the theater, but this sometimes spoiled some good comedy. The censorship of George Colman the Elder's *The Election of the Managers* in 1784 provides an interesting example. The election held in the City of Westminster constituency during the general election of 1784 aroused great public interest for two quite different reasons. It was, on the one hand, a very vigorously fought and a very close contest. The three candidates were Lord Hood and Sir Cecil Wray for the government, and Charles James Fox for the opposition. Voting began on 1 April and went on until 17 May, when Hood and Fox were declared the winners. But Wray, only two hundred and thirty-five votes behind Fox in a poll of nearly twenty thousand, demanded a scrutiny of the votes by the House of Commons. The inquiry did not end until 3 March 1785, when the original results were confirmed (although the figures were slightly altered).[52] The uncertainty of the outcome in itself assured an unusually interesting election. But the personalities involved also kept public attention at its peak for a period of several weeks. And it was the politicians' supporters as much as the politicians themselves who were responsible for this. In particular, there were two eminent ladies from polite society who took it upon themselves to get embroiled in the hurly-burly of electioneering. Georgiana, the beautiful and elegant duchess of Devonshire, became an active canvasser for Fox, and the duchess of Rutland came out in support of Fox's opponents. It was the duchess of Devonshire who was in the limelight most of the time. Wearing a fox's tail to proclaim her political allegiance, and ready to spend freely her currency of charm, embraces, and kisses for promises of votes, she bribed and badgered the voters of Westminster to support her favorite, ignoring the indignities and abuse she had to suffer from the followers of Hood and Wray.[53] But impartial observers were not impressed by the lady's antics. "We are sorry," said the

Critical Review in April 1784, "when the behaviour of a lady of high rank is rendered the subject of public discussion, especially when strongly taxed with the charge of levity and indecency."[54] George Colman the Elder saw it in a different light. With a foresight which would have done credit to Foote, Colman set to work on a play which would exploit the public interest in the election generally and in the activities of the duchess in particular.

Colman called his new piece *The Election of the Managers*. It was based on an imaginary election contest between the three patent theater managers—Holly and Ivy from Drury Lane and Covent Garden, and Bayes from the Little Theatre. Appropriately, Holly and Ivy had joined forces against Bayes, just as Hood and Wray opposed Fox. But Colman did not press the parallels between his theater managers and the politicians too far. That there were three candidates in an election, with two of them pledged against the third, was enough to show the audience what he was getting at. Once this was established, the celebrities of the Westminster election could appear. Among the several introduced, including authors, booksellers, a tailor, a printer, and an attorney, there were three who would have been instantly recognized. The first was a remarkable man, called Tom Twopenny by Colman, who owned a public house in Wardour Street and was a fervent supporter of Fox. His name was Sam House and his canvassing for Fox during the election added to the notoriety he had already won in Westminster, both by his dress (he never wore a hat or stockings) and by his bizarre recreations, which included keeping an aviary and, on one occasion, diving off Westminster Bridge at high tide.[55] But the characters probably most eagerly anticipated by the audience were Mrs. Buckram (the tailor's wife), supporter of Holly and Ivy, and Mrs. Dimple, supporter of Bayes. The highlight of the play is a direct confrontation between the two ladies when they accuse each other of using unfair canvassing tactics.

By 18 May Colman had finished the play and a copy was sent for licensing. The allusions to well-known individuals and to memorable incidents during the election must have been obvious to Larpent. He could have banned the whole thing, and in some ways it is surprising he did not. Apart from the personalities involved, the play exposes some of the more blatant election irregularities, such as bribery and the use of imaginary names in the voting lists, and also offers provocative comment on the power of the press, including the touchy question of the reporting of parliamentary debates. But the Examiner was content to remove only the more critical references to the election and the direct and obvious allusions to the part played in it by the two duchesses.[56]

Most of the deletions relative to the duchesses occur in the confrontation scene between Mrs. Dimple and Mrs. Buckram, where the biting sarcasm, so well captured by Colman, was regrettably reduced by the censorship. The italicized words are those marked for omission in both licensing manuscripts (except "personal" in Mrs. Buckram's first speech which is underlined for emphasis in the original).

Mrs. Buckram. "Trust to Nature."! pretty Natural! you don't trust ev'n to the Money in your pocket, without promising more for which in the mean time you often give your *personal* security—and there is not a Voter qualified to take his seat in the twelve penny Gallery, on whom you have not lavish'd your guineas, your tears, *ogles, kisses and embraces* ["& attractions" substituted].

Mrs. Dimple. Oh, if *kisses &c.* ["they" substituted], are bribes not used by my opponent, it is because no Voter would go through the penance and drudgery of giving or taking them from her. As to personal security you may justly complain, if mine is thought more acceptable since, your own, Mrs Buckram must be allowed to be so much more than sufficient.

Mrs. Buckram. Your own favors almost go a begging—*did not a Cheesemonger only seem to wish for a Kiss, and did not you bid him take it?* And did not you but last night, on your Canvass, dance a reel & hornpipe, at the door of an Alehouse in the Haymarket to the grinding of the Barrel Organ, and the Music of the Marrowbones and Cleavers.

Mrs. Dimple. And have not you done all in your power in the same way, and for the same purposes; have not you shaken your round sides and jolly figure in Quadrille & Cotillons with boys of eighteen, and prigs from behind the Counter, at every hop in Westminster?—*Besides, which, because Ladies of Quality of superior abilities have plays at their houses, have not you exposed yourself in Calista, and*

131

> *Juliet, Philly Nettletop and Lady Temple? and even hinted*
> *that the celebrated Melpomene and Thalia of the Stage,*
> *were both jealous of your Abilities.*[57]
>
> Mrs. Buckram. *And have not you on your Canvass, realized the fiction of*
> *the Theatre—been the true Juliet of every Prentice, and*
> *the actual Desdemona of every Chimney sweeper.*

The allusions to the activities and characters of the two ladies would doubtless have been instantly understood by most of the audience. Larpent's censorship was obviously intended to protect them from public laughter and (bearing in mind Mrs. Buckram's final speech) scandal. But it is odd that he thought the allusion to the duchess of Devonshire's offer of a kiss to a cheesemonger improper while allowing the audience to guffaw at the thought of her cutting a caper outside an alehouse.

In the summer of 1790 there arose another of those high-society scandals which in the eighteenth century, as now, provided such diversion and profit to the paragraph writers, pamphleteers, and gossips. The real or supposed sins and misdemeanors of the great have always proved irresistibly fascinating to the less elevated members of society; the higher the rank and the more personal the offense, the greater the interest. Prurient and degrading such interest might often be, but scandal, like death, is a powerful leveler, and in a class-ridden society such as existed in eighteenth-century England, to torment the great was to reduce them, if only briefly, to the common rank or even lower. The scandal, not a particularly sensational one, that began in 1790 lasted for a year or more and concerned three families, those of General John Gunning, George Spencer, fourth duke of Marlborough (a former Lord Chamberlain), and John Campbell, fifth duke of Argyll. General Gunning was the only brother of the famous Gunning sisters, renowned for their beauty and advantageous marriages (one of them, Elizabeth, was the wife of Argyll). The general's daughter, also named Elizabeth, was the central figure in the scandal.

Because so many people gave so many different accounts of what actually happened, the details of the scandal are sometimes obscure. But the main fact, submerged as it was (in Horace Walpole's words) in an "extraordinary tissue of effrontery, folly, and imposture,"[58] eventually proved to be that Elizabeth Gunning, through a series of

132

forged letters, had deceived her family and friends into thinking that Marlborough's son, the marquis of Blandford, had proposed marriage to her. When the truth came out the people involved hurled any number of accusations, recriminations, and threats among themselves, and several abusive paragraphs, pamphlets, and even books were published to satisfy the public appetite for news and comment on the scandal.

Charles Stuart took the most appropriate course by writing a farce about it all and called it *She Would Be a Duchess*. The licensing copy of the play (LA 915) is endorsed by Larpent, "taken from the Spanish, August 13th 1791 *prohibited*." The circumstances surrounding this suppression are rather unusual and certainly irregular. It seems that General Gunning heard about Stuart's farce before the Examiner had time to license it and the general immediately protested both about the title and the content of the play. The Lord Chamberlain, Salisbury, agreed with him and insisted first that the title be altered, and secondly that General Gunning be allowed to censor the play himself! (*The Times*, 15 August 1791.) George Colman (the manager who submitted the play for licensing) and Stuart had, of course, little choice. They submitted to the general's censorship even though he was hardly the best person to judge between justified and libelous ridicule of his family. We do not know if he claimed the two-guinea fee for doing the Examiner's job for him, but he went through the manuscript of *She Would Be a Duchess* with great care, marking with small crosses those speeches which alluded in any way to the Gunninghiad (as Walpole called the affair).

There are altogether some two dozen cuts made by the general in the thirty-page manuscript. According to Larpent's note this amounted to a suppression of the farce, but Colman somehow managed to extract an actable script from what Gunning had left him and the play was produced as *The Irishman in Spain* at the Little Theatre on 13 August 1791. A report in the *Morning Post* for 15 August 1791 says that the general did not complete the censorship until late in the evening of 12 August, "when he so completely gutted it, that neither actors nor author knew it again." Not surprisingly, it had a poor reception. Oulton says it "was dismissed by the audience with great disapprobation,"[59] and *The Times* (15 August) reported an indifferent reception until some references to the British constitution gave great offense and the farce was hissed off the stage. Only one performance was given and then the play was more carefully revised and reduced to one act. All the allusions to the Gunnings were, of course, omitted, and the political references were also dropped. Very little new material was added. This new *Irishman in Spain* was submitted for a license by Wrighten, the Little Theatre prompter, on 30 August (LA 917) and it was performed, again without success, on 2 September.[60]

The further down the social scale one found oneself, the more difficult it became to secure the Lord Chamberlain's protection from ridicule in the theater, but a member of Parliament was important enough to have the Examiner's ear—even for such a trivial reason as that described by Thomas Morton when he appeared before the 1832 Select Committee on Dramatic Literature. Part of the exchange between Morton and the committee was as follows:

Can you recollect any [phrases] that were erased from your plays?—No, I cannot, I remember Mr. Larpent objecting to the word gammon being put into a play of mine.
On what ground?—He said there was a gentleman in Hampshire who had been very much hurt by a play of O'Keefe's; I think it is in Wild Oats; "What is your name?"—"Gammon." "Then you are the Hampshire hog." This rather hurt his feelings; and if it offended an individual's feelings, there was of course no harm in removing the word.
Mr. Gammon happened to be acquainted with Mr. Larpent?—I suppose he represented it was disagreeable to him. I never had a very important alteration made.[61]

"Mr. Gammon" was Sir Richard Grace Gammon, M. P. for Winchester, and Morton's memory was correct about the Gammon used by O'Keeffe. The words he quotes occur in II. i of *Wild Oats; or, The Strolling Gentleman*, acted at Covent Garden on 16 April 1791. The play of his own to which Morton was referring is *The Way to Get Married*. Mrs. Larpent's diary shows that this was received for licensing on 8 January 1796. A few days before the play was acted at Covent Garden (23 January), Mrs. Larpent records that "Sr Richard Gammon employed much of Mr L's time owing to a fancy that his name (made for punning) was improperly introduced into the new play—Strange are the various means whereby self importance acts!" Sir Richard had probably got to know of the use of his name in Morton's play from someone attending the rehearsals at Covent Garden and had approached Larpent directly. Since he then took up "much of M^r L's time" it is not unlikely that Larpent at first did not give him a sympathetic hearing. But Gammon had his way in the end.

A potentially much more serious case of this kind arose on 7 May 1777 when *The School for Scandal* was temporarily suppressed. Sheridan himself spoke of the matter in the House of Commons many years later during a debate on the Seditious Meetings Bill (3 December 1795). He told the House that "The night before the piece was to be performed, he was much surprised to hear from the prompter that a licence was refused."[62] Apparently, the character of Moses, the Jew, was taken to be a portrayal of Benjamin Hopkins, the government-supported opponent of John Wilkes in the election for the office of Chamberlain of the City of London in the summer of 1777. Hopkins was reputed to have "lent money to young men in an usurious manner" (*The Times*, 4 December 1795), and it was felt by the Examiner that to allow Moses to appear at Drury Lane would emphasize this blemish on Hopkins' character and so damage his chances of success against Wilkes. However, Sheridan went to see Lord Hertford, the Lord Chamberlain, the following day and explained the satire to be of a general nature, and not "of personal obloquy or ridicule . . . ." Hertford apparently "laughed at the affair and gave the license."[63] *The School for Scandal* was then free to be acted, as planned, on that same evening, 8 May.[64]

As a final example of the censorship of personal satire in this period it is worth mentioning the case of Dr. John Hill, the notorious quack, if only to show that it was not always necessary to be a prince, peer, or M. P. to win the Lord Chamberlain's sympathy. On 20 March 1753 Fielding's farce, *The Mock Doctor*, was revived at Drury Lane. A new prologue had been written by Christopher Smart for the occasion. *The Mock Doctor* was a pre-1737 play and thus was not sent for licensing; the prologue, however, was new and so was read by the Examiner. Although it does not refer by name to Hill, the audience would have been in no doubt that he was the mock doctor about to be ridiculed. The prologue was suppressed.[65]

Playwrights and mimics, like the poets and novelists, sometimes ridiculed individuals who deserved to be ridiculed. But on the whole they were not inspired by a social conscience to satirize individuals for the general improvement of mankind. Mostly they simply wanted to please their audiences, and a person was often selected as a subject for ridicule with regard only to the amount of entertainment that might be extracted from him. People guilty of nothing more than unusual or eccentric behavior were thought fit subjects for public mockery; whether or not the ridicule was morally or socially justifiable was scarcely a relevant issue. Inevitably, this caused suffering and distress, and when the Lord Chamberlain cried halt to it we should be thankful for the sake of the victims that he did. There is no need to shed too many tears over the denial of freedom of expression to someone like Samuel Foote. Foote made large profits out of quite harmless people and caused several of them much suffering; it is to the credit of the Lords Chamberlain that they sometimes displayed more humanity than Foote and some of his contemporaries seemed capable of.

Yet this is not to say that the Lord Chamberlain's censorship was the proper way of controlling personal satire in the drama. A system of precensorship directed by one man was bound to give rise to unfair and biased rulings.[66] The aristocratic and wealthy brought a pressure to bear on the Lord Chamberlain which was difficult to resist and no single individual should have had to face such onerous responsibilities. A thorough reform of the legal system to bring the law of libel within the practical reach of all members of society and to make it an effective punishment and deterrent was obviously needed. Just as obviously, such reform was unlikely to occur.[67] Until it did, the most easily accessible legal protection available to people who were satirized in plays rested with the Lord Chamberlain. He and his Examiner of Plays gave or withheld this protection sometimes fairly, sometimes unfairly, always arbitrarily. But whatever justice or injustice their decisions created it remained intolerable that dramatic literature should have been subjected to such capricious restrictions, restrictions imposed, of course, on playwrights alone.

Profaneness and Immorality on the English Stage a Century After Collier

MORAL CENSORSHIP

A number of theater historians have discussed the growth of the moral and sentimental strain in the British theater of the second half of the eighteenth century. One of them, James Lynch, has written:

> We may . . . characterize the audiences between 1737 and 1777 in respect to their moral tone in two ways: first, that in spite of their numerous exclamations against the licentiousness of the drama, they often welcomed the very plays that when performed gave the theatre of the period much of its immoral color; and second, that the later decades, judged by both new and revived drama, show a greater demand by the audiences for plays of unquestionable morality. It is apparent that in moral matters there had earlier been a period of indecision that was later supplanted by one of assurance and greater certainty.[1]

As far as sexual morality was concerned, the development described by Lynch took the form of purging the old plays of their indelicacies of situation and language[2] and keeping the new ones in line with the stricter moral standards of the London audiences. The job was done well, not well enough to please everyone's tastes (complaints about double entendres and obscenity in old and new plays could still be read in the newspapers and periodicals of the early 1800s), but Hazlitt could claim with some conviction in his "Lectures on the English Comic Writers of the Last Century" (1819) that

> we seem afraid to trust our eyes or ears with a single situation or expression of a loose tendency, as if the mere mention of licentiousness implied a conscious approbation of it, and the extreme delicacy of our moral sense would be debauched by the bare suggestion of the possibility of vice.[3]

It is generally accepted that the reaction against the exploitation of sexual comedy and displays of immoral behavior in the drama arose mainly from the increasing presence of a sober-minded and (outwardly, at least) respectable middle-class element in the theater audiences. The changes effected in the drama by this presence were often the subject of discussion in the plays themselves. Dangle's complaint in *The Critic* (1781) is well known: "Now, egad, I think the worst alteration is in the nicety of the audience.—No double entendre, no smart innuendo admitted; even Vanburgh and Congreve oblig'd to undergo a bungling reformation!" (I. i); and a character in Hough's comic opera, *Second Thought is Best* (1778) had already said much the same thing:

> Fashion, Sir, justifies the propriety of actions, and reconciles them to reason. I have known the time, when a double entendre might be delivered from the stage, and create a risibility in the features of a chaste and polite audience: but tempora, mutantur! the times are changed, and the fashions so alter'd, that a lady of easy virtue, or no virtue at all, will almost expire at a speech, that does not contain as much morality as Tillotson's sermons.   (Act II)

The influence of audiences on the moral reform of the drama in the second half of the eighteenth century is of prime importance. But other theatrical factors were involved as well. Harry Pedicord has made us aware, for example, of the importance of Garrick's managerial cooperation with his audiences in removing the moral blemishes of earlier times from the repertory of Drury Lane.[4] John Beard, too, was under pressure from the moment he took over the management of Covent Garden in 1761 to follow Garrick's example—"the public have reason to expect a reformation in this point, under the management of the decent Mr. Beard," said the *Gentleman's and London Magazine* in 1762.[5] We should also remember that most playwrights during and after Garrick's time did not merely respond to the changing tastes of their audiences, they actively encouraged the new morality. Cumberland, for example, held it a "matter of conscience and duty in the dramatic poet . . . to give no false attractions to vice and immorality, but to endeavour . . . to turn the fairer side of human nature to the public . . . ." He condemned Congreve and Farquhar for having made "vice and villany so playful and amusing," and found Shadwell's comedies "little better than a brothel."[6] It is, Cumberland pronounced, "much better, more justifiable and infinitely more charitable, to write nonsense and set it to good music, than write ribaldry, and impose it upon good actors."[7] A depressing, but not untypical viewpoint. There were, moreover, some performers who would not speak "ribaldry" on the stage. Mrs. Siddons, for example, refused to speak the original epilogue (by Colman the Elder) to Robert Jephson's tragedy, *Julia*, in April 1781 because she found it indelicate, and a new one (by John Courtenay) had to be written for her.[8]

Audience, manager, playwright, and even actor were thus generally united in the task of cleansing the English drama of its indelicacies and obscenities. A fifth element in the theatrical world, the Lord Chamberlain's censorship, sometimes overlooked by historians of the theater, also played its part in promoting and maintaining a reformed drama. The censorship was not extensively used and did not need to be when almost everyone associated with the theater was agreed that plays ought to be free from immorality. Indeed, by the second decade of the nineteenth century the pressure from all quarters in favor of moral propriety in plays was so great that the censor had very little to worry about. Shakespeare had been bowdlerized twice by 1818 and six years previously James Plumptre had provided the same service for lesser playwrights in *The English Drama Purified: Being a Specimen of Select Plays, in which all the Passages that have Appeared to the Editor to be Objectionable in Point of Morality, are Omitted or Altered* (Bowdler was a subscriber). In March 1812 a play was hissed off the stage in Bath when the line "there is only a poor gentlewoman in labour" was spoken (Genest, 8: 324), and in 1815 Byron, of all people, when he was on the Drury Lane Committee, objected to Thomas Dibdin's using the word "ravish" too frequently in one of his plays.[9] There was precious little chance for dramas like Shelley's *The Cenci* (1819), aptly described by one critic as "an unmitigated affront to popular morality,"[10] when "labour" and "ravish" were taboo words. This kind of prudish intolerance of any sexually suggestive theme or language in plays was so strong by the early nineteenth century that very seldom did the Examiner find it necessary to censor anything on moral grounds, for his job had nearly always been done for him.

There appears to be only one post-1800 play in the Larpent collection which contains more than the deletion of an odd word or two for moral reasons. This is an anonymous tragedy called *The Inquisition of 1650; or, Eugene and Maria* (LA 1906) which was denied a license on 26 January 1816 (Larpent's account book). A passage in which Pedro, a chief inquisitor, threatens to rape Maria is marked for omission in the manuscript, as is this speech in which Pedro describes Maria to a colleague:

> Her neck so finely tapered to the swell,
> Where rose two piramids of virtuous love;
> That ever & anon did ambling play
> As if in token of their innocence.—
> Withal a waist for dalliance shaped,
> And arms & limbs whose slender mould
> Gave each & all true beauties symmetry.

Noel Perrin, in his lively account of Bowdlerism, has noted that "With the turn of the nineteenth century, a new literary morality appeared in England."[11] The effect of this new morality on dramatic literature was severe, but before the turn of the century playwrights had more frequently ignored the Collier-like, censorious prudishness of their audiences and had written of sexual matters with a freedom and lightheartedness (and sometimes crudeness) we do not normally associate with the drama of the mid- and late eighteenth century. When such plays were accepted for production by the managers the Lord Chamberlain's Examiner of Plays usually intervened.

Three Larpent plays were refused licenses by the Examiner on moral grounds. Each play had to be revised before permission to perform it was granted. The three plays are conveniently spread over a period of thirty years (1743; 1761; 1772) and an examination of the deletions and changes made in the manuscripts reveals what was officially regarded as morally unsuitable for the London stage in these years.

On 25 January 1743 Lady Frances Seymour Hertford informed her son, Lord Beauchamp, that Henry Fielding had written a new comedy. She also told him that the play had run into trouble with the Examiner and had been refused a license, not, she wrote, because

140

it was "a reflecting one" (i.e. libelous), but because of its "immorality."[12] The comedy was *The Wedding Day*, which was eventually performed, after the objections of the Examiner had been attended to, at Drury Lane on 17 February 1743. It ran for six nights with Garrick in the leading part.

Lady Hertford believed that Fielding succeeded in getting *The Wedding Day* licensed only "by suffering his bawd to be carted," the bawd being Mrs. Useful, who was, says Lady Hertford, Fielding's favorite character in the play.[13] It is true that Mrs. Useful was partially reformed by the Examiner, but the licensing manuscript of *The Wedding Day* (LA 39) shows that other morally questionable aspects of the play had to be removed or toned down before the license was granted. The manuscript contains, as Arthur H. Scouten has briefly pointed out, "many question marks, and deletions of suggestive, passionate, and physiological references."[14] It is probably assuming too much to think that the Examiner was responsible for all of the queries and deletions, but many of the differences between the manuscript text and the printed (1743) text can safely be attributed to his intervention.

The Wedding Day concerns the amorous adventures of Millamour, a likable but, for most of the play, unscrupulous rake. His activities bring him into contact with several desirable young women and some rather less desirable old procuresses, including Mrs. Useful. By later standards even the censored version of the play contained a good deal of indecent dialogue and immoral social philosophy, and some of Fielding's contemporaries found it objectionable too. "I think we are corrupt enough already without having any new commendations of it," wrote Lord Beauchamp to his mother, expressing regret that *The Wedding Day* had been licensed at all,[15] and few respectable women came to see the sixth and final performance of the comedy.[16] But there would have been much more to complain about had the Examiner not raised his objections.

We can best see the kind of changes that had to be made in the play by comparing passages in the 1743 printed text (in *Miscellanies*, 2, almost certainly the acting text) with the same passages as they appear in their original form in the Larpent manuscript where parts of them are marked for deletion or alteration.

Apart from the deletion of vocabulary considered to be too erotic in the context in which it appears in *The Wedding Day* ("lusciously," "panting," or even "body"), most of the censorship is directed at Millamour and Mrs. Useful. Mrs. Useful's profession has led her to adopt a rather cynical view of life and in her more bitter moods she can be severely critical of society, too critical for the Examiner in the following cases. Mrs. Useful advises the recently married Clarinda to leave her husband and give herself to Millamour (III. iii). Clarinda's reaction to this, "What! with the loss of my honour?" provokes a cynical reply from Mrs. Useful. In the printed text all we get is:

> The Loss of your Honour! No, no—You may keep your Honour still; for every Woman hath it till she is discovered.

But Fielding had originally given Mrs. Useful a rather more forceful speech:

> The Loss of a Figg.—I would as soon grieve at the loss of a Queen Elizabeth Ruff—they have both no value but when in Fashion.—pray what do you think this Honour was—Why it was a Specious Covering for an Intrigue—as the other was for the Neck. But the present Age desires no covering for either—Besides you may keep your Honour still—for every woman has it till she is discover'd.

A large X appears in the margin alongside this speech in the manuscript. Mrs. Useful's bawdy wit also suffers from the censorship. A few lines further on from the speech just quoted, Mrs. Useful continues to urge Clarinda to leave her husband: "E'en do it without thinking of it—Let the poor Man [i.e. Millamour] owe the continuing of his Life to my Entreaties." The manuscript version (underlined for omission) reads: "E'en do it without thinking of it—Let one Man owe the Continuing of his Life to my Entreaties—As Heaven knows many have the beginning." And near the end of the play the Examiner deprived the Drury Lane audience of a fine exchange between Millamour and Mrs. Useful. In V. viii in the printed text Millamour suddenly turns against Mrs. Useful, despite the good service she has rendered him. The scene ends with Millamour threatening to expose her so that "every wretched Maid shall curse thee, every honest Woman despise thee . . . ." She is "a more mischievous Animal than a Serpent," and he demands that "A publick

Mark of Infamy should be set on every such Wretch, that we might shun them as a Contagion." In the manuscript version the scene ends somewhat differently. In place of Millamour's out-of-character social moralizing we get an almost hysterical appeal to Mrs. Useful to help him conquer Clarinda, followed by a splendidly aloof reply from the bawd (both marked for deletion):

Mill: Lead me again to the Attack, thou best of Bawds, let me but Succeed, I'll rob Churches & Palaces to build an Hospital to thy Profession.

Useful: I thank you kind Sir, but our Profession are pretty well provided for already.

In the manuscript text of *The Wedding Day*, as in the printed text, Millamour finally repents his rakish life, but the censorship insured both that the repentance was quicker and firmer and that Millamour's earlier sexual impulses were moderated somewhat. Before his repentance Millamour's personal philosophy of life is one of unashamed sexual hedonism. He explains it to his friend, Heartfort, in II. ii: "What is Life worth without Pleasure? And what Pleasure is there out of the Arms of a Mistress? All other Joys are Dreams to that. Give me the fine, young, blooming Girl,—Cheeks blushing,—Eyes sparkling. Give me her, *Heartfort*—" Thus the printed version. But Millamour's erotic fantasies are more detailed in the manuscript version, most of which is underlined for omission:

what is life worth without pleasure, and what pleasure is there out of the Arms of a Mistress. All other Joys are dreams to that. Give me the fine, Young, Blooming Girl. Cheeks Blushing, Eyes Sparkling, Breasts heaving, Arms Embracing,—Give me her Heartford [*sic*], and when I can do nothing else in her Arms, let me Expire in them. And so slide Gently from one Heaven to another.

In addition to the mild eroticism the Examiner probably detected a touch of profanity in the final sentence. A later (III. viii) boast by Millamour that out of his house "no Maid, Wife, or Widow of what Condition Soever goes, without being treated with proper Civility," is also underlined in the manuscript and is omitted from the printed text altogether.

But despite the enforced cuts and changes, the censorship of *The*

143

Wedding Day represented little more than a half-hearted attempt to remove some of the more indecorous language and make Millamour a more morally acceptable hero. Much remains that would not have been tolerated by the time Garrick was managing Drury Lane.[17]

Joseph Reed's farce, *The Register Office*, for example, was quite severely censored in 1761 although the censored scenes were, on the whole, much less indelicate in language and subject matter than many in *The Wedding Day*. The farce was aimed at exposing the abuses practised by some of the managers of London's register offices (forerunners of Britain's employment exchanges, founded by Henry Fielding). Yet when Garrick and James Lacy submitted it for licensing on 7 March 1761 (under its original title, *The Universal Register Office*) it was dismissed by the Examiner (now Edward Capell, acting as Chetwynd's deputy) with a curt "not thought fit to be acted" (LA 189).

The farce consists of a series of interviews between the register office manager, Gulwell, and prospective employers and employees. The employers include bawds, lords, and ladies whose intentions in seeking employees are neither very proper nor very moral. Mrs. Snarewell, for example, a religiously-minded bawd, frequents Gulwell's establishment in the hope of securing a few innocent country girls to join her line of business. Like that of her counterpart in *The Wedding Day*, Mrs. Snarewell's language displeased the Examiner. Her expressions of faith and devotion occasion some fine double entendres which are marked for omission in the licensing copy. She complains at one point of a very restless night, caused by her rheumatism:

I never expected to live till morning, I assure you—Poor Mr Watchlight the Tallow Chandler, was call'd twice out of Bed to *pray with me*—the dear Man was so fervent in his *Prayers*, & so earnest in his *Ejaculations*, that I receiv'd great Comfort and Consolation—I was so easy, so compos'd, so resign'd after *I had made my peace with Heaven* . . . .

The italicized words were objected to by the Examiner, and again we notice the profanity produced by the association of sexual contentment with religious experience. Later in the farce the register office is visited by Lord Brilliant, who seeks a housekeeper with amatory as well as domestic interests. While Gulwell conducts another interview, Lord Brilliant retires into a back room where, Gulwell tells him, he will find "Rochester's Poems, & the Memoirs of a Woman of Pleasure to entertain you . . . ." This reference to undesirable literature is marked for omission.[18] Another character who seeks Gulwell's assistance is an Irishman, who has lost his previous job with an Irish farmer because he insisted on yoking the mules to the plough by their tails—"every body knows the Strength of a Mule & a Woman lies in the Tail," he says; "& a Woman" is underlined.

There are many more marginal queries and underlinings of impious references to "the spirit," "salvation," and "providence," and of bad language, such as "son of a whore" and similar phrases in LA 189. But despite the censorship, Garrick and Lacy evidently considered Reed's farce too good to drop altogether. Not long after *The Universal Register Office* was refused a license the managers submitted a revised version of the farce, now called simply *The Register Office* (LA 196). It is clear from this second manuscript that the Examiner's objections to the first had, to some extent, been heeded. For example, Mrs. Snarewell's speech about Mr. Watchlight, quoted above, reads rather differently in LA 196:

poor Mr Watchlight, the Tallow-Chandler, was call'd twice out of bed to comfort me—the dear Man was so fervent in his Discourse, and so earnest in his Exhortations, that I receiv'd great Comfort & Consolation—I was so easy, so compos'd, so resign'd, after I had made my Peace . . . .

Several other speeches are altered in accordance with the Examiner's wishes in this new version and some of the material marked for deletion in LA 189 is simply omitted from LA 196. One character, in fact, is entirely discarded. This is Lady Wrinkle, whose reasons for using the register office are similar to Lord Brilliant's. She is looking for an "obliging" manservant, preferably a handsome six-footer, whose duties, it would appear, will go beyond those normally expected of a manservant. Although the Lady Wrinkle scene is not marked in LA 189 for omission in its entirety, it seems that the Examiner let it be known that while it was not improper for a male aristocrat (Lord Brilliant) to have sexual designs on his servants,[19] he could not allow such insinuations to be made against a Lady.

Indelicacies and profanities of language and situation do not feature nearly so prominently in LA 196 as they do in LA 189. But, rather surprisingly, there remain in the second manuscript a number of passages clearly marked for omission in the original one. Even after he had censored the first version of *The Register Office* the Examiner still had to delete a number of the same passages again in the second version. Phrases like "upon my Soul" and "Son of a Whore" are again censored, as is the frequent use of "damn'd" and the description of one character's wife as a "bitch." Gulwell's reference to Rochester's poems and Cleland's novel appears again in LA 196, only to be marked once more for omission. Longer passages are censored too. The following exchange between Mrs. Snarewell and Gulwell is all marked for omission (virgins are in short supply and Mrs. Snarewell is afraid that she will not be able to satisfy her customers):

Snare. . . . I have promis'd a Virgin to Mr Zorobabel Habakuk to-night.
Gul.   You must palm some of your freshest Commodities on him for one.
Snare. Palm some of your freshest Commodities quotha! Lard help you, Mr Gulwell! you are vastly mistaken!—He is too knowing in these Matters to be impos'd on in any such Manner—It would be as difficult to deceive my little Israelite in that point, as a Jury of Matrons—Besides, he pays the Price of Virginity, & I assure you I am a Person of more Honour & Conscience, than ever endeavour to fob him off with a Counterfeit—Conscience should be us'd in all our Dealings—No! no! I have too strong a Sense of Religion, to be guilty of such a heinous Imposture—

But the censorship did not lead to a total ban on this revised version of *The Register Office*. LA 196 was duly licensed and the farce was produced at Drury Lane on 25 April 1761, soon to become a stock eighteenth-century afterpiece. It was also published in 1761. The text of the first edition uses both manuscript versions and includes the Lady Wrinkle scene. Much of the censorship of both manuscripts is ignored in the printed text, although in some instances impious or indelicate expressions deleted in the manuscripts appear in altered form or not at all in the text. It is certainly not true to say, as T. B Shepherd does, that the published play is unexpurgated.[20]

It is apparent from the two manuscripts of *The Register Office* that Lady Wrinkle never appeared in the acted version of the farce. This is confirmed by a note in the 1761 text (at the foot of the list of

146

Thomas Rowlandson, "The Registry Office." *Henry E. Huntington Library and Art Gallery*

Dramatis Personae) which also indicates that Mrs. Snarewell too was "*not* permitted *to be play'd.*" Evidently the partial censoring of Mrs. Snarewell's lines in the two manuscripts was finally considered inadequate and the bawd had to be cut altogether. This rather annoyed Genest (4: 613), who thought "the Licenser . . . ought to have been ashamed of himself for objecting to Mrs. Snarewell after having licensed Mrs. Cole—." In fact, as we have seen,[21] Mrs. Cole (who bears close similarities to Mrs. Snarewell) suffered from the censorship herself.[22]

The Examiner's censorship of *The Register Office* was designed principally to keep immoral characters (female ones, anyway) off the stage and to prevent the remaining characters from using indecent or profane language. The censorship was a more thorough and more effective job than that done on *The Wedding Day* and well illustrates the Examiner's awareness of and reaction to the growing strength of the middle-class reforming element in the theater of the 1760s.

Still more extensive and severe moral censorship occurred some eleven years after *The Register Office* was licensed in the case of Kane O'Hara's farce, *The Golden Pippin*, a burlesque of the mythological "Judgment of Paris." There are again two Larpent manuscripts to consider. The first version of *The Golden Pippin* (LA 330), in three acts, was submitted for licensing by Colman from Covent Garden on 5 February 1772. It is marked "forbid the 17th. Febry. 1772." LA 339 is a shortened (two acts) and considerably revised version of the burletta, submitted on 9 October 1772 and licensed without any trouble although it was not performed until 6 February 1773.

In LA 330 only one passage is marked for deletion in Edward Capell's neat hand and moral censorship is not involved. Capell wanted some brief but impolite references to royalty and aristocracy removed from the play. But this was obviously not the sole cause of the play's being "forbid." By comparing the unlicensed LA 330 with the licensed LA 339 we can see that numerous alterations and omissions had to be made on moral grounds before Capell was prepared to allow *The Golden Pippin* to be performed.

The changes occur throughout the whole of the burletta and range from the rewriting of single lines to the complete omission of whole scenes. In Act I of LA 330, for example, Erynnis steals the treasured

golden pippin from the Dragon, who is, understandably, annoyed
about it:

> Fe. . .Fa. . .Fum
> If up with her I come,
> I'll claw Erynnis' bum
> And make her pelt my drum.

In LA 339 the Dragon's threat in line three of this is changed to the
less suggestive but (all things considered) rather more severe, "I'll
strike Erynnis dumb." And in Act III of LA 330 Paris forthrightly
and eagerly suggests to Juno: "Gad, Ma'am, let's cuckold Jove! 'tis
what he merits." In LA 339 this becomes a euphemism more suited
to eighteenth-century polite society: "Gad, Ma'am, let's use your
husband as he merits." Some longer speeches and songs are completely rewritten to make the language, if not the content, more
decorous. For example, Paris' direct declaration of his likes and dislikes in Act III of LA 330 takes on a lyrical gentility in LA 339.

> Dem your savage Trade of Fighting,
> Moi a Cadet for the Wars?
> Think you, Beaux Garcons delight in
> Blood and Bruises, Maims, and Scars?
>   On a Sofa—down derry, derry,
>   On a Sofa,
>   Tout nos Combats.
>
> (LA 330)

> Let Heroes delight in the Toils of the war,
> In maims, blood, and bruises and blows;
> Not a sword, but a Sword knot rejoices the Fair,
> And what are rough Soldiers to Beaux?
> Away then with Laurels! come Beauty and Love,
> And silence the trumpet and drum;
> Let me with soft myrtle my brows bear inwove
> And tenderly combat at home.
>
> (LA 339)

The main difference between the two manuscripts is simply that a
good deal of the text of LA 330 is omitted altogether from LA 339.
The first scene of Act II in which Momus molests and attempts to

seduce Iris disappears; so does a further scene in Act II between Oenone and Paris (in which Oenone asks Paris to marry her and "make me an honest woman") and the opening scene of Act III which includes a warning by Momus to Jupiter not to make advances to Iris.

> No more of your Tricks, my old Privateer,
> Of my little Frigate steer wide and clear,
>   If once I smoke your fun,
> My Seamanship you soon shall know,
>   I'll lower as sure as a Gun,
>   The top and top Gallant of Juno.
> We'll rout you, flout you, horn you, scorn you,
>   Riot, and revel, and play,
>   Poor Jove in sad taking,
>   Shall rue Cuckold making,
>   When he has the worst of the Lay.

Later in Act III nearly three pages of conversation between Paris and Venus are omitted. The conversation is mainly concerned with the promises of carnal pleasures and gambling successes made by Venus to Paris if he awards her (rather than Pallas or Juno) the golden pippin. The enjoyment of Helen is but one of the delights Paris can look forward to:

> She's so buxom and fresh,
> Such a sweet bit o' flesh,
>   Ads [?] life you've no Idea,
> How She's form'd to delight,
> Both the Touch and the sight,
> She's a Peerless Dulcinea.[23]
>
> Smooth and white as an egg,
> And as right as my legg,
>   High train'd, knows all her paces,
> She's an Olio of Joy,
> Say the word, jolly Boy,
>   And you're smack—in her good Graces.

Suggestive passages of this sort made in plain English in LA 330 are, interestingly enough, altered or omitted in LA 339, whereas some similar passages couched in foreign or unfamiliar language are allowed to remain. Thus while Paris' direct invitation to Juno to cuckold Jove is disguised in LA 339, the following invitation (Paris to Juno again) is untouched:

> Sweet Revenge there is a Clue to,
>   Wou'd you take a Fool's advice,
> Me voici tout pret—Cornuto,
>   We may dub him in a trice.
>   Dans le Bon ton—Down derry, derry!
>   Dans le Bon ton
>   Sur le Gazon.

This is a diverting example of a principle that occurs time and again in the history of censorship—that educated people are less susceptible to moral "corruption" than the uneducated.

Clearly, then, despite the absence of Examiner's deletions in LA 330, the original text of *The Golden Pippin* was subjected to a heavy moral censorship. Quite likely Capell communicated his objection to the whole tone of the burletta by letter to Colman rather than enumerating his specific objections in the text. The one passage he did mark in LA 330 (mentioned above) seems to have led G. W. Stone, Jr. to the conclusion that *The Golden Pippin* was denied a license on political grounds,[24] but this, considering the sort of revision the burletta underwent before a license was granted, can hardly have been the case.[25]

As a final example of Capell's moral censorship, one might quote R. Crompton Rhodes's *Harlequin Sheridan* (Oxford, 1933), p. 145:

When Sheridan in 1777 submitted the manuscript of *A Trip to Scarborough* to the Lord Chamberlain's office, the Deputy Licenser of Plays, Edward Capell, placed brackets round a cynical comment of Berinthia, "No man worth having is ever true to his wife, or ever was, or ever will be so." Against it he wrote austerely "This ought to be suppressed." No doubt it was explained to him that this line was Vanbrugh's, and not Sheridan's, and that for seventy years it had been spoken in *The Relapse* [Act III] and was, indeed, still being spoken by Mrs. Bellamy at Covent Garden. Accordingly, this pious expression of opinion must have been disregarded, for the sentence stands unaltered in the printed copy of 1781 [Act III], and all the other editions.

To this we need only add that the licensing manuscript of *A Trip to Scarborough* is LA 426; that Capell wrote "soften'd," not "suppressed"; and that the printing of the words Capell objected to is no indication that they were spoken on stage.

Compared to the kind of sexual themes, language, and subject matter one finds in other literature in the later years of the eighteenth century, the sexual content of the period's plays is hardly worth mentioning. Even the uncensored versions of the plays discussed in this chapter pale into sexual insignificance when set against publications like Wilkes's and Potter's *An Essay on Woman* (1763), *Harris's List of Covent-Garden Ladies* (1788-93), or the host of popular eighteenth-century pornographic works in verse and in prose, many of them illustrated.[26] Fielding, Sterne, and Smollett enjoyed and exploited a far greater sexual freedom in the novel than was permitted in the theater. We should not, however, be surprised at this discrepancy between the freedom enjoyed by nondramatic authors and the limitations imposed on a playwright so far as sexual matters are concerned. The gap between what can be spoken or acted on the stage and what can be printed has always been a wide one (although it is narrowing nowadays) and merely demonstrates that the spoken word and acted event carry a greater immediate impact than the printed word alone and thus in the eyes of officialdom warrant greater control. As Thomas Holcroft pointed out in his preface to *Duplicity* (1781), "Were the humour of Smollett, which never fails to excite laughter in the closet, spoken upon the stage, it would frequently excite universal disgust." Eighteenth-century moral reformers like Wilberforce and Hannah More were genuinely concerned about the corrupting influence of immoral literature, and, reading some of it, one can appreciate their concern. But one can hardly see the job of the Examiner of Plays in the same terms as one sees the reformers' attempts to suppress pornography. Notwithstanding some contemporary opinion to the contrary, there was little chance of anyone being morally corrupted by any of the plays the Examiner was called on to license, including those he felt obliged to censor. His task was rather to prevent in the theater the flouting of middle-class standards and ideals; sexual matters could no longer be treated with Jacobean frankness or Restoration flippancy. The Examiner of plays was the theatrical equivalent of the literary bowdlerizers. In addition, we can see in the Examiner's censorship the seeds of the Victorian notion that sex, although its existence cannot always be denied, is nonetheless something one should not admit to finding enjoyable. Even Venus is not allowed to describe the pleasures of physical love. In a word, the Examiner was there to prevent not corruption, but embarrassment and offense, just as he was there also to prevent political embarrassment and offense to government. With sex, as with politics, he had some measure of success, but there were always those who believed that the war against licentiousness or suggestiveness or plain bawdiness in the theater could and should be conducted with more earnestness than even the censor displayed.[27] To this extent the official censorship was always one step behind some segments of public opinion in the eighteenth and early nineteenth centuries. But the increasing restrictions imposed by the censorship on the use of sexual humor in comedy indicate that the Examiner of Plays was generally in accord with the mounting public opposition to indelicacy and indecency in the drama. Playwrights and managers were too, but on the rare occasions when playwright and manager failed to exercise a sufficiently strict voluntary control, the official guardian of the theatrical public's moral sensitivity was always ready to do his duty.

RELIGIOUS CENSORSHIP

A student of Biblical drama in England has said that

theatrical censorship throughout the eighteenth century . . . was aimed primarily at political attacks on the government and was only casually concerned with religious indiscretions. We must assume, therefore, once again that the absence of biblical drama from the stage during this period was due less to legal prohibition than to a tacit assumption that the dramatization of scriptural themes was in some sense profane.[28]

All the evidence I have found supports the accuracy of these statements. Biblical themes, as Roston points out,[29] reached the English stage during this period by way of oratorios. These were normally submitted for licensing, but since the themes and librettos were mostly taken directly from the Bible the question of censorship did not arise (even though some of them, like Handel's *Jephtha* and *Susanna* dealt with rather sensuous themes).

Profanity was a crime under common law in England,[30] and there were extra safeguards to insure that it did not occur in the theater. An Act of 3 Jac. I. c. 21, for example, specified that "if in any stage play, interlude, or shew, the name of the holy trinity, or any of the persons therein, be jestingly or profanely used, the offender shall forfeit 10*l*; one moeity to the king and the other to the informer."[31] Another safeguard was written into the patents granted to theaters after the Licensing Act. Part of the Newcastle patent for 1787 reads:

no Representation [shall] be admitted on the stage by Virtue or under Couler of these our Letters Patent whereby the Christian Religion in general or the Church of England may in any manner suffer reproach. Strictly inhibiting every degree of Abuse or Misrepresentation of Sacred Characters tending to expose Religion itself and to bring it into contempt and that no such Character be otherwise introduced or placed in any other Light than such as may enhance the just esteem of those who truly answer the end of their sacred Function.[32]

In actual fact the only sort of profanity eighteenth-century Examiners of Plays were likely to meet in a new play was a "damn" or an "Egad" or some similar oath from a country squire or gentleman about town. Sometimes these were censored, but not consistently. The *Monthly Review* in February 1763 criticized Arthur Murphy's farce *The Citizen* for approaching "too near the borders of prophaneness: LORD OF HEAVEN! is, surely, an expression too solemn, too awful, for the trivial occasion on which it was introduced, in this ludicrous scene!"[33] Complaints of this sort were not, however, very common before the end of the eighteenth century and Examiners tended not to be unduly sensitive about mild profanities. George Colman, Examiner from 1824 onwards, was different. He set out, says his biographer, to "purge the drama . . . even of the most innocent and reverent mention of the deity or the celestial beings, all prayers, invocations, and appeals for heavenly guidance, help, or blessing."[34] John Larpent was not so fanatical, but in the first quarter of the nineteenth century he began to experience the public pressures to which Colman later so willingly responded.

The moral propriety which became increasingly strong in the early years of the nineteenth century was closely allied to a new sense of religious propriety. Divines like James Plumptre and devout laymen like Thomas Bowdler were concerned with purging literature of religious as well as moral blemishes. Plumptre was concerned that the censorship of drama, when exercised at all—which was, he thought, rarely—was aimed only at "checking *political* liberties," whereas "The honour of God is left to shift for itself."[35] His misgivings were shared by many of his contemporaries. The *Morning Chronicle* reminded playwrights on 10 October 1808 of "the risk to which they expose themselves and the performers by their mock prayers and familiar use of the name of the Deity," the risk being prosecution under the James I statute mentioned above. Genest complained (8: 550) that Larpent had failed to censor "two indecent allusions to the Scriptures" in Daniel Terry's *Guy Mannering* (Covent Garden, 12 March 1816), and Rowland Hill wrote as energetically as anyone on the subject of profanity in plays:

To enumerate all the reprobate expressions used in plays would be endless. I mention not only their frequent calling on the name of God, sometimes with more *mock* solemnity, and at other times by the trifling terms "EGAD!"—"DAMME!" but also their very profane imprecations for damnation on themselves and others, *sworn out at full length.*—The reader will bear with me, if I mention but one other—enough to chill the very blood of those who have any regard to the sacred name of Christ—I mean the word, "ZOUNDS!" Can any thing be more horrid, when their filthy ribaldry is sanctioned by their swearing by *the wounds* of God, our holy Saviour and Redeemer? Can the lovers of HIS NAME be the admirers or hearers of language, so infernally blasphemous and profane!!![36]

Despite threats of legal action in this world and damnation in the next, playwrights in the early nineteenth century continued to draw upon religious subjects quite openly. That is, while they bowed very readily to demands for moral propriety they seemed much more reluctant to abandon the rich pickings of religion. Oaths and profanities continue to be uttered by their characters, the scriptures are alluded to in low farces, and, above all, the clergy are mocked relentlessly. This last factor occupied much of John Larpent's time, but he censored and suppressed plays on other religious grounds too. In a musical burletta called *Lovers of All Sorts* (LA 2136, Adelphi, 7 January 1820 as *Lovers on All Sides*) the following little exchange occurs between a chambermaid and her mistress's lover:

155

Courtall.   I say Jenny, do you ever hear her talk of me? eh you little witch?

Jenny.   Um, a little.

Courtall.   What did she say? eh, quick tell me, why dont you speak?

Jenny.   Why you know Sir, Chambermaids are sometimes like Balaams ass, they can't speak till they see the angel. (*holds out her hand.*)

Larpent deleted the speech about Balaam's ass and wrote to the Adelphi's acting manager, William Lee, about it. Lee replied (in a letter bound with LA 2136) that he had complied with the Examiner's wishes and "omitted the passage altogether . . . as I am most anxious to preserve the strictest proprity [*sic*] in the representations at the theatre I direct." Barlow at the Olympic theater was equally anxious to preserve propriety. In an anonymous piece called *Grey the Collier* (LA 2173, Olympic, 3 November 1820) a gang of ruffians, led by Grey, robs a church. In the course of the robbery Grey murders the local squire's daughter who happens to be in the church playing the organ at the time. Grey eventually is killed in an explosion in a mine, but so far as Larpent was concerned poetic justice was inadequate compensation for the sacrilege that had occurred, and the church robbery and murder had to be omitted. Barlow commented on Larpent's order in a note dated 27 October 1820, bound with the licensing manuscript of *Grey the Collier*:

I am very sorry we have had the misfortune to submit any thing to you which should be disapproved on such very strong grounds as those you have named—I should not have submitted it to you, if the *moral justice* of the whole had not . . . counteracted all implications of Sacrilege and impiety;—I submit however with great deference to your superior discretion & . . . the scene of the murder is removed.—& the intention of Sacrilege Diverted. . . . With many thanks for your kind & prompt consideration.

The Examiner was no less kind and prompt in protecting the clergy of any denomination from all kinds of satire in the early years of the nineteenth century. This must have been a disappointment to Francis Place, who wrote very sensibly on the subject of criticism of the church and its ministers in the drama:

No harm whatever could result from the most unlimited indulgence in respect to the church and the clergy of all denominations; some good might result from exposing cant, and fraud and hyprocricy; its tendency would be to make the clergy more discreet, and more attentive to their business. Of all men the clergy ought to be the most exposed to castigation for their vices, the most open to ridicule for their follies . . . .[37]

But Place, in religious as in political matters, was not a man of his time, and the more typical view was that the clergy's special status in society should guarantee them virtual immunity from criticism, especially in a public theater. One of the most frequent jokes about the clergy in the Larpent plays has to do with their fondness for drink, but the Examiner did his best to keep such jokes off the stage. Thus in a comedy by his successor, George Colman, Larpent decided that a speech about a village vicar would have to be omitted: "Mr Owlet, the Vicar, dines early; he always takes his three Pints. And, if by this time he knows the funeral service from the Apocrypha, his head is stronger than it used to be."[38] Similarly, a drunken parson who, among other things, is liberal with his blessings because they cost nothing, and who enjoys a cup of ale to whet his "sacred whistle," was eliminated by the censorship from G. Fox's pantomime *The House That Jack Built; or, Harlequin Tattered and Torn* (LA 2269, Olympic, 26 December 1821). He was replaced by an apothecary; and Reeve, Barlow's fellow lessee at the Olympic, wrote at the same time to Larpent to assure him that he "would not willingly be instrumental to the production of any piece that had a tendency to impropriety," as well as to confess that he felt "a little mortified at your having occasion to point out the necessity of an alteration." Another cooperative theater administrator was Samuel Arnold at the Lyceum. He wrote to Larpent on 1 July 1822 to confirm that some lines in George Macfarren's comic opera *Gil Blas* to which the Examiner had "so reasonably objected" had been expunged from the play.[39] The lines were spoken by Gil Perez, a drunken priest who believes in the restorative powers of alcohol (for himself as well as his flock) and merely suggests that "it behoves a good Priest (*pious* like myself) to avert all men's sorrows, and why should I not be my own pastor?" (LA 2301, Lyceum, 15 August 1822).

Larpent met with no resistance in these cases, but when he used the censorship to protect Methodist preachers from ridicule in Theodore Hook's farce, *Killing No Murder*, he found Hook less eager to congratulate him for his responsible guardianship of religious propriety than some managers had been. The play was sent for licensing from the Little Theatre in the Haymarket by James Winston on 20 June 1809 (LA 1582), but several alterations were demanded before it was licensed for performance on 21 August 1809. The bulk of the censorship was directed at a scene in which one Apollo Belvi gives an account of how, at Swansea, he became a Methodist preacher in order to win the hand of Hephzibah, the daughter of a Methodist minister—"So I preached and I preached—la, how I did preach!—till at last I preached myself plump into the heart of my young saint . . . ." The wedding date is fixed, but on the eve of the marriage Hephzibah gives birth to a son, seemingly Apollo's, and the ceremony is called off.

In a preface to the 1809 text of the play (with the suppressed scene printed separately at the end) Hook describes his reaction to and interpretation of the censorship. The night before the scheduled first performance Hook heard that his play had been refused a license. He was told that the refusal was on political grounds, but he later heard that it had to do with the play's "immorality." So he decided to visit Larpent, who received him, Hook says, with "a chilling look" and told him that the second act of *Killing No Murder* was a most "indecent and shameful attack on a very religious and harmless set of people." And so Hook's hope of "turning into ridicule the ignorance, and impudence of the self-elected pastors who infest every part of the kingdom," was foiled. Hook goes on to claim that Larpent told him that the government did not want the Methodists ridiculed, but Hook later discovered that the Examiner was "not only a rigid methodist himself,[40] but . . . even built a little tabernacle of his own." He was wrong on both counts, but having established to his own satisfaction Larpent's personal reasons for censoring the play Hook concludes his preface with a fierce attack on the Methodist movement.

LA 1589 is a copy of the 1809 edition of *Killing No Murder* with a number of manuscript notes and corrections, some of them in the preface, almost certainly by Larpent. Some of Hook's statements about his meeting with Larpent are denied, including those regarding government policy about the Methodists and Larpent's having built his own tabernacle. But this personal dispute between censor and author did not spread beyond the pages of Hook's preface. *The Times* announced on 28 June 1809 that a license for *Killing No Murder* was not forthcoming, but little interest and no controversy was generated by the announcement. In the early nineteenth century feeling ran high in some quarters against the Methodists and one finds much abuse of them in the press as fools, bigots and hypocrites. They were also known, of course, as enemies of the theater, and the *Theatrical Inquisitor* declaimed in 1812 that "The widely-spreading influence of this people is indeed alarming, and the effects are almost too terrible for belief."[41] But whatever Larpent's own religious views, his protection of churchmen was both consistent and unbiased; Welsh Methodist and Spanish Catholic alike were shielded from satire in the English theater.

Churchwomen, too, were protected. A license was refused outright to James Wild's short afterpiece, *Maids; or, The Nuns of Glossenbury*, submitted for licensing from the Lyceum on 26 May 1812 (LA 1721). *Maids* is a dismal thing, set at the time of the dissolution of the monasteries. Two soldiers find their way into a convent and make advances and even proposals of marriage to some very receptive nuns. The nuns display carnal and wordly desires unworthy of their calling and their unseemly behavior presumably caused the suppression of the play. And in John Howard Payne's play, *Mrs. Smith; or, The Wife and the Widow* (LA 2356; Little Theatre, 18 June 1823) a widow, speaking of her ambitions for a second marriage, says "If I stumble this time, I deserve to fall—now I know what's what, and have my senses about me. Charles has graces which would convert a whole nunnery to matrimony." A note at the end of the licensing manuscript describes this as a "very coarse speech" and it is marked for omission.

David Mayer has noted that a sharply satirical, and uncensored, portrait of a clergyman appears in the pantomime *Harlequin and Poor Robin; or, The House that Jack Built* (LA 2388; Covent Garden, 26 December 1823). Mayer suggests, and it is a plausible suggestion, that Larpent's "feeble condition" shortly before his death a few weeks later prevented him from censoring the satire.[42] But given good health, Larpent was as efficient as ever in detecting and suppressing disrespectful portraits of clergymen and religious improprieties of all kinds.

159

7

Stage Censorship and Society, 1737-1824

Others write plays so inconsiderately, that after they have appeared on the stage, the actors have been forced to fly and abscond, for fear of being punished, as it has often happened, for having affronted kings, and dishonoured whole families. These, and many other ill consequences, which I omit, would cease, by appointing an intelligent and judicious person at court to examine all plays before they were acted, that is, not only those which are represented at court, but throughout Spain; so that, without his licence, no magistrate should suffer any play to appear in public. Thus players would be careful to send their plays to court, and might then act them with safety, and those who writ would be more circumspect, as standing in awe of an examiner that could judge of their works. By these means we should be furnished with good plays, and the end they are designed for would be attained, the people diverted, the Spanish wits esteemed, the actors safe, and the government spared the trouble of punishing them.[1]

So wrote Cervantes in Spain at the beginning of the seventeenth century. By the end of the first quarter of the nineteenth century in England, public opinion, including, on the whole, theatrical opinion, had settled firmly in favor of a system very similar to that described by Cervantes. When the 1832 Select Committee on Dramatic Literature met, some witnesses, it is true, spoke out against precensorship of drama, and many valid objections to it were raised. George Bolwell Davidge, for example, considered an Examiner of Plays to be unnecessary, since it was unlikely that the public "in these enlightened times would tolerate anything offensive,"[2] and if a theater should present anything offensive it stood, in any case, to lose its license. Davidge also thought it wrong that plays should be subject "to the opinion of an individual; for there are scarcely two people to be found in the world who think exactly alike; and sometimes the licencer might think one way, and the public might think very differently."[3] The playwright Douglas Jerrold, some of whose plays had been censored by George Colman, also thought precensorship of plays was unnecessary, on the grounds that managers were sensible and responsible enough not to "overstep any bounds of decorum . . . ."[4] John Payne Collier, although he thought the system of licensing plays was "advantageous" and had "as a whole from 1737 to the present time . . . been fairly exercised,"[5] nonetheless believed that the Lord Chamberlain ought not to have unlimited power over the drama. Aggrieved playwrights should have the right of appeal, perhaps to a court of law.[6] Francis Place, the radical politician, was, not surprisingly, strongly against the censorship. When asked if the abolition of censorship might not bring political plays into the theater, he bluntly replied, "Yes; and there ought to be."[7] "Do you mean to state that, in your opinion," the committee asked, "there ought to be no limit to any political allusions in a play, or any indecency or immorality, which might be produced at a theatre, other than the limit which would be imposed upon it by the judgment of the audience?" To which Place answered, "Yes, I think no other restriction is necessary."[8]

But those witnesses who criticized the censorship system were in a minority. The general feeling among witnesses, most of whom were connected in some way with the theater, was that the system established in 1737 should continue to operate. The committee accepted this view and in their report no changes were recommended. Place had admitted that his attitude toward the censorship, although shared, he claimed, by "many well-read and intelligent men," was not the general opinion, and in electing to recommend the retention of precensorship the committee undoubtedly reflected public feeling on the matter. This feeling was perhaps summarized by Francis Ludlow Holt when, in 1816, he defended the 1737 Licensing Act (in its censorship aspects) as "a salutory regulation of the morality and decency of public exhibitions, and if it can be said at all to interfere with the liberty of the press, it is an interposition well warranted by the interests of the public morals and peace."[9]

One difficulty faced by the critics of the censorship in 1832 was that they were not supported by any tradition of opposition to government control of the drama. They could not refer to any sustained efforts during the past several decades to rid the theater of the Lord Chamberlain and his Examiner of Plays. Indeed, to find any sort of serious attack on the censorship it is necessary to go back nearly a century, to the time of the Licensing Act itself.

Lord Chesterfield, of course, had had the opportunity and the talent to voice early and comprehensive criticism of the act. His famous speech in the House of Lords[10] has justly been praised for over two centuries for its eloquence. We should praise Chesterfield, too, for so precisely identifying the injustices created by the act. His criticism of the system which gave the Lord Chamberlain such power over the "poets and players" was never satisfactorily answered:

Do not let us subject them to the arbitrary will and pleasure of any one man. A power lodged in the hands of one single man, to judge and determine, without any limitation, without any controul or appeal, is a sort of power unknown to our laws, inconsistent with our constitution. It is a higher, a more absolute power than we trust even to the King himself; and, therefore, I must think, we ought not to vest any such power in his Majesty's lord chamberlain.[11]

Chesterfield's speech was easily the most informed and thoughtful attack made on the Licensing Act in the eighteenth century. It was quickly followed by a new edition of Milton's *Areopagitica* with an unacknowledged preface by James Thomson. Neither the Licensing Act nor, indeed, the stage at all, is mentioned by Thomson, but the point of the preface and of the republication of the *Areopagitica* was very obvious:

I hope it will never be this Nation's Misfortune to fall into the Hands of an Administration, that do not from their Souls abhor any thing that has but the remotest Tendency towards the Erection of a new and arbitrary Jurisdiction over the Press: or can otherwise look upon any Attempt that way, than as the greatest Impiety, the cruellest, the wickedest, the most irreligious thing that can be imagined.[12]

Then, in 1739, appeared Johnson's essay, *A Complete Vindication of the Licensers of the Stage from the Malicious and Scandalous Aspersions of Mr. Brooke*, which was prompted by the suppression of Henry Brooke's *Gustavus Vasa*. *A Complete Vindication* covers much the same ground as Chesterfield's speech, but whereas Chesterfield attempted to sway the government with cool eloquence, Johnson assaulted it with scathing irony. The Examiner gave Brooke no reason for banning *Gustavus Vasa*, but "Is it for a poet to demand a licenser's reason for his proceedings? Is he not rather to acquiesce in the decision of authority, and conclude, that there are reasons which he cannot comprehend?"[13] Will the "pernicious sentiments" banished from the stage be printed and thus "more studiously read, because they are prohibited?" Then let us hope to "succeed in our design of extending the power of the licenser to the press, and of making it criminal to publish any thing without an IMPRIMATUR."

How much would this single law lighten the mighty burden of state affairs! With how much security might our ministers enjoy their honours, their places, their reputations, and their admirers, could they once suppress those malicious invectives which are, at present, so industriously propagated, and so eagerly read; could they hinder any arguments but their own from coming to the ears of the people, and stop effectually the voice of cavil and inquiry![14]

Did Brooke think his play unjustly banned? But even his prologue

is filled with such insinuations, as no friend of our excellent government can read without indignation and abhorence, and cannot but be owned to be a proper introduction to such scenes, as seem designed to kindle in the audience a flame of opposition, patriotism, publick spirit, and independency; that spirit which we have so long endeavoured to suppress, and which cannot be revived without the entire subversion of all our schemes.[15]

Fielding, too, in the *Champion* of 10 December 1739, "defended" the Licensing Act, and encouraged the executive "to perform their parts with the utmost vigilance, and to take the most effectual care that no infringements be made in so invaluable a law."[16] Pope can also be counted as one of the eminent opponents of the Licensing Act, although in print he limited himself to just a few lines of gentle criticism:

> There sunk Thalia, nerveless, cold, and dead,
> Had not her Sister Satyr held her head:

164

Nor cou'd'st thou, CHESTERFIELD! a tear refuse,
Thou wept'st, and with thee wept each gentle Muse.[17]

One might have expected some opposition from Swift, too, for he surely could not have approved of Walpole's introducing censorship to silence his critics. But Swift was old and in Ireland when the Licensing Act was passed, and, if he had spoken out against it, he would doubtless have been reminded that he had himself proposed in 1709 a stage censorship system differing from Walpole's only in its greater severity.[18]

The opposition expressed against the Licensing Act by individual and gifted writers was backed for several months by some segments of the press and public. It seems clear that London theatergoers were unhappy both about the reduction in the number of theaters regularly open to them after the act became law,[19] and about the censorship. But it is difficult to be sure to what extent the feeling was directed against the censorship alone. The *London Evening Post* commented on 28 January 1738 that it was "remarkable that the new Comedy call'd The Nest of Plays[20] . . . and the new Farce call'd The Coffee House[21] . . . which are the two first that have been perform'd since the Act of Parliament took Place, obliging all Plays, Farces, &c. to be licens'd before play'd, were both damn'd by the Town." But a writer in the *Daily Advertiser* for 30 January denied that the unfavorable reception accorded these plays had anything to do with the new licensing methods; they were damned because "they Both were Most Damnable Things, and on no other Account whatsoever."[22] But the preface to *The Nest of Plays* quite firmly attributes the opposition to the performance to "*some People, who, it seems, were determined, as they themselves declared, to silence without any Distinction, the* first Fruits *of that* Act *of* Parliament *which was thought necessary for the Regulation of the* Stage." Miller, on the other hand, was under the impression that *The Coffee-House* was damned solely because it was thought to contain some personal reflections.[23] Miller's next play, *Art and Nature*, acted at Drury Lane on 16 February 1738, was also damned on the first night, and a correspondent in the *Daily Advertiser* for 22 February 1738 implied that this was again a protest against the Licensing Act.[24] Another play which was acted but once in the months immediately following the Licensing Act was William Shirley's tragedy, *The Parricide; or, Innocence in Distress*. It was

165

damned at Covent Garden on 17 January 1739 because it was, says Shirley in the published text (1739), "a New Play, and had been Licensed."

Silencing a play seems an odd way of protesting against legislation that was itself intended to silence plays, and for an author to say that his play was damned because of the Licensing Act was a convenient way of sidestepping the question of the play's merit.[25] But that there was a degree of feeling against the new censorship is beyond doubt. A French visitor to England at this time, the Abbé Le Blanc, declared that the new law "occasioned an universal murmur in the nation, and was openly complained of in the public papers: in all the coffee-houses of London it was treated as an unjust law, and manifestly contrary to the liberties of the people of England."[26] And an old man looking back in 1775 on the year of the Licensing Act remembered that "every person . . . of wit and taste, as well as multitudes of good sense and examples of virtue, objected against its passing into a law, as being an infringement of British liberty . . . ."[27] Moreover, if there had not been opposition, the government newspaper the *Daily Gazetteer*, would not have spent so much time in the spring and summer of 1737 defending the licensing of plays. Numerous paragraphs were published in May, June, and July to explain why censorship was necessary, and just as many articles appeared in the opposition press (principally the *Craftsman, Common Sense,* and *Fog's Weekly Journal*) to explain why it was both unnecessary and undesirable. The normal *Gazetteer* line was that the theater had abused its freedom by encouraging indiscriminate political satire which brought his Majesty's ministers into disrepute and hence threatened the constitutional authority of government.[28] The basic opposition view was that if ministers behaved in a foolish or corrupt manner, they ought to be criticized, and this was very different from preaching sedition.[29] The *Craftsman* and the *Daily Gazetteer* continued their dispute about politics and drama until the resignation of Walpole removed the main cause of the controversy.

Opposition to the censorship clauses of the Licensing Act also came from the playwrights, but it was opposition of a mild kind. One of the complaints was that the censorship added an extra hazard to the already difficult task of getting a play produced. Thomas Cooke, in the preface to his tragedy, *The Mournful Nuptials; or, Love the*

Cure of all Woes, published in 1739, outlines some of the difficulties faced by a playwright:

The treating with an injudicious, and sometimes an insincere, manager, the necessity of hearing the petulant remarks of actors . . . and the attendance at rehearsals, are severer tryals of human patience than they who have never had occasion to make them can well conceive.

To these difficulties is now added "another fiery ordeal," the Lord Chamberlain's office, "which may prove severer than the former, by blasting all the fruits of the labours passed." But Cooke is mainly concerned to defend the use of satire in literature and to criticize those who have recently moved to restrict its use in the drama. He predicts that as a result of the new restrictions the public will be "deprived of many excellent pieces,which would otherwise be exhibited." (Much of this preface was reprinted in the *Craftsman* of 6 April 1745.)

Two anonymous writers of this period made brief and rather lighthearted complaints against the censorship. The author of the unacted farce, *The Informers Outwitted* (1738), says he did not offer it to the theaters because now the "*Inspectors, and the L—d C—n*" have been added to the many hands through which a play must pass before a decision to act it can be taken, the process "would perhaps *take up several years.*" The author of another unacted farce, *Mock-Preacher* (1739), says he had no intention of introducing it to the stage; "therefore I give myself no Concern, about its being licensed, which is a great Satisfaction to me; for I dread the Thoughts of having my Works go through the Hands of Mr. *Odell*; tho' he is an old Friend—"

In addition to those whose plays were actually refused a license in these early years of the censorship's operation, one playwright who had just cause to complain was James Ayres. He had hopes that his ballad-opera, *Sancho at Court; or, The Mock-Governor*, might be suitable for a London production. Since Ayres was in Trinity College, Dublin, John Torbuck, the printer and bookseller, undertook to treat with Fleetwood at Drury Lane on his behalf. After some shortening of the text, Fleetwood said "*he believ'd it would do, provided it pass'd the Chamberlain's Office.*" Torbuck expressed surprise at Fleetwood's comment: "*Why, Sir, says I, I don't see any Reflexion on the Government in it . . . . 'tis true there are some free*

Strokes, but then they are general, and are not levelled at any particular Party or Person." To which Fleetwood replied: *"that's very true; but we can't judge how the Licencer may interpret Things; however I'll put it on the Trial, and if it passes it shall be acted."* The play was sent for licensing, but for nearly eight months Torbuck heard nothing from Fleetwood. *"At length,"* he says, *"being tired with Attendances and waiting, I desired my Copy again; but was told I could not have it, it being left at a Place not then to be come at."* Where this "Place" was, Torbuck does not say, but it sounds very much as if it was the Lord Chamberlain's office. The conclusion that Torbuck drew from these experiences was that the difficulties faced by a playwright—*"the Approbation of the Players, the Licensing-Office and the ill-natur'd Critic, not to say any thing of the Publick"*—gave him little chance of success.[30]

The only serious criticism of the censorship to come from the playwrights at this time was from Henry Brooke[31] and Thomas Cooke, both of whom were associated with the political opposition to Walpole. For the rest, the censorship was not much more than a minor irritation, a lesser grievance than the many others playwrights constantly complained about.

For the period of nearly five years between the passing of the Licensing Act and the resignation of Walpole, there existed a fairly constant amount of criticism of the new procedure for licensing plays. That much of the criticism, especially from the press, was really directed at Walpole rather than at the censorship, is shown by the rapid decline in interest in dramatic censorship that took place after Walpole had gone. Also, of course, after five years the censorship had established itself as a normal part of theatrical life and audiences and playwrights became less conscious of it. For managers the censorship was never a great burden. There were always plenty of plays, old and new, available and if the Lord Chamberlain should happen to refuse his license to a new piece, it was no problem to find another.

From 1742 until as late as the Joint Committee of the House of Lords and House of Commons investigation of theater censorship in 1909, there was no organized or sustained opposition to the system of play licensing established in 1737. The pattern that developed after 1742, of individual and isolated protests against the censorship, continued until the end of the nineteenth century. Even then Shaw was saying that "few things would surprise me more than to meet a representative Englishman who regarded my desire to abolish the Censor otherwise than he would regard the desire of a pickpocket to abolish the police."[32] In the eighteenth and early nineteenth centuries nearly all the protests came, understandably enough, from the authors of suppressed plays. Some of the more publicized ones— from Henry Brooke, Samuel Foote, Lady Wallace, and Theodore Hook, for example—have been discussed in previous chapters. The point that should be stressed here is that in none of the protests from the playwrights do we find a direct call for the abolition of the precensorship of drama. The protests are not as a rule against the system of censorship; they are against the unjustified application of the system in particular cases. The protestors seek relief for their personal grievances; they do not attempt to speak for their profession. Thus even Charles Macklin readily concedes that the Lord Chamberlain "has a right to prohibit," insisting only that a prohibition must not arise from "caprice, or enmity, or partiality,"[33] as Macklin evidently thought it had in the case of *The Man of the World.*

William Shirley had more reason to berate the censorship system than almost anyone else in the eighteenth century. When his *Electra* was banned, most unjustly, in 1765, his reputation, his honor, and his purse suffered. Not only did he lose the profits from the production of *Electra*, but his prospects as a playwright suffered. Beard, the Covent Garden manager, had liked *Electra*, but after it had been refused a license he would not consider another play Shirley had written some years earlier. But despite all this, the tone of Shirley's protest against the censorship (in the 1765 edition of *Electra*) is very moderate. True, he describes the Licensing Act as a "source of real grievance," and he concludes his remarks by telling those who hold "such unlimited power" over the drama to mind "how they exercise hereafter, lest injuries are thereby heedlessly extended far beyond any means of compensation they can possibly apply." But Shirley adheres to his earlier promise not to comment on "the nature of such power, or any methods of executing it." Instead, he expresses his "abhorrence" of "any prostitution of the stage to the serving of unworthy purposes, and every cause of deviation from the wise ends of its institution; which were . . . to polish the manners and improve the morals of the people."

Frederick Reynolds, whose play, *The Bastille*, was banned in 1789, refrained from writing personal satire if he did not have the permission of the subject of the satire, for otherwise the play "must have been suppressed by the licenser"; and he regrets that dramatists have to "bow submissively" to "despotic decisions, and anomalous opinions, of managers, actors, editors, reviewers, licensers, and last, not least, cockney auditors . . . ."[34] But the suppression of *The Bastille* elicited no objection from Reynolds that we know of.

Press campaigns against the censorship, such as that carried on by the *Craftsman* before 1742, were almost nonexistent later in the century. Occasionally, the press would take up a particular playwright's cause, as the *Morning Chronicle* did in Foote's case when *The Trip to Calais* was suppressed. And from time to time a review or a theatrical column would make a passing comment about a particularly arbitrary instance of censorship or about the inhibiting effect of the censorship in general. The *London Review*, for example, once encouraged Hugh Downman to write something for the stage, saying that he may possibly "succeed better than those whose productions have suffered so much by the curtailing of lord chamberlains, and the correction and metamorphosing of managers."[35]

The only attempt at sustained criticism of the censorship after 1742 that has come to light is that in the *Monthly Mirror* in the 1790s. The first issue of this periodical appeared in December 1795. The preface promised a "more minute investigation than has generally been given" to the theater. This, readers were told, would include "A Series of Letters to the Licencer." In a letter to the Lord Chamberlain in this first issue, "Honestus" indicated his intention of writing these letters to the Examiner, "wherein I mean to explain the use, necessity, and duties of such a character: his influence on dramatic writing in general: and the qualifications requisite to the due discharge of his office."[36] The scheme was ambitious and worthwhile; but the achievement failed to live up to the promise. The first Letter appeared in January 1796 and is interesting.[37] Honestus expresses astonishment that so much power should rest in the hands of one man. Foreigners, too, he says, are surprised at this, but they would be still more surprised if they realized that Englishmen "sit tamely under the exercise of his [the Examiner's] authority, and so far from regretting their subjection, never think proper even to inquire into the nature of the office." Honestus doubts whether "*one twentieth* part of the British nation have any idea of what a LICENSER is." Some think the office purely nominal, others that it is beneficial to the interests of the stage. But Honestus believes, and hopes to prove, that "not only the DRAMA, but *men* and *manners* in general, are very materially affected and injured by his authority," and he promises to tell the Examiner how he should discharge his duties. This was a good introduction to the series. Mrs. Larpent thought her husband "much abused" by it,[38] but it asked important questions about the theater that had not been asked for fifty years. The *Monthly Mirror* showed a lack of urgency about answering them, however. Seven months passed before the next Letter appeared in September.[39] It opened in a very moderate tone. It is, Honestus tells the Examiner—sounding rather like a *Daily Gazetteer* writer of the late 1730s—"necessary that the legislative authority should be secure from the wanton attacks of faction and disloyalty. To prevent, therefore, the propagation of seditious sentiments, through the medium of the public stage, the appointment of a situation like yours, I grant, was expedient . . . ." But an error was made, according to Honestus, both in giving such a job to one man and in allowing the selection of this man to be on such an uncontrolled basis. The Examiner gets his job not because he is likely to perform his duties well, but because the Lord Chamberlain wishes to oblige him with the salary and fees attached to the office. The "blundering supervisor" thus appointed may be quite unqualified for the job:

Ignorance may start objections to one passage, and caprice to another, till the piece be thought unfit for representation, or permitted to be acted only in such a state as that inevitable condemnation must ensue.

No one knows what abilities an Examiner of Plays is supposed to possess:

The qualifications of a LICENSER are not defined like those of a physician, a lawyer, or any other professional character; he goes through no examination before his formal instalment into office: he has no claims to make but those of his patron; interest, not merit, is his initiation and his warranty.

These critical observations by Honestus, although not backed up by any detailed examples, were perfectly fair and were worth developing. In the November issue of the *Monthly Mirror*[40] a third Letter was promised for December, but it did not appear. In fact, Letter II proved to be the end of the series. There were perhaps two reasons why the Letters were discontinued. The editor may have realized that 1796, with England losing the European war, was a somewhat tactless time to raise the issue of freedom of speech in the theater; or, more likely, there was not very much interest shown in the series by the *Monthly Mirror*'s readers.

One of the most noticeable features about attitudes toward the censorship of plays in the eighteenth and early nineteenth centuries is lack of interest or concern, often in places where one would most expect to find it. In the numerous pamphlets published at regular intervals debating the usefulness or danger of the theater to society, censorship is hardly mentioned. For those God-fearing individuals who were opposed to the theater on religious grounds, nothing short of complete abolition would do; for those who found the theater socially valuable, the important censors were public opinion and the managers. In most of these debates the Lord Chamberlain's censorship was simply not an important issue one way or the other.[41] In the intense discussions in the early nineteenth century about the "freedom" of the theater, writers were interested not in freedom from censorship, but freedom from the monopoly on legitimate drama enjoyed by the patent houses. Theater audiences occasionally became agitated when the censorship prevented them from seeing a particular play or hearing a prologue, but there was never anything in London to compare with the rioting crowds in Paris on 13 June 1783 when the king suppressed *Le Mariage de Figaro*.[42] There is precious little evidence to support Theodore Hook's contention that English audiences in 1809 had a "detestation" of the Examiner's "arbitrary and strained prerogative."[43] The newspapers and periodicals, although often noisy in defense of their own freedom of speech, never granted the theater that same right. The censorship or suppression of a play was usually glossed over in the way that the

European Magazine reviewed the production of Charles Stuart's *The Irishman in Spain,* which had been heavily censored by General Gunning: "This Farce was originally advertised under the title of *She would be a Duchess,* which alarming some individuals of high rank, the piece was much altered, and its title changed."[44] There is no direct mention of the censorship, no discussion of it, and no objection to it.

Another segment of British society which zealously defended freedom of speech was the legal profession. William Blackstone, for example, summed up the widely accepted view of what was meant by the "liberty of the press":

The liberty of the press is indeed essential to the nature of a free state: but this consists in laying no previous restraints upon publications, and not in freedom from censure for criminal matter when published. Every freeman has an undoubted right to lay what sentiments he pleases before the public: to forbid this, is to destroy the freedom of the press: but if he publishes what is improper, mischievous, or illegal, he must take the consequence of his own temerity. To subject the press to the restrictive power of a licenser, as was formerly done . . . is to subject all freedom of sentiment to the prejudices of one man, and make him the arbitrary and infallible judge of all controverted points in learning, religion, and government.[45]

All of what Blackstone says could well have been applied to the theater but it was not, by Blackstone or anyone else.

Many people who wrote about the theater in the eighteenth and early nineteenth centuries expressed the view, in spite of the existence of precensorship, that the drama was not under adequate control and that much was said and seen on the stage that ought to have been left unsaid and unseen. It was not the practice as a rule to criticize the Lord Chamberlain or the Examiner directly (as James Boaden criticized Larpent for licensing Colman's *The Iron Chest*),[46] but in many paragraphs there was the implication that they were not being strict enough. Complaints about immorality, licentiousness and offensive language were common. Often, Restoration plays were the cause of complaint. The *Public Ledger* review of the performance of Congreve's *Love for Love* at Drury Lane on 14 November 1771 is not untypical. The play is condemned for its "vein of licentiousness, so dangerous in its tendency, and so unsuitable to the present professed chastity of the times." It should be "consigned to oblivion."[47] The Lord Chamberlain had the power to do just this, but, oddly enough, he never did so. New plays, too, were not adequately controlled according to some people. *The School for Scandal* was described as "more dangerous to the manners of society, than it can possibly tend to promote its pleasure," by a writer in the *Gentleman's Magazine*,[48] and the anonymous author of *Thoughts on the Entertainments of the Stage* spoke for many of his contemporaries in 1786 when he said, disapprovingly, that "in general it must be acknowledged, that they [i.e. plays] abound with oaths and curses, with profane jests, and lewd discourses."[49] If this were the case, then John Larpent was not doing his job properly. It was perhaps a like feeling that led John Galt to ask in 1814:

The stage has, in England, become almost as great an organ of public instruction as the pulpit. Is it proper that there should be no law to regulate what is taught from it, except the notions of one obscure solitary individual, the reader of plays in the Lord Chamberlain's department?[50]

Not surprisingly, James Plumptre wanted the censorship tightened up, especially in the provinces, where he thought that local magistrates should be empowered to act as censors, a suggestion which, if implemented, would have had disastrous consequences for provincial theaters.[51] Plumptre also believed that all plays, not just new ones, should be subject to censorship, and he advocated the establishment of a "Dramatic Institution" where old plays could be cleansed of "all indecency, profaneness and immorality . . . ."[52]

Some playwrights had reason to complain because their plays had been suppressed. But what of those playwrights who were not so directly involved with the censorship? In the present century, before the abolition of precensorship of the drama, we became accustomed to hearing complaints from playwrights about the oppressive effect the censorship had on their work. In the period covered by this study there was no such feeling prevalent among the playwrights. To be sure, even those who normally had nothing to fear from the censorship were well aware of its existence, and were sometimes even a little worried or deterred by it. Horace Walpole, for example, worried (unnecessarily as it turned out), that the new epilogue he had written for a performance of Rowe's *Tamerlane* on 4 November

1746 might be suppressed,[53] and Oliver Goldsmith wrote later in the century of a playwright's work having to be "strained through a licenser" before it could be presented to the public.[54] But most writers, including several whose plays were censored or suppressed, expressed no objection to the censorship at all. When Sheridan, for example, opposed the Seditious Assemblies Bill in the Commons in 1795 on the grounds that it deprived people of their liberty, he was reminded that he had never felt it necessary to "seek the alleviation of such a restraint on dramatick freedom."[55] Sheridan was by no means alone in this. Indeed, support for censorship was rather more common than opposition to it among playwrights. Joseph Holman, author of *The Robbers*, suppressed in 1799, not only accepted Larpent's decision, he defended it.[56] At about the same time, Mrs. West urged strict government control of plays, and another playwright of that period, Thomas Morton, lived long enough to express his support for censorship to the 1832 committee. He told them that the political "licentiousness" of Fielding's *Pasquin* had made control of the drama "absolutely necessary" in 1737,[57] and when asked if he thought "the censorship of the licenser . . . any obstacle to the well-being of the stage," he replied, "I think it is highly essential to the well-being of the stage that such an officer should be appointed."[58]

Spasmodic and restrained criticism, apparent indifference, demands for stricter application, silent acceptance, firm support: these were the various attitudes toward the censorship of plays between 1742 and John Larpent's death in 1824. The opposition generated between 1737 and 1742 could not be maintained after Walpole's resignation, and thereafter the authority of the Lord Chamberlain and his Examiner was not seriously questioned for another hundred and fifty years.

This acquiescence in a state of affairs which has now been abolished as an intolerable burden on the theater seems odd. Why did so few people in a period very sensitive about freedom of speech, object to the obvious restriction on the playwrights' liberties? Or, to put it another way, what was there about the theater in the eighteenth and early nineteenth centuries that made nearly everyone feel that it had to be strictly controlled? The brief answer to these questions is that the drama, and literature in general, of that time had, or were considered to have, considerably more influence on the

John Larpent. *Courtesy Mr. Douglas de H. Larpent*

tone and quality of life than they are thought to have nowadays. Broadly speaking, all censorship at all times has been based on the assumption that there is a direct relationship between what people hear, see, or read, and how they behave, or might behave, thereafter. Its only justification has been that to allow certain types of literature to be freely available would, sooner or later, have a harmful effect on society. One of the main reasons why such strong objections have been raised in recent years to all forms of literary censorship is that the assumption that literature can have this sort of influence or effect has been seriously questioned and by some rejected. "It is not," according to the Arts Council of Great Britain, "for the State to prohibit private citizens from choosing what they may or may not enjoy in literature or art unless there were incontrovertible evidence that the result would be injurious to society. There is no such evidence."[59] Now earlier times, rightly or wrongly, relied more on general observations of the way life was lived around them than on "evidence" of the statistical kind. Their observations told them that what people read at home or saw in the theater could and did influence their behavior. There might be disagreements over whether a particular play or novel was likely to be influential in a good or bad way; but most people were agreed that words, read or spoken, were never simply neutral.

As regards the theater, some persons believed, perhaps rightly, that the extent of its influence on the behavior of people was exaggerated. In his familiar prologue for the opening of the Drury Lane season in 1747, Johnson stressed that "The stage but echoes back the public voice; / The drama's laws, the drama's patrons give." The drama follows, not leads. And another great man of the age, Jean-Jacques Rousseau, said much the same thing in a more elaborate way. In his *Lettre à M. d'Alembert*, published in 1758, he wrote that we ought not to ascribe to the theater "le pouvoir de changer des sentiments ni des moeurs qu'il ne peut que suivre et embellir." And,

Je voudrois bien qu'on me montrât clairement et sans verbiage par quels moyens il [the drama] pourroit produire en nous des sentiments que nous n'aurions pas, et nous faire juger des êtres moraux autrement que nous n'en jugeons en nous-mêmes.[60]

But despite the pronouncements of great men, it was the common belief that the drama did a lot more than simply reflect or follow public taste and manners.

> What equal Method can be found to lead, or stimulate the Mind, to a quicker Sense of Truth, and Virtue, or warm a People into the Love, and Practice of such Principles, as might be at once a Defence, and Honour to their Country?[61]

This, said Cibber, the drama could do. The sentiment echoed through the eighteenth century. Fifty years after Cibber, Thomas Holcroft is saying the same thing:

> The theatre . . . has a most powerful and good influence on morals . . . . the soul, imbibing virtuous and heroic principles, is roused and impelled to actions that honour not only individuals but nations, and give a dignity to human nature. Those who can doubt this are to be pitied.[62]

"Of all recreations it [the stage] is the most rational, and teaches morality much more effectually than the pulpit," says one of Holcroft's characters.[63] High praise, but also heavy responsibility. For if the drama was capable of fostering so much good, it was also necessarily capable of promoting much that was bad. Thus John Hawkesworth justified his extensive expurgation of Dryden's *Amphitryon* on the grounds that a less carefully revised version of the play might have left it "so vicious in the very constituent parts, as to sully, and, perhaps corrupt almost every mind, before which it had been represented."[64] Comments like these were not the preserve of the fanatical opponents of the theater; they came from practically anyone who was interested in the well being of the theater. Plays, undoubtedly, could be a danger to society.

The evidence? To prove that the drama had been directly responsible for corrupting wide areas of English society was difficult even for the religious enemies of the theater. But *The Beggar's Opera* often took some of the blame for the rising crime rate in London, and many people could give individual instances of the harmful consequences of a play or plays. The story of how a group of young Germans in Fribourg tried to emulate the deeds of the outlaws in Schiller's *Die Räuber* was well known,[65] and Charles Dibdin was convinced that German playwrights "have tainted the manners of

178

Europe, and in particular of England, with productions which violate probability, wound morality, terrify instead of delight, menace instead of conciliate, in short, which among every outrageous and monstrous doctrine, teach filial ingratitude, encourage adultery, and circulate such revolting and scandalous tenets as thirty years ago would have been spurned at by an English audience with ineffable indignation."[66] An argument frequently heard in early nineteenth-century religious tracts against the theater was that Eustace Budgell's suicide in 1737 (drowning in the Thames) was prompted by Cato's suicide in Addison's play. "What Cato did, and Addison approved/ Cannot be wrong," Budgell's suicide note is said to have read. Governments, however, were more worried about sedition than suicide, and the impact of plays like *The Beggar's Opera* in London in 1728, *Mahomet* in Dublin in 1754, or *Le Mariage de Figaro* in Paris in 1784, could have left them in no doubt that the drama was capable of producing an immediate and, to a governmental way of thinking, alarming effect. That, after all, is why there was a Licensing Act.

Most eighteenth- and early nineteenth-century theatergoers would have agreed with Joanna Baillie's proposition that "The theatre is a school in which much good or evil may be learned."[67] The theaters, therefore, were too important to be left to themselves. "On the virtues, and manners of a people, depends the prosperity of a state: these will be influenced by the theaters; the concern is therefore of a public nature; and the government only can prudently be entrusted with the care of them."[68] So declared an anonymous writer in 1759. His own and later generations would have approved both of the conclusion and of the logic used to arrive at it.

Thus the period's acceptance of dramatic censorship can be explained. The arguments advanced to show why dramatic censorship was necessary could also be used to explain why all literature, and even the press, ought to be subject to some form of government control. In fact, a censorship did operate against nondramatic literature and the press in the eighteenth and early nineteenth centuries.[69] But it was a postcensorship in these cases, not, as with the drama, a precensorship. That is, the government had no regular machinery for censoring a novel or a newspaper before it was published. Nor was there any widespread public demand that they should have. It remains to explain, then, why it was thought that the drama alone should bear the extra restraint of precensorship.

The author of *The Usefulness of the Stage to Religion, and to Government* asked, "Cannot the Press spread its poison as far as the Stage, and be attended with the same mischievious Consequence?" (p. 25). And the 1832 Committee wanted to know why plays should be precensored and not books. John Payne Collier went part of the way to providing an answer to both questions:

> For this reason: first of all for the old maxim, that what is objectionable is presented to the eyes; next, because it is presented to the eyes and ears in the most attractive manner; and also, thirdly, because what is presented to the eyes and ears, instead of being offered to one reader, as in the case of a book, is presented to hundreds or perhaps thousands of persons at once.[70]

James Sutherland has perhaps made the point more clearly than Collier managed to do on the spur of the moment. Speaking particularly of personal satire in the theater, but making a valid general point at the same time, Sutherland says:

> there its [i.e. the satire's] explosive qualities are greatly increased by the presence of an audience in whom excitement is easily generated. Readers are scattered up and down the country; an audience is concentrated in one place, and as the feelings of each individual are communicated to his neighbour the mass emotion may rapidly become overwhelming.[71]

The combination of words and action is a more potent force than spoken words alone, and more potent still than printed words. Or, as Colley Cibber, following Jeremy Collier, says:

> I doubt it will be very difficult, to give a *printed* Satyr, or Libel, half the Force, or Credit of an *acted* one. The most artful, or notorious Lye, or strain'd Allusion that ever slander'd a great Man, may be read, by some People, with a Smile of Contempt, or at worst, it can impose but on one Person, at once: but when the Words of the same plausible Stuff, shall be repeated on a Theatre, the Wit of it among a Crowd of Hearers, is liable to be over-valued, and may unite, and warm a whole Body of the Malicious, or Ignorant, into a Plaudit. . . .[72]

With an individual reader, Cibber continues, "the Poison has a much slower Operation, upon the Body of a People, when it is so

180

retail'd out, than when sold to a full Audience by wholesale."[73]
Printed words, whether we think of the Bible or of *Das Kapital*, can,
in the long term, have an immense effect on societies and nations. But
since books are usually read privately and individually, the process is
bound to be a prolonged one. A play, on the other hand, can provoke
an immediate and spontaneous reaction from many hundreds of people at the same time, as did *The Playboy of the Western World* with
riots in Dublin in 1907 and New York in 1911.

The question of violence and mob behavior in the theater is of
some relevance to the consideration of precensorship of the drama.
Harry Pedicord has shown that the theaters of the eighteenth century
were not such riotous and disorderly places as has sometimes been
supposed,[74] but we can be sure that the fear of the mob, that "mass of
ignorance, presumption, malice, and brutality," prevented more people than just Smollett's Matt. Bramble from going to plays.[75] The
prologue for the opening of Covent Garden on 20 September 1773
describes the scene Mr. Bramble wished to avoid:

> Oft have we seen, with Sadness and Surprize,
> Th' assembl'd House in sudden Tumult rise;
> Loud crack'd the Floor, the trembling Seats gave way,
> And truncheon'd Heroes shudder'd at the Fray.[76]

Violent incidents—like the attempted assassination of George III at
Drury Lane on 15 May 1800[77]—were sometimes triggered by factors quite extraneous to the play being acted at the time. Disagreements between audience and management (often about admission
prices); opposition to certain actors from time to time; fights and
feuds within the audience itself; these were some of the causes of riots
of varying degrees of seriousness. But sometimes a speech or a scene
in a play could cause trouble in the audience. Often it was of a
political nature. The seriousness of these incidents should not be exaggerated, but they do reflect what could have been a real danger in a
time of unruly theater audiences. Violent social upheaval, or the
threat of it, was never long absent from British politics—the '45, the
Wilkite mobs, the Gordon riots, naval mutiny, threats of invasion,
revolutionary societies, the Peterloo massacre, and so on. And when
Britain looked abroad, to America and France, the message was
revolution. One of the features of the French theater during the last

181

decade of the eighteenth century was its involvement in political affairs. The riotous and violent scenes that regularly erupted in Parisian theaters during the 1790s were the inevitable result of political allusion and innuendo in the plays.[78] London theater managers were, on the whole, responsible and cautious men, sometimes overcautious. But occasionally plays were chosen for production which, if acted, would almost certainly have caused violence of some kind—*Richard the Second* and *Runnamede*, for example. Plays like these, had they been acted even once in this age of political violence, could have turned the theater into a violent political arena. The prevention of this was, at least, some justification for the censorship.

Precensorship of the drama, then, was defended and accepted in the eighteenth and early nineteenth centuries on the grounds that what went on in the theater was too important in its political, social, moral, and religious consequences to allow the drama its freedom. The argument that a free theater, openly and provocatively discussing important issues of the time, would be, despite the risks, valuable to society, carried little weight. So in 1824 George Colman inherited from John Larpent a respected and valued office, an office which granted successive Examiners the right to exercise very considerable influence over the English theater. Yet among their many concerns one subject remained largely irrelevant—the quality of dramatic literature. Examiners did not, of course, deliberately set out to discourage the writing of good plays, but their determined efforts to prevent the involvement of drama in social and political discussion inevitably dealt the drama a crippling blow. Denied the stimulus of personal or social satire, of participation in religious or moral debate, and, above all, of engagement in political controversy, the drama limped forward, seriously handicapped. The censors' defense of the social order evolved at the expense of the drama. To blame the censorship alone for its debility would be to oversimplify a complex issue, but no art form is likely to develop and thrive under the kind of restrictions evidenced by the Larpent plays. Ultimately what the censorship of these plays charts is the paradox of a society creating unprecedented potential for the theater as a force in its affairs, but lacking sufficient confidence in its own stability to accord to playwrights the freedom to exploit that potential—for the benefit of dramatic literature and the theater or, indeed, for the true benefit of society.

APPENDIX

Lords Chamberlain and Examiners of Plays, 1737-1824

Periods of Office

LORDS CHAMBERLAIN[1]

1. Charles Fitzroy, Duke of Grafton, 14 May 1724—6 May 1757.
2. William Cavendish, Duke of Devonshire, 16 May 1757—28 October 1762.
3. George Spencer, Duke of Marlborough, 22 November 1762—April 1763.
4. Granville Leveson-Gower, Earl Gower, 22 April 1763—10 July 1765.
5. William Henry Cavendish Bentinck, Duke of Portland, 10 July 1765—26 November 1766.
6. Francis Seymour Conway, Marquis of Hertford, 29 November 1766—10 April 1782; 9 April 1783—26 December 1783.
7. George Montagu, Duke of Manchester, 10 April 1782—9 April 1783.
8. James Cecil, Marquis of Salisbury, 26 December 1783—14 May 1804.
9. George Legge, Earl of Dartmouth, 14 May 1804—10 November 1810. [Office vacant, 10 November 1810—7 March 1812]
10. Francis Ingram Seymour, Marquis of Hertford, 7 March 1812—11 December 1821.
11. James Graham, Duke of Montrose, 11 December 1821—13 April 1827.

EXAMINERS AND DEPUTY EXAMINERS OF PLAYS[2]

1. William Chetwynd, 10 March 1738—6 October 1778 (Examiner).
2. Thomas Odell, 10 March 1738—24 May 1749 (Deputy).
3. Edward Capell, 23 May 1749[3]—24 February 1781 (Deputy).
4. John Larpent, 20 November 1778—18 January 1824 (Examiner).
5. James Trail, February 1781 (?)—1782(?) (Deputy).

---

[1] Pp. 25-29, above, should be consulted for further details.

[2] Pp. 29-35, above, should be consulted for further details.

[3] His salary was paid from this date. His appointment received royal confirmation on 7 November 1749.

Notes

Introduction

[1] Michael Foote, M.P., speaking in the debate on the second reading of the Theatres Bill (1968), House of Commons, 23 Feb. 1968 *(Hansard,* vol. 759, no. 67, c. 854).

[2] Richard Brinsley Sheridan, M.P., speaking in the debate on the Seditious Meetings Bill, House of Commons, 3 Dec. 1795 *(The Parliamentary History of England, from the Earliest Period to the Year 1803,* London, 1806-20, 32: 441).

[3] Nicoll, *A History of English Drama,* 3: 19.

[4] James J. Lynch, *Box, Pit, and Gallery: Stage and Society in Johnson's London* (Berkeley and Los Angeles, 1953), p. 222.

[5] There are a number of reliable accounts of the early history of English theatrical censorship. For pre-Restoration censorship the following studies are indispensable: E.K. Chambers, *Notes on the History of the Revels Office under the Tudors* (London, 1906), especially pp. 71-80; Virginia C. Gildersleeve, *Government Regulation of the Elizabethan Drama* (New York, 1908); Evelyn May Albright, *Dramatic Publication in England, 1580-1640* (New York and London, 1927), especially pp. 94-197; and *The Dramatic Records of Sir Henry Herbert,* ed. Joseph Quincy Adams (New Haven, 1917). There are also two interesting chapters on censorship under Charles I and II in Frederick S. Boas, *Shakespeare & the Universities, and Other Studies in Elizabethan Drama* (Oxford, 1923). Accounts of censorship during the Restoration period can be found in Nicoll, *A History of English Drama,* 1, Appendix A, passim, and *The London Stage,* Part 2, 1: xxxix-xliii, and the sources cited there. The index to *The London Stage,* Part 1, is very useful in tracing particular instances of censorship between 1660 and 1700. There is a useful summary of government control of the stage in the early eighteenth century in *The Critical Works of John Dennis,* ed. E.N. Hooker (Baltimore, 1939-43), 1: 509-10. For this period see also Alfred Jackson, "The Stage and the Authorities, 1700-1714 (As Revealed in the Newspapers)," *Review of English Studies,* 14 (1938), 53-63.

[6] I have given an account of the 1968 legislation in my article, "The Abolition of Theatre Censorship in Great Britain: The Theatres Act of 1968," *Queen's Quarterly,* 75 (Winter, 1968), 569-83.

[7] [Walley Chamberlain Oulton], *The History of the Theatres of London* (London, 1796), 2: 89.

[8] For some examples of serious political plays which were never submitted for licensing see below, p. 191, note 38; and p. 194, note 6.

[9] *Observer* 29 (*The British Essayists,* ed. Lionel Thomas Berguer, London, 1823, 38: 189-90).

[10] Donald Thomas, *A Long Time Burning, The History of Literary Censorship in England* (London, 1969), p. 251.

[11] Lynch, pp. 53, 164.

[12] Lucyle Werkmeister, *A Newspaper History of England, 1792-93* (Lincoln, Nebraska, 1967), p. 316. Genest (9: 125) tells us that during a performance of *The Beggar's Opera* at Bath on 15 Jan. 1821 the actresses who portrayed Macheath's women of the town "were so delicate, that, tho' they repeated the dialogue, they took care the audience should not hear it . . . ."

[13] See, for example, pp. 70, 84-85, 192 *n*.18, 204 *n*.25.

[14] F. Fowell and F. Palmer, *Censorship in England* (London, 1913) and Richard Findlater, *Banned! A Review of Theatrical Censorship in Britain* (London, 1967). C.M.G.'s *The Stage Censor, an Historical Sketch: 1544-1907* (London, 1908) is what the title says it is. John Palmer's *The Censor and the Theatres* (London, 1912) is an eloquent argument against censorship but contains little historical background.

[15] Dougald MacMillan, *Catalogue of the Larpent Plays in the Huntington Library* (San Marino, 1939). See also George Sherburn et al., "Huntington Library Collections," *Huntington Library Bulletin*, 1 (1931), 49-50.

[16] *Catalogue of Additions to the Manuscripts. Plays Submitted to the Lord Chamberlain 1824-1851* (London, 1964).

[17] Ibid., p. vi.

[18] See MacMillan, p. vi and note, and the present writer's article, "Some New Larpent Titles," *Theatre Notebook*, 23 (Summer, 1969), 151.

[19] See, for example, *The London Stage*, Part 4, 1: clxxi, and Part 5, 1: clxxi.

[20] This practice was not peculiar to Larpent. See the page of an early eighteenth-century acting copy of Beaumont and Fletcher's *The Prophetess*, reproduced in *The London Stage*, Part 2, 2, between pp. 766 and 767. Trying to identify Larpent's handwriting on the basis of one three-letter word is a chancy business.

[21] MacMillan transcribed many of these on the cards he used when compiling his *Catalogue*. He did not publish the transcriptions, but he kindly allowed me to consult the cards at the Huntington Library.

[22] Collier's personal copy of *Biographia Dramatica*, in which he and the sixth duke of Devonshire made MS notes, is now in the Huntington Library. Of the anonymous *The Triple Discovery* (LA 1282) Collier writes: "It was perhaps never performed as Larpent objected to many passages." But the deleted passages in the MS are of such an inoffensive nature that it is quite impossible to believe that they were censored.

[23] Augustan Reprint Society Publication no. 116.

[24] Peter Thomson, "Thomas Holcroft, George Colman the Younger and the Rivalry of the Patent Theatres," *Theatre Notebook*, 22 (1967-68), 165-66.

[25] See J.F.P.'s [Jean F. Preston] note on the Larpent diaries in the *Huntington Library Quarterly*, 32 (Nov., 1968), 81. I have given some account of the theatrical content of Mrs. Larpent's diaries and journal in my articles, "The Censor's Wife at the Theatre: The Diary of Anna Margaretta Larpent, 1790-1800," *Huntington Library Quarterly*, 35 (Nov., 1971), 49-64, and "Anna Margaretta Larpent, The Duchess of Queensberry and Gay's *Polly* in 1777," *Philological Quarterly*, 51 (Oct., 1972), 955-57.

[26] See, for example, Richard Findlater, *Comic Cuts* (London, 1970).

[27] For speculations about the paucity of dramatic talent, particularly during the Romantic

186

period, see Nicoll, *A History of English Drama*, 4: 57; Richard M. Fletcher, *English Romantic Drama 1795-1843* (New York, 1966); U.C. Nag, "The English Theatre of the Romantic Revival," *Nineteenth Century*, 104 (1928), 384-98; and Dewey Ganzel, "Patent Wrongs and Patent Theatres: Drama and the Law in the Early Nineteenth Century," *Publications of the Modern Language Association*, 76 (1961), 384-96.

[28] *The Artist*, 14 (13 June 1807), 16.

Chapter 1. Licensing of Plays: Theory and Practice

[1] The events leading up to the Licensing Act, including earlier government efforts in the 1730s to regulate the stage, are described by P. J. Crean, "The Stage Licensing Act of 1737," *Modern Philology*, 35 (1937-38), 239-55; and Arthur H. Scouten, *The London Stage*, Part 3, 1:xlviii-li. See also F. T. Wood, "Goodman's Fields Theatre," *Modern Language Review*, 25 (1930), 443-56; and Kenneth D. Wright, "Henry Fielding and the Theatres Act of 1737," *Quarterly Journal of Speech*, 50 (1964), 252-58.

[2] The King's Opera House in the Haymarket was not affected by the act and remained open. Plays in the provinces continued to be acted under the jurisdiction of the local justices, although there is no authority given for this procedure in the 1737 act. See Cecil Price, *The English Theatre in Wales* (Cardiff, 1948), p. 12; and Sybil Rosenfeld, *Strolling Players and Drama in the Provinces, 1660-1765* (Cambridge, 1939), pp. 7-9. It was not until 1788, by the Act of 28 George III c. 30, that justices were given the power to license theatrical representations in the provinces, and then strict conditions were laid down (Rosenfeld, p. 2). When patents were granted to the more important provincial theaters it was made clear that plays presented in them were subject to the censorship in the same way as the London theaters. The Bristol theater patent of 1799, for example, specified that only those plays "as have already been or shall hereafter be Licensed by the Chamberlain of our Household" can be acted (P.R.O. L.C. 7/9, f. 22v).

[3] The best account is by Scouten in *The London Stage*, Part 3, 1:li-lx. The standard work on the establishment, maintenance, and termination (in 1843) of the Drury Lane and Covent Garden monopoly is Watson Nicholson's *The Struggle for a Free Stage in London* (Boston, 1906, reprint New York, 1966).

[4] I quote from the act as it is published in Danby Pickering, *The Statutes at Large* (Cambridge, 1762-69), 17: 140-43.

[5] The phrase, "other entertainment of the stage," is not defined in the act, but in practice it meant anything for which a script could be provided.

[6] *The Parliamentary History of England, from the Earliest Period to the Year 1803* (London, 1806-20), 10: 328-41.

[7] The "Alphabetical Catalogue," now in the Carl H. Pforzheimer Library in New York, is described in my article, "Some New Larpent Titles," *Theatre Notebook*, 23 (Summer, 1969), 150-57.

[8] *The London Stage*, Part 4, 3: 1859.

[9] James Boaden, *Memoirs of the Life of John Philip Kemble* (London, 1825), 1: 306.

[10] R. B. Peake, *Memoirs of the Colman Family* (London, 1841), 2: 438-39.

[11] Sir Henry Herbert, when he was master of the revels, used to indicate his permission to

187

act a play by writing a short note at the end of the MS, but he does not seem to have issued a separate license. (*Dramatic Records of Sir Henry Herbert*, ed. Joseph Quincy Adams, New Haven, 1917, facing p. 48.) Charles Fleetwood used the verb "license" in one of the very first application notes sent to the Lord Chamberlain, but he may not have been using the word in a precise sense. See above, p. 19. Separate licenses were issued at least as early as 1761, as indicated in a letter from Edward Capell to the Examiner of Plays, William Chetwynd, 8 March 1761 (Folger MS, Y.c. 458 (1)).

[12] Enthoven Collection, D. L. file, 1791. The only license that I have seen published is that for Mrs. Inchbald's farce, *The Hue and Cry* (1791) in *The London Stage*, Part 5, 1, between pp. cxliv and cxlv. This too is in the Enthoven Collection (D.L. file, 1791), as is the license for William Linley's comic opera, *The Honey Moon* (D.L. file, 1797). The Enthoven Collection also contains licenses for some nineteenth and twentieth-century plays.

[13] Peake, 2:438-39.

[14] See, for example, how James Ayres' *Sancho at Court* was dealt with by the Lord Chamberlain's office, below, pp. 167-68.

[15] J. T. Kirkman, *Memoirs of the Life of Charles Macklin* (London, 1799), 2:279.

[16] Sidney C. Isaacs, *The Law Relating to the Theatres* (London, 1927), p. 23, note (o). *The Times*, 13 March 1912.

[17] See below, pp. 132-34.

[18] *Memoirs of Mrs. Inchbald*, ed. James Boaden (London, 1833), 1:163-64. The date of the incident is about 1782, but I have not been able to identify the play in question.

[19] See below, p. 81.

[20] John Adolphus, *Memoirs of John Bannister* (London, 1839), 1:342-43.

[21] See *The Times* 10 April 1797. The address is printed there.

[22] Adolphus, 1:50.

[23] In August 1775, acting in *The Rehearsal*, Foote made some unscripted comments about the recent suppression of his play, *The Trip to Calais*. The *Public Ledger*, noting this, reminded Foote on 8 August of the penalties allowed by the Licensing Act for speaking unlicensed lines.

[24] Tate Wilkinson, *Memoirs of His Own Life* (Dublin, 1791), 1:148.

[25] John O'Keeffe, *Recollections of the Life of John O'Keeffe* (London, 1826), 2:316.

[26] *Gray's Inn Journal*, 10 Nov. 1753.

[27] See below, pp. 116-17.

[28] Preface to *The Mournful Nuptials; or, Love the Cure of all Woes* (London, 1739).

[29] *Report from the Select Committee on Dramatic Literature: with the Minutes of Evidence*, House of Commons, 2 August 1832, p. 69, para. 1046.

[30] Ibid., p. 32, paras. 384-85; p. 180, paras. 3230-31.

[31] That is, theaters operating under magistrates' licenses, not royal patent. In theory they were not permitted to perform legitimate drama, a privilege zealously, but ineffectually, guarded by the patent theaters. At the popular Penny Gaffs in the 1830s as many as a dozen new short pieces would be performed in a week—obviously the Lord Chamberlain never got to look at these.

[32] P.R.O. L.C. 7/4, unbound, unfoliated documents.

[33] Robin Estill, "The Factory Lad: Melodrama as Propaganda," *Theatre Quarterly*, 1: (Oct.-Dec., 1971), 23.

[34] P.R.O. L.C. 1/42, f. 136.

[35] The five principal sources I have used to obtain information about the Lords Chamberlain are Joseph Haydn, *The Book of Dignities* (London, 1890); G.E.C. [George Edward Cokayne], *The Complete Peerage* (London, 1910-59); *DNB*; Beatson's *Political Index*; and James E. Doyle, *The Official Baronage of England* (London, 1886), which here, and in the Appendix, unless otherwise stated, I follow for precise dates of commencement and termination of appointments.

[36] Benjamin Victor, *The History of the Theatres of London and Dublin, from the Year 1730 to the Present Time* (Dublin, 1761), 1:111, 155. In Ireland the lord lieutenant operated the same kind of irregular and haphazard censorship as had existed in England before the Licensing Act.

[37] Ibid., 1:44n.

[38] *Dublin Journal*, 2-6 Nov. 1762.

[39] P.R.O. L.C. 5/25, f. 74: "On Wednesday the 9th of April 1783 the Earl of Hertford received his Staff of Office as Lord Chamberlain of His Majisty's Houshold."

[40] George III, *The Correspondence of King George the Third, From 1760 to December 1783*, ed. Sir John Fortescue (London, 1927-28, reprint, London, 1967), 2, passim.

[41] Horace Walpole, *Horace Walpole's Correspondence with the Rev. William Cole*, ed. W. S. Lewis and A. Dayle Wallace (London and New Haven, 1937), 1:237n. [*The Yale Edition of Horace Walpole's Correspondence*, ed. W. S. Lewis (London and New Haven, 1937-   ), vol. 1].

[42] Horace Walpole, *Horace Walpole's Correspondence with George Montagu*, ed. W. S. Lewis and Ralph S. Brown, Jr. (New Haven and London, 1941), 1:235 [*Yale Edition*, vol. 9].

[43] Philip Dormer Stanhope, *The Letters of Philip Dormer Stanhope, 4th Earl of Chesterfield*, ed. Bonamy Dobrée (London, 1932), 6: 2667.

[44] See my article, "Horace Walpole, Unofficial Play Censor," *English Language Notes*, 11 (Sept., 1971), 42-46.

[45] Hertford resisted a demand from ambassadors to Roman Catholic countries in 1775 to suppress performances of Dryden's *The Spanish Fryar* (*Morning Chronicle*, 25 August 1775).

[46] The MS letter is bound with one of the licensing MSS of *The Man of the World* (LA 500) and is quoted in full by Dougald MacMillan, "The Censorship in the Case of *The Man of the World*," *Huntington Library Bulletin*, no. 10 (1936), 84-85.

[47] Doyle (2: 453) gives 7 April, but Hertford's first spell as Lord Chamberlain did not end until 10 April.

[48] Doyle (3: 253) gives 20 Dec., but Hertford's second spell as Lord Chamberlain did not end until 26 Dec.

[49] Staffordshire Record Office, D(W) 1778/V/688. Documents concerning Dartmouth's appointment as Lord Chamberlain are in Dartmouth MSS, D/1778/I.ii/1666.

[50] *The Manuscripts of the Earl of Dartmouth*, 3 (London, 1896), p. 291 [Historical Manuscripts Commission, 15th Report, Appendix, Part 1].

[51] See Watson Nicholson, *The Struggle for a Free Stage in London,* p. 431.

[52] There is bulky official correspondence on this subject in the Public Record Office.

[53] British Library Add. MS 38,254, ff. 93v-94.

[54] L. C. 5/161, ff. 8-9. Grafton was not in fact "impower'd" by the Licensing Act to appoint an Examiner of Plays.

[55] Richard John Smith Collection of playbills, newspaper cuttings, etc., 21: f. 149.

[56] "The Censorship in the Case of Macklin's *The Man of the World,*" p. 88 and note; *Catalogue of the Larpent Plays in the Huntington Library* (San Marino, 1939), p. v.

[57] "The Chetwynd Manuscript of *The School for Scandal,*" *Theatre Notebook,* 6 (1951-52), 10-12.

[58] John Nichols, *Illustrations of the Literary History of the Eighteenth Century* (London, 1817-58), 1:468n.

[59] *Burke's Genealogical and Heraldic History of the Peerage, Baronetage & Knightage,* ed. L. G. Pine, 102nd ed. (London, 1959), p. 447.

[60] "The Censorship in the Case of Macklin's *The Man of the World,*" p. 88.

[61] David Garrick, *The Letters of David Garrick,* ed. David M. Little and George M. Kahrl (London, 1963), 1:332 and note.

[62] P.R.O. L.C. 5/161, f. 9.

[63] Nicoll, *A History of English Drama,* 2:284.

[64] Ibid., 2:243.

[65] P.R.O. L.C. 5/161, f. 310.

[66] Wilbur L. Cross, *The History of Henry Fielding* (New Haven, 1918, reprint 1963), 2:246.

[67] P.R.O. L.C. 5/161, ff. 312-13.

[68] Pegge's "Brief Memoirs," Nichols, *Illustrations of the Literary History of the Eighteenth Century,* 1:468.

[69] *The Court and City Register* (London, 1769), p. 76.

[70] An appreciation of Capell as editor of Shakespeare is given by Alice Walker, "Edward Capell and his Edition of Shakespeare," in *Studies in Shakespeare,* ed. Peter Alexander (London, 1964), pp. 132-48.

[71] Pegge's "Brief Memoirs," Nichols, 1:467.

[72] See below, p. 135.

[73] Pegge's "Brief Memoirs," Nichols, 1:468n.

[74] Ibid.

[75] Boaden, *Memoirs of the Life of John Philip Kemble,* 1:xviii.

[76] British Library, Add. MS 33,056, f. 146 (Trail's allowance warrant, 1765).

[77] Letters to him in this capacity are British Library Add. MS 38,242, ff. 98, 195 (1807-08).

[78] *The Annual Register . . . for the Year 1778* (London, 1779), p. 224.

[79] Horace Walpole, *Horace Walpole's Correspondence with Sir Horace Mann,* ed. W.

S. Lewis, Warren Hunting Smith, and George L. Lam (London and New Haven, 1955-67), 6: 449 [*Yale Edition*, vol. 22].

[80] *The Court and City Register* (1769), p. 76. Capell was then a groom of the privy chamber in the same department and perhaps knew Larpent.

[81] P.R.O. L.C. 5/25, f. 16.

[82] P.R.O. L.C. 5/59, f. 24 is a copy of a warrant for payment of liveries to Larpent, dated 8 Feb. 1777.

[83] See F. Seymour Larpent, *The Private Journal of F. Seymour Larpent*, ed. Sir George Larpent, 2nd ed. (London, 1853).

[84] This information on the Larpents, unless otherwise stated, is derived from *DNB*.

[85] The fees Larpent received for licensing plays between 1801 and 1824 are recorded in his account books for those years (Huntington MS 19926, 2 vols.). The amounts range from a low of £57.15.0 in 1801 to a high of £165.18.0 in 1821.

[86] Successive editions of *The Royal Kalendar* in the early 1800s indicate that Larpent was a deputy clerk and a secretary in the Privy Seal Office. His son John was also a deputy clerk.

[87] The Larpents were friends of the Bowdlers for many years, but there is disappointingly little in the diaries about their conversations, which surely must have touched on censorship from time to time.

[88] See Lewis Namier, *The Structure of Politics at the Accession of George III*, 2nd. ed. (London, 1965), pp. 389-401.

[89] The children of a later Examiner, William Bodham Donne, are said to have helped their father in his censorship duties. See James F. Stottlar, "A Victorian Stage Censor: The Theory and Practice of William Bodham Donne," *Victorian Studies*, 13 (1969-70), 255.

[90] See below, pp. 95-98 for a full discussion of *Richard the Second* and its suppression.

[91] MS letter bound with LA 2331, dated 8 Jan. 1823.

[92] *Literary Panorama*, 4 (1808), 302.

[93] Thomas Gisborne, *An Enquiry into the Duties of the Female Sex*, 9th ed. (London, 1813), p. 95n.

[94] An interesting criticism of Larpent was once made by James Boaden. Of George Colman's *The Iron Chest* (D. L., 12 March 1796), based on William Godwin's novel, *Things as They are; or, The Adventures of Caleb Williams* (1794), Boaden writes: "Innocence, persecuted by power, and a chivalrous honour conducting to the most atrocious baseness, were incidents of sufficient interest to furnish a play; and if poor Larpent did not, or could not, see the libellous mischief of the whole business—how it endangered all that ennobled our nature, and sullied the purity even of our tribunals,—why, then he was as a licenser more than 'sand blind, high gravel blind,' and the state must run the peril, which its dramatic guardian of the night did not apprehend" (*Memoirs of the Life of John Philip Kemble*, 2:154-55).

[95] Sir Martin Arthur Shee, *Alasco* (London, 1824), p. xi.

[96] Martin Arthur Shee, *The Life of Sir Martin Arthur Shee* (London, 1860), 1:369.

[97] F. Fowell and F. Palmer, *Censorship in England* (London, 1913), p. 161.

[98] *Censorship in England*, pp. 164-65. Mrs. Larpent's judgment of Sheridan's play was made on 14 Jan. 1800.

[99] A good example of Larpent's efficiency has recently come to light with the publication of *Drury Lane Journal: Selections From James Winston's Diaries, 1819-1827*, edited by Alfred L. Nelson and Gilbert B. Cross (London, 1974). On 6 November 1822 at 10 a.m. Larpent received the licensing copy of a play by J. H. Payne; three hours later he had licensed it.

Chapter 2. Censorship of Political Drama, 1737-1745

[1] For a detailed discussion of the political drama of the early eighteenth century, see John Loftis, *The Politics of Drama in Augustan England* (Oxford, 1963).

[2] Thomas Davies, *Dramatic Miscellanies* (London, 1784), 1: 151-54.

[3] John Percival, first earl of Egmont, *Manuscripts of the Earl of Egmont, Diary of Viscount Percival, afterwards first Earl of Egmont*, ed. R. A. Roberts (London, 1920-23), 3: 83. [Historical Manuscripts Commission, no. 63.]

[4] Thomas Davies, *Memoirs of the Life of David Garrick*, 3rd ed. (London, 1781), 2: 34.

[5] Advertisement for the printed text of *Agamemnon*, *Daily Post*, 24 April 1738, and other newspaper advertisements for the play.

[6] See Léon Morel, *James Thomson* (Paris, 1895), p. 126: "Il [the Prologue] contenait, à la fin, d'expression de quelques vagues sentiments politiques et une allusion fort inoffensive à la censure. La censure se vengea en exigeant la suppression des derniers vers."

[7] Davies, *Memoirs of. . . Garrick*, 2: 35.

[8] *Daily Gazetteer*, 12 April 1739.

[9] For a concise account of the Anglo-Spanish disputes, see Basil Williams, *The Whig Supremacy, 1714-1760*, 2nd ed., rev. C. H. Stuart (Oxford, 1962), pp. 207-10.

[10] Douglas Grant, *James Thomson* (London, 1951), p. 246; *DNB*, s.v. Mallet, David.

[11] Mallet's *Mustapha*, Brooke's *Gustavus Vasa*, Thomson's *Edward and Eleonora*, and Aaron Hill's *Caesar*. *Caesar* was eventually acted at Bath ca. 1753 as *The Roman Revenge*.

[12] *James Thomson (1700-1748) Letters and Documents*, ed. Alan Dugald McKillop (Lawrence, Kansas, 1958), p. 127.

[13] *Diary of. . . Earl of Egmont*, 2: 339.

[14] Ibid., 2: 390.

[15] See, for example, the issue of 28 April 1739.

[16] Davies, *Memoirs of. . . Garrick*, 2: 33.

[17] *The Politics of Drama*, p. 151.

[18] *Daily Post*, 17 March 1739.

[19] *Daily Post*, 22, 23 March.

[20] *Gentleman's Magazine*, 9 (April, 1739), 210.

[21] Sir John Hawkins, *The Life of Samuel Johnson*, ed. Bertram H. Davis (London, 1962), p. 43.

[22] See issues of 12 April, 15, 21, 24 May 1739.

[23] Charles Dibdin, *A Complete History of the English Stage* (London, n.d. [1797-1800]), 5: 167.

[24] The procedure was not, of course, new. Gay is said to have earned about £1,200 from the publication of *Polly* after it had been suppressed in 1728. See William Henry Irving, *John Gay, Favorite of the Wits* (Durham, North Carolina, 1940), p. 273.

[25] Alan D. McKillop, "Thomson and the Licensers of the Stage," *Philological Quarterly*, 37 (1958), 452.

[26] R. W. C[hapman], "Brooke's *Gustavus Vasa*," *Review of English Studies*, 1 (1925), 460-61, and 2 (1926), 99.

[27] *James Thomson . . . Letters and Documents*, p. 129.

[28] Herbert Wright, "Henry Brooke's 'Gustavus Vasa,'" *Modern Language Review*, 14 (1919), 174n.

[29] The MS sent to the Examiner is marked "forbid to be acted by the Ld Chamberlain the 26th March 1739." (LA 12.)

[30] But Jean B. Kern's suggestion that the dedication was partly responsible for the suppression cannot be accepted. The dedication was not, of course, intended to be spoken on the stage and so was not included with the text sent for licensing. Hence the decision to refuse the license was made in ignorance of the dedication. See Jean B. Kern, "The Fate of James Thomson's *Edward and Eleonora*," *Modern Language Notes*, 52 (1937), 501-02.

[31] The *Gentleman's and London Magazine*, 31 (June, 1762), 322-27.

[32] *The Works of James Thomson* (London, 1762), 1: xx.

[33] Nicoll, *A History of English Drama*, 2: 23; Scouten, *The London Stage*, Part 3, 1: liii; Richard Findlater, *Banned!* (London, 1967), p. 48; Loftis, *The Politics of Drama*, p. 150n; McKillop, "Thomson and the Licensers of the Stage," p. 452.

[34] Apart from Loftis in a brief note in *The Politics of Drama*, p. 150n.

[35] *The London Stage*, Part 3, 1: liii.

[36] Williams, *The Whig Supremacy*, p. 210.

[37] Many years later, Charles Macklin found much to criticize about the political levee in *The Man of the World*, a much-censored play. See below, pp. 77-78. The levee was a frequent satiric target in the eighteenth century. There is a useful note on the subject in F. Homes Dudden, *Henry Fielding, His Life, Works, and Times* (Hamden, Connecticut, 1966), 1: 202n.

[38] Both William Hatchett's *The Chinese Orphan* (1741) and Robert Morris's *Fatal Necessity* (1742) are impressive attacks on Walpole, but neither play was acted or even submitted for licensing.

Chapter 3. Censorship of Political Drama, 1745-1789

[1] Macklin's *King Henry VII*, D. L., 20 Jan. 1746, a failure; Cibber's *Papal Tyranny in the Reign of King John*, C. G., 15 Feb. 1745, altered from Shakespeare.

[2] Dennis' *Liberty Asserted* and *A Plot and no Plot*; Ford's *Perkin Warbeck*; Cibber's *The Non-Juror*; Lee's *Massacre of Paris*; Fielding's *The Debauchees; or, The Jesuit Caught*.

[3] Benjamin Victor, *Original Letters, Dramatic Pieces, and Poems* (London, 1776), 1: 118.

[4] See Mary E. Knapp, *Prologues and Epilogues of the Eighteenth Century* (New Haven, 1961), chapt. 6.

[5] "It cannot sure be a Principle of Liberty, that would turn the Stage into a Court of Enquiry, that would let the partial Applauses of a vulgar Audience give Sentence upon the Conduct of Authority, and put Impeachments into the Mouth of a *Harlequin?*" (*An Apology for the Life of Mr. Colley Cibber, Comedian,* 2nd ed., London, 1740, pp. 236-37).

[6] Charles Dibdin, *A Complete History of the English Stage* (London, n.d. [1797-1800]), 4:411.

[7] Benjamin Victor, *The History of the Theatres of London* (London, 1771), pp. 132-33; Joseph Cradock, *Literary and Miscellaneous Memoirs* (London, 1828), 1:202.

[8] Tate Wilkinson, *Memoirs of His Own Life* (Dublin, 1791), 3:239.

[9] Horace Walpole, *Horace Walpole's Correspondence with George Montagu,* ed. W. S. Lewis and R. S. Brown, Jr. (New Haven and London, 1941), 1:381*n*. [*The Yale Edition of Horace Walpole's Correspondence,* ed. W. S. Lewis (New Haven and London, 1937-), vol. 9.]

[10] Richard Brinsley Sheridan, *The Letters of Richard Brinsley Sheridan,* ed. Cecil Price (Oxford, 1966), 3:220.

[11] Richard Brinsley Sheridan, *The Speeches of the Right Honourable Richard Brinsley Sheridan,* ed. "A Constitutional Friend" (London, 1816), 3:19-20.

[12] The best account of the incident is in Esther K. Sheldon, *Thomas Sheridan of Smock-Alley* (Princeton, 1967), pp. 197-205.

[13] *B. D.,* 2:191-92. The *Monthly Review* noticed the propaganda aspect of the play: "Our connexion with Portugal . . . the favourable light in which the court of Lisbon is here placed to our view; but above all, the pacific sentiments, the idea of a monarch who places his glory, not in that military spirit which operates to the destruction of mankind, but in cultivating the arts of peace; are all circumstances which unite to stamp this play with the character of a political performance" (*Monthly Review,* 28, Jan., 1763, 67).

[14] *The London Stage,* Part 4, 1: clxi; James J. Lynch, *Box, Pit, and Gallery: Stage and Society in Johnson's London* (Berkeley and Los Angeles, 1953), p. 255.

[15] Lynch, p. 255.

[16] Horace Walpole, *Memoirs of the Reign of King George the Third,* ed. G. F. Russell-Barker (London and New York, 1894), 1:249.

[17] Neville MS diary. Quoted in *The London Stage,* Part 4, 2:1259.

[18] For the censorship of *The Man of the World,* see below, pp. 77-78. There is an interesting paragraph in the *North Briton* no. 45 (23 April 1763) about politics and the theater at this time. In his speech to Parliament after the Peace of Paris had been concluded, the king defended the treaty on the grounds that the war had been expensive to Britain: "The minister cannot forbear, even in the *King's Speech,* insulting us with a dull repetition of the word economy. I did not expect so soon to hear that word again, after it had been so lately exploded, and more than once by a most numerous audience, *hissed* off the stage of our *English* theatres."

[19] Unidentified newspaper cutting, Mathews Collection, Victoria and Albert Museum, dated (in manuscript) 6 June 1771; but the date is not that of Garrick's performance for he did not play Hastings in 1771. The performance referred to is almost certainly that of 13 December 1769.

[20] *Memoirs,* 1:201-02.

194

[21] *The Bourbon League* is LA 210. The license application is dated 8 March 1762 and the MS is marked "forbid." The play was never performed or printed.

[22] The action of *The Bourbon League* takes place in a country town on the coast of Kent. The inhabitants fear a French invasion, especially since the French have concluded a treaty with Spain (previously neutral). Anti Catholic feeling runs high in the town and a local magistrate, Sir Credulous Caution, refuses to allow his daughter, Clarinda, to marry a local boy, Freeman, because he is suspected of harboring French sympathies. The real papist, however, is the trusted and respected schoolteacher, Plausible, who himself has designs on Clarinda. After the excitement produced by a false alarm of a French invasion has subsided, the true identity of Plausible is discovered by a drunken Irishman, and Freeman, no longer suspected by Sir Credulous, is allowed to marry Clarinda.

[23] I base my account of *Electra's* unfortunate history on Shirley's address "To the Reader" in the published text (1765).

[24] The Jacobite rebellion of 1745 was still a sensitive issue—at least so far as the censor was concerned—as late as 1806, when Charles Kemble's *The Wanderer; or, The Rights of Hospitality* (adapted from Kotzebue) was denied a license by John Larpent (see Kemble's preface to the 1808 edition of the play). *The Wanderer* depicted the escape of Charles from Scotland after Culloden, and Kemble could not get the play licensed until he turned Charles into a Swedish prince and moved the action to Sweden. The revised *Wanderer* was then acted at Covent Garden on 12 Jan. 1808; the original *Wanderer* was later revived as *The Royal Fugitive* at Covent Garden on 26 Nov. 1829.

[25] Lewis Namier and John Brooke, *The House of Commons 1754-1790* (London, 1964), 1:73-80.

[26] LA 384. Capell's letter to Garrick is bound with the MS.

[27] For a detailed discussion of the censorship, see Dougald MacMillan, "The Censorship in the Case of Macklin's *The Man of the World*," *Huntington Library Bulletin*, no. 10 (1936), 79-101.

[28] Quoted by MacMillan, p. 97.

[29] Ibid., p. 96.

[30] Ibid., pp. 99-101.

[31] Robert Anderson, ed., *The Works of the British Poets, with Prefaces, Biographical and Critical* (London, 1792-1807), 11:1028. Nicoll, 3:391, says *Runnamede* was "probably" given in Edinburgh in 1784. Anderson (p. 1028) is quite certain it was acted there, but gives no date. There is a Larpent MS of *Runnamede* (LA 684). It is dated 1784 and is presumably the text of the Edinburgh production. The MS of the 1783 text has not survived. It is likely, however, that the 1783 published text followed the text of the suppressed version, and that the MS for the Edinburgh production was altered from the 1783 version. The Larpent MS of 1784 and the 1783 published text are identical in many places, but some speeches printed in 1783 were discarded in 1784, probably in accordance with Larpent's objections.

[32] Steven Watson, *The Reign of George III, 1760-1815* (Oxford, 1960), p. 244.

[33] Quoted in *The London Stage*, Part 4, 1:210.

[34] Horace Walpole, *Memoirs of the Reign of King George the Second*, ed. Lord Holland, 2nd ed. (London, 1847), 3:251. An attempt was also made to prohibit the play's publication.

³⁵ Unidentified newspaper cutting in the British Library (James Winston Collection). The prologue, which is indeed critical of new government taxes, is printed in the 1784 text of *Aerostation*.

³⁶ Preface to *Seduction* (1787).

Chapter 4. Suppression of Political Comment

¹ The fullest discussion of French theatrical censorship in this period is in Marvin Carlson's *The Theatre of the French Revolution* (Ithaca, New York, 1966).

² *The Life of Thomas Holcroft, Written by Himself. Continued . . . by William Hazlitt*, ed. Elbridge Colby (London, 1925), 2: 101.

³ See the *True Briton*, 30 Jan. and 1 Feb. 1793 (where it is claimed that the exceptionable passages had been expunged from performances of the play) for attacks on Mrs. Inchbald, and *The Times*, 4 Feb. for her reply. Mrs. Inchbald's answer to the *True Briton* is also given in *Memoirs of Mrs. Inchbald*, ed. James Boaden (London, 1833), 1: 311. A correspondent in the *Morning Chronicle*, 1 Feb. 1793 quotes the speech which caused the trouble: "'There is never a theft, nor a fraud committed, that you do not *take the offender's part*, shake your head, and exclaim, *Provisions are so scarce!* and no longer ago than last Lord Mayor's Day, when you were told that Mr. Alderman Ravenous was ill with an indigestion, you endeavoured to soften the matter by exclaiming, *Provisions are so scarce!*'"

⁴ *The Life of Thomas Holcroft*, 2: 247-48. There is a detailed analysis of the political aspects of Holcroft's plays in G. J. Scrimgeour's unpublished Ph.D. thesis, "Drama and the Theatre in the Early Nineteenth Century" (Princeton University, 1968), pp. 296-316.

⁵ *The Life and Times of Frederick Reynolds* (London, 1826), 2: 132. See Theodore Grieder's useful "Annotated Checklist of the British Drama, 1789-99," *Restoration and Eighteenth Century Theatre Research*, 4 (May, 1965), 21-47, where he identifies those plays which had a patriotic intent.

⁶ Similarly prorevolutionary plays like *The Fall of Robespierre* which Coleridge and Southey wrote in 1794, and Southey's *Wat Tyler*, also 1794, would unquestionably have been denied licenses had they been submitted for production.

⁷ The beautiful Carline, fleeing from the lustful and tyrannical commandant of the island of St. Marguerite, takes refuge in a convent. But soon disillusioned with the idea of a chaste life, she strikes a bargain with the commandant and he rescues her from the nuns and takes her to his castle. There she meets the prisoner in the iron mask, learns his identity—he is in fact her foster brother—and, because she has learned the truth, is herself imprisoned. But by this time the townsfolk have had enough of the tyrant and form a "Committee of Insurrection." The castle is attacked, the prisoners released (the man in the iron mask turns out to be of royal blood) and the commandant executed. The story of "The Man in the Iron Mask" (variously identified as the brother or son of Louis XIV, the duke of Monmouth, Molière and others) who was imprisoned by Louis XIV and forced to wear a black velvet mask to conceal his identity even from his jailers (Voltaire seems to have created the legend that the mask was of iron) had already been revived by *The Times*. An article about him appeared in September (28th) and others followed, three of them immediately succeeding the production of *The Island of St. Marguerite* (14, 17, 18 November). *The Times* also did its best to

196

stimulate interest in St. John's opera by printing a number of short items about it on 7, 17, 29, 31 October and 7 November.

[8] Quoted from Collier's annotated copy of *Biographia Dramatica* by Dougald MacMillan, *Catalogue of the Larpent Plays in the Huntington Library* (San Marino, 1939), p. 140.

[9] *The Life and Times of Frederick Reynolds*, 2: 54. According to a paragraph in the *Dublin Chronicle* for 7 Nov. 1789, both Covent Garden and Drury Lane had been officially warned on 28 October that no representations of the fall of the Bastille or any "representation founded on any of the recent transactions in France," would be allowed. See J. H. Stewart, "The Fall of the Bastille on the Dublin Stage," *Journal of the Royal Society of the Antiquaries of Ireland*, 74 (1954), 80.

[10] The letters are bound with LA 870 and LA 1058. The offending passage (not included in printed editions of the play) is as follows: "What in England,—oh, there I prophecy wonders, nay, almost impossibilities—In 1790 the Lawyers will become honorable—The Bench of Bishops charitable—The men of fashion sensible, the Physician useful, and the two houses of Parliament witty and entertaining—But you shall hear . . . ."

[11] *The Times*, 30 November.

[12] *The Maid of Normandy* was published in 1794, but the licensing MS has not survived. In his preface to a later play, *The Fatal Sisters* (1797), Eyre resigns himself to the thought that the suppression of *The Maid* "no doubt was regulated by prudential motives." In her diary for 14 April 1794 Mrs. Larpent records her view of the play:

A Strange Absurd Jumble of C. Corde killing Marat. The Prison of ye French Royal family introduced, their Sufferings, ridiculous attempt at simplicity in the young Kings Conversation. One part perfectly ridiculous. His mother tells him God is his Father, he Alas has no Other. The Boy asks if God will take him on his knee & fondle him. In short it is as devoid of poetry and judgment as it can be & highly improper just now were it otherwise.

A few years later, in 1804, a play called *The Death of the Queen of France* was submitted for licensing from Norwich (LA 1413). Although shorter, this is practically the same play as Eyre's. Larpent again prohibited the performance.

[13] A. W. Ward and G. P. Gooch, eds., *The Cambridge History of British Foreign Policy 1783-1919*, (Cambridge, 1922), 1: 374.

[14] Genest claims (8: 245-46) that William Dimond's history play, *The Royal Oak*, was temporarily denied a license in June 1811. The play (LA 1681) deals with Charles I's escape from Cromwell after the battle of Worcester and is very proroyalist ("Knaves and cowards may deny their sovereign; but brave and honest men will always glory to acknowledge him"). I have not been able to confirm Genest's claim about the temporary suppression, but any play at this time about deposed kings was sure to be greeted warily by Larpent.

[15] I have given an account of the censorship of O'Keeffe's play in my article, "A Case of Political Censorship at the Little Theatre in the Haymarket in 1794: John O'Keeffe's *Jenny's Whim; or, The Roasted Emperor*," *Restoration and Eighteenth Century Theatre Research*, 10 (Nov., 1971), 34-40.

[16] But it is hard to see why the Examiner felt it necessary to object to some songs in a piece written by T. J. Dibdin to celebrate the efforts of the Dutch people to liberate themselves from French rule after Napoleon's defeat at the battle of Leipzig in October 1813. The piece

was called *Orange Boven; or, More Good News* and was submitted for licensing from Drury Lane on 4 December 1813 (LA 1788). A note in the Drury Lane prompter's book for 8 December 1813 tells what happened then: "The new Divertisement of Orange Boven was advertised, but at 1/2 p one o Clock a Prohibition was brought by Mr Larpent the Licensing Clerk on acc^t of his having had only 5 Days given him to read *One Act*" (Folger MS W.b. 381). The management hastily posted a handbill to explain to the public why *Orange Boven* would not be played that evening, but the reason for the prohibition had nothing to do with the time Larpent needed to read the piece. The real reason, although Larpent was reluctant to admit it, is revealed by the deletions in the licensing manuscript and has to do, as Dibdin says in his *Reminiscences* (London, 1827, 2: 23), with some songs "which were thought too personal against Bonaparte." Three songs satirizing Napoleon's career and character are expunged in the manuscript. The satire is all pretty innocuous and it is odd that Larpent felt it necessary to shield the French emperor from criticism at this time.

[17] *Cobbett's Parliamentary Debates*, 14 (1st series), c. 481.

[18] See the advertisement at the end of Lewis's *Venoni* (1809). The monody is LA 1568 and was published in *The Life and Correspondence of M.G.L.* [by Mrs. Margaret Baron-Wilson] (London, 1839), 1: 378-80.

[19] James Plumptre, *Four Discourses on Subjects relating to the Amusement of the Stage* (Cambridge, 1809), p. 41.

[20] The story can be found in David Hume's *The History of England* (London, 1811-13), 3: 7.

[21] See the well-known passage in his letter to Southey, 3 Nov. 1794 (Samuel Taylor Coleridge, *Collected Letters of Samuel Taylor Coleridge*, ed. Earl Leslie Griggs, Oxford, 1956-59, 1: 122). For English adaptations and translations of *Die Räuber* see B. Q. Morgan, *A Critical Bibliography of German Literature in English Translation*, 2nd ed. (London, 1938, reprint, 1965), pp. 420-21, and L. A. Willoughby, "English Translations and Adaptations of Schiller's 'Robbers,'" *Modern Language Review*, 16 (1921), 297-315. Also of interest are Thomas Rea, *Schiller's Dramas and Poems in England* (London, 1906), pp. 7-27, Theodore Grieder, "The German Drama in England, 1790-1800," *Restoration and Eighteenth Century Theatre Research*, 3 (Nov., 1964), 39-50, and Margaret W. Cooke, "Schiller's 'Robbers' in England," *Modern Language Review*, 11 (1916), 156-75.

[22] Folger MS W.b. 67 (63-63v).

[23] A similar case against the German drama is made in the famous attack in the *Anti-Jacobin; or Weekly Examiner*, no. 30 (4 June 1798).

[24] The MS of *The Whim* is LA 1093. It is dated 7 September 1795 and "Prohibited from being acted" is written on the MS in Larpent's hand. LA 1104 is a printed copy of the play (Margate, 1795). This is almost identical to the MS and is obviously not a second application for a license. A few of Lady Wallace's comments in her "Address to the Public" are underlined, but there are no marks in the text itself.

[25] Larpent seems to have thought that judges deserved special protection. The original title of J. G. Holman's comic opera, *Abroad and at Home* (C. G. 19 Nov. 1796) was *The King's Bench*, but Larpent is said to have objected to this, presumably because he thought the dignity of the court and its judges would be affronted by this use of the court's name. (See *B.D.*, 2: 2; Genest, 7: 305; Nicoll, 3: 271-72; and MacMillan, *Catalogue of the Larpent Plays*, p. 190.) Titles of plays were considered by Larpent to be of some importance. He

would not license Mrs. Inchbald's comedy, *I'll Tell You What*, until he had been given the title (*Memoirs of Mrs. Inchbald*, 1: 200). See also a cutting from the *Monthly Mirror* in the Enthoven Collection, Victoria and Albert Museum: "*Aurelio and Miranda*, a play by Mr. Boaden.—This drama, taken professedly from the romance of The Monk, was to have been called *Ambrosio*, but the licencer objecting to the *name*, the title was altered to that of *Aurelio and Miranda*. We see no good ground for this objection; for if any danger were apprehended from a play derived from a work that has, by some, been considered as licentious, how could the alteration in question counteract its pernicious tendency? or, if the licencer dreaded the further publicity of the novel, how could it conceal the fact beyond the first night? We notice this circumstance, because we think the capricious exercise of an important duty is injurious both to individuals and to the public." (D. L. file, 29 Dec. 1798.) It was said that the original title of J. R. Planché's *Amoroso, King of Little Britain* (D. L., 21 April 1818) was *Amoroso, King of Pimlico* and that Larpent insisted on a change because of some personal allusion in the earlier title. But Planché claims to have known nothing of the Pimlico title or its prohibition (*The Recollections and Reflections of J. R. Planché*, London, 1872, 1: 25-26*n*).

[26] For the censorship of Holcroft's and O'Keeffe's plays, see Stewart S. Morgan, "The Damning of Holcroft's *Knave or Not?* and O'Keeffe's *She's Eloped*," *Huntington Library Quarterly*, 22 (1958), 51-62, and Leonard W. Conolly, "More on John O'Keeffe and the Lord Chamberlain," *Notes and Queries*, n.s., 16 (May, 1969), 190-92.

[27] Larpent refused to change his mind about licensing *The Two Farmers* even after Dibdin called at his home (then in Bedford Square) to remonstrate with him; see *The Reminiscences of Thomas Dibdin*, 2: 25. (References to corn monopolists are deleted in the MS of Theodore Hook's farce, *The Garland*, LA 1445.) Dibdin also found just cause for complaint against Larpent when his successful musical entertainment, *Il Bondocani; or, The Caliph Robber* was suppressed on the thirty-third night of its run at Covent Garden (having opened there on 15 November 1800) because of an allusion to the resignation of Pitt, who left office on 3 February 1801 because the king was unwilling to make concessions to the Irish Catholics after the Act of Union (see *Reminiscences*, 2: 25-26).

[28] See Moore's preface to the 1811 edition of his play, as well as the Larpent MS.

[29] *The Duke's Coat; or, the Night after Waterloo: A Dramatick Anecdote, prepared for Representation on the 6th September, at the Theatre Royal, Lyceum, and Interdicted by the Licenser of Plays* (London, 1815).

[30] For a detailed discussion of the licensed text of Byron's play see Thomas L. Ashton, "The Censorship of Byron's *Marino Faliero*," *Huntington Library Quarterly*, 36 (1972), 27-44.

[31] Leigh Hunt, *The Descent of Liberty* (London, 1815), p. vi.

[32] Edward Bulwer Lytton, *England and the English*, ed. Standish Meacham (Chicago, 1970), pp. 305-06.

[33] Ernest Bradlee Watson, *Sheridan to Robertson. A Study of the Nineteenth-Century London Stage* (Cambridge, Mass., 1926), p. 5.

[34] Christopher Murray, "Elliston's Coronation Spectacle, 1821," *Theatre Notebook*, 25 (1970-71), 63.

[35] David Mayer III, *Harlequin in His Element: The English Pantomime, 1806-1836* (Cambridge, Mass., 1969), p. 246.

[36] Ibid., p. 50.

³⁷ Ibid., p. 6.

³⁸ Michael R. Booth, *English Melodrama* (London, 1965), pp. 123-24, 136.

³⁹ See Robin Estill, "The Factory Lad: Melodrama as Propaganda," *Theatre Quarterly*, 1 (Oct.-Dec., 1971), 22-26. This issue of *Theatre Quarterly* contains an interesting series of articles on "People's Theatre in Nineteenth Century Britain."

⁴⁰ Leslie H. Meeks, *Sheridan Knowles and the Theatre of His Time* (Bloomington, Ind., 1933), p. 39. An account of Knowles' political activities is given in Richard Brinsley Knowles, *The Life of James Sheridan Knowles* (privately printed, 1872), pp. 76-84

⁴¹ Richard M. Fletcher, *English Romantic Drama 1795-1843. A Critical History* (New York, 1966), p. 145.

⁴² *The Life of James Sheridan Knowles*, p. 68.

⁴³ William Archer, *William Charles Macready* (London, 1890), p. 53.

⁴⁴ See below, pp. 127-28.

⁴⁵ William Hazlitt, *Dramatic Essays*, ed. William Archer and Robert W. Lowe (London, 1895), p. 188. Passages omitted in the representation of *Virginius* are marked, as usual, with inverted commas in the printed text.

⁴⁶ James Winston, *Drury Lane Journal: Selections from James Winston's Diaries*, ed. Alfred L. Nelson and Gilbert B. Cross (London, 1974), p. 76.

⁴⁷ The *Courier*, 11 Nov., 1823; *John Bull*, 17, 24 Nov.; the *Real John Bull*, 16 Nov.; *The Times*, 19 Nov., for example.

Chapter 5. Censorship of Personal Satire

¹ Doth a man stutter, look a-squint, or halt?
Mimics draw humour out of Nature's fault:
With personal defects their mirth adorn,
And hang misfortunes out to public scorn.

Charles Churchill, *The Rosciad*, lines 401-04 (*The Poetical Works of Charles Churchill*, ed. Douglas Grant, Oxford, 1956, p. 14).

² "BOSWELL. 'Did not he [Foote] think of exhibiting [mimicking] you, Sir?' JOHNSON. 'Sir, fear restrained him; he knew I would have broken his bones. I would have saved him the trouble of cutting off a leg; I would not have left him a leg to cut off.'" (James Boswell, *Boswell's Life of Johnson*, ed. G. B. Hill, revised by L. F. Powell, Oxford, 1934-50, 2:95. Foote lost a leg in a riding accident in 1766.) Robert Walpole is said to have "Corrected . . . with his own Hands very severly" an actor who ad-libbed some lines against himself and the excise tax (*The London Stage*, Part 3, 1:clxvii).

³ The most useful studies of Foote and his plays are Mary Belden's *The Dramatic Work of Samuel Foote* (New Haven, 1929) and Simon Trefman's *Sam Foote, Comedian, 1727-1777* (New York, 1971).

⁴ Charles Dibdin, *A Complete History of the English Stage* (London, n.d. [1797-1800]), 5:143.

⁵ If Fielding's *Miss Lucy in Town* (1742) was suppressed, as has generally been supposed, then it antedates *The Author* on both these counts by several years. But it is doubtful if the

stories about the suppression of *Miss Lucy* are accurate. Charles B. Woods has argued convincingly that they are not, in his article, "The 'Miss Lucy' Plays of Fielding and Garrick," *Philological Quarterly*, 41 (1962), 294-310.

⁶ Thomas Davies, *Memoirs of the Life of David Garrick*, 3rd ed. (London, 1781), 1:201.

⁷ Ibid., 1:201-02. Adolphus describes Apreece as "a worthy Welsh baronet from whom he [Foote] had received hospitality and favours" (*Memoirs of John Bannister*, London, 1839, 1:67), and Dibdin says he was "a person of fortune not in any respect deserving of public or private reprehension for any breach of honour, liberality or moral rectitude ..." (*Complete History of the English Stage*, 5:146). Davies adds (1:202) that Apreece was "greatly respected for his good-nature, and readiness to do acts of kindness."

⁸ Davies, *Memoirs*, 1:202-03.

⁹ *Town and Country Magazine*, 9 (Oct., 1777), 599-600.

¹⁰ William Cooke, *Memoirs of Samuel Foote* (London, 1805), 1:80; Davies, *Memoirs*, 1:203.

¹¹ Davies, *Memoirs*, 1:203.

¹² Printed in the *Monthly Mirror*, 7 (Jan., 1799), 39-41.

¹³ Tate Wilkinson, *Memoirs of His Own Life* (Dublin, 1791), 1:251. Wilkinson suggests that Mrs. Clive's real disappointment lay in losing the part of Mrs. Cadwallader more than in any sympathy she had for Foote (1:252).

¹⁴ Ibid., 1:250.

¹⁵ Wilkinson, *Memoirs*, 1:279. Wilkinson is inaccurate. They had seen it on 1 February 1758.

¹⁶ Ibid., 1:280.

¹⁷ Ibid., 1:281.

¹⁸ *Strolling Players and Drama in the Provinces, 1660-1765* (Cambridge, 1939), passim. However, a planned performance of *The Author* in York in 1765 had to be cancelled when Apreece's son threatened to break up the theater if the play was acted (Wilkinson, *Memoirs*, 3:76-79).

¹⁹ *The Dramatic Work of Samuel Foote*, pp. 81-106. Although the attack on the Methodists caused all the trouble, it was by no means the main theme of *The Minor*. Mr. Squintum (George Whitefield) is not even one of the *dramatis personae* and is referred to by other characters not more than six or seven times. Mrs. Cole, the bawd used by Foote to ridicule Whitefield and his teachings, makes only three appearances, two of them very brief. Those who went to see the play expecting a continual mockery of the Methodists would have been disappointed. Most of the action of the play concerns the efforts of a disguised father, Sir William Wealthy, to discover the true character of his apparently dissolute son, Sir George. But the plot, as in so many of Foote's works, is of no great importance. Characters are introduced mainly to allow Foote to mimic well-known people of the day. For the identification of some of these, see Belden, pp. 82-83.

²⁰ The earliest recorded appearance of *The Minor* is for 9 Nov. 1759 when Foote read some of the play at L. T. H. as part of a Comic Lecture. (*The London Stage*, Part 4, 2:755.) The following day he left for Ireland, taking *The Minor* with him, and played it at the Crow St. theater, Dublin, on 28 Jan. 1760 in its original two-act version. (Cooke, *Memoirs of Samuel Foote*, 1:96.) It was first produced in its familiar three-act version at L.

T. H. on 28 June 1760 and during the summer season appeared thirty-five times. Its first performance at D. L. was 22 Nov. 1760 and at C. G. 24 Nov. 1760. The licensing copies for the Little Theatre and C. G. performances have not survived. LA 177 contains the license application for D. L. only, dated 20 Nov. 1760. ⎰

[21] Foote doubtless derived the name "Squintum" from the fact that Whitefield had a deformity in one eye. Albert M. Lyles, *Methodism Mocked* (London, 1960), ch. 8, has information on other satirical attacks on Whitefield by his contemporaries. Foote's *The Orators, The Mayor of Garratt* and *The Devil upon Two Sticks* contain satirical references to the Methodists.

[22] See *The Life and Times of Selina Countess of Huntingdon*, "By a Member of the Houses of Shirley and Hastings" [i.e. Aaron Crossley Hobart Seymour] (London, 1844), 1:209.

[23] David Garrick, *The Private Correspondence of David Garrick*, ed. James Boaden. (London, 1831-32), 1:120.

[24] Horace Walpole, *Horace Walpole's Correspondence with George Montagu*, ed. W. S. Lewis and Ralph S. Brown Jr. (New Haven and London, 1941), 1:326-27 [*Yale Edition*, vol. 9].

[25] Belden, Part II, ch. 3, passim, discusses the more important ones.

[26] Joseph A. Byrnes has noted in "Four Plays of Samuel Foote," Ph.D. diss. (New York Univ., 1963), p. 185, that "The influence of this anonymous *Letter to David Garrick* may be reflected in the deletions to be noted in the Larpent manuscript. With only two exceptions, every such deletion is of a word or phrase to which specific exception was taken in that pamphlet."

[27] A note kept with the Larpent text shows that Garrick suggested alternative readings for two passages. His suggestion for this one was: "All will come to it sooner or later—as Mr. Squintum says Regeneration is not the work of a Day—no no no—"

[28] Garrick thought it should be abbreviated to, "I was wish'd to Mr. Squintum & I became as you see a New Creature."

[29] Dougald MacMillan, *Catalogue of the Larpent Plays in the Huntington Library* (San Marino, 1939), p. 31.

[30] A review of *The Minor* in the *London Chronicle* for 22-25 Nov. 1760 lists some of the substitutions.

[31] It had over twenty full performances. On three occasions at least the epilogue was performed separately, once, at D. L. on 29 May 1761, by a four-year-old boy (*The London Stage*, Part 4, 2:870). Either the censorship of the epilogue was ignored for these performances or a new version had been written, for the few remaining lines in the censored version hardly justified a separate performance. Byrnes doubts if the epilogue, "or any substantial part of it," was ever omitted from performances of *The Minor*, and he also believes that C. G. may have used a full, uncensored, text for their production ("Four Plays of Samuel Foote," p. 170).

[32] There is no Larpent MS of *The Trip to Calais*. The revised version of the play, *The Capuchin*, was submitted for licensing on 6 August 1776 and is LA 413. The two plays were published together in 1778 as *A Trip to Calais. . . . To which is annexed, The Capuchin. . . . Altered from the Trip to Calais.*

[33] See also Charles Pearce, *The Amazing Duchess* (London, n.d. [1911]), and Elizabeth Mavor, *The Virgin Mistress . . . . The Life of the Duchess of Kingston* (London, 1964).

[34] Miss Chudleigh had secretly married Augustus John Hervey in 1744. The marriage was never legally dissolved, but in 1770 she married Evelyn Pierrepoint, 2nd duke of Kingston.

[35] *Town and Country Magazine*, 7 (May, 1775), 259.

[36] Throughout August 1775 the *Morning Post*, the *Public Ledger* and other newspapers continued to criticize and abuse Foote. Only Woodfall's *Morning Chronicle* offered him much support.

[37] *An Authentic Detail of Particulars relative to the late Duchess of Kingston* (London, 1788), p. 41.

[38] Ibid., p. 43.

[39] Ibid., p. 55.

[40] The *Morning Chronicle*, 3 August 1775. The letter was reprinted in most of the other London papers. According to a report in the *Morning Post* on 4 August 1775, Foote also wrote to the king about the suppression of his play, "praying for the royal interposition in favour of his piece, assuring his Majesty, that the satire contained therein was general and not calculated to disturb the peace or reputation of any individual whatever: The King returned no answer."

[41] Horace Walpole, *The Last Journals of Horace Walpole during the Reign of George III from 1771-1783*, ed. A. Francis Steuart (London, 1910), 1:472.

[42] Had *The Trip to Calais* been licensed and performed at the time of the duchess' trial there is a good chance that the courts would have intervened to suppress it anyway. That, at any rate, is what happened in similar circumstances some years later with a play called *The Gamblers*. On 24 Oct. 1823 one William Weare brutally murdered John Thurtell after a dispute about gambling debts. The case attracted a great deal of publicity and before Weare's trial began the Surrey put on *The Gamblers* which re-created the murder. After only two performances the play was halted by order of the Court of King's Bench, although shortly after Weare's conviction and execution (9 Jan. 1824) the play reopened (12 Jan.). And at the Coburg a play called *The Gamblers; or, The Murderers at the Desolate Cottage* seems to have been censored by the local magistrates because of its obvious allusions to the murder. (See *The Gamblers*, n.d. [1824]; *The Drama; or, Theatrical Pocket Magazine*, 5 (July 1823-March 1824), 192; *The Times* Oct. 1823-Jan. 1824; and H. Chance Newton, *Crime and Drama* (London, 1927), pp. 96-97. Newton gives an entertaining account of the Surrey *Gamblers*, but erroneously says that it was suppressed by the Lord Chamberlain.)

[43] There is a detailed account of the trial in the *Town and Country Magazine*, 8 (Dec. 1776), 693-96.

[44] P.R.O. L.C. 7/4, unbound, unfoliated documents.

[45] Newspaper cutting, Enthoven Collection, Victoria and Albert Museum, dated (in manuscript) 1 (?) June 1817, placed in C. G. file, 2 June 1817.

[46] See Steven Watson, *The Reign of George III 1760-1815* (Oxford 1960), pp. 304-05.

[47] It is bound, together with Wrighten's note to Larpent, with the Larpent MS of *The Learned Lady* (LA 842). The play was not published.

[48] The first half of the title as well as some allusions to the king's illness were deleted from the licensing manuscript of *Madness Rules the Hour; or, A Budget of Blunders* (LA 1612).

[49] *Annual Register*, 64 (1822), 236-37.

[50] A concise summary may be found in Spencer Walpole, *A History of England from the Conclusion of the Great War in 1815* (London, 1912), 2: 147-50.

[51] See also Christopher Murray's interesting article, "Elliston's Coronation Spectacle, 1821," *Theatre Notebook*, 25 (1970-71), 57-64: "No matter what the play, allusions to Caroline's case were found by the audience" (58).

[52] For details see Loren Reid, *Charles James Fox* (London and Harlow, 1969), pp. 193-213.

[53] See Iris Leveson Gower, *The Face Without a Frown: Georgiana Duchess of Devonshire* (London, 1944), chaps. 7-8 and *Georgiana*, ed. the Earl of Bessborough (London, 1955), ch. 7 [letters to and from the duchess about the election].

[54] *Critical Review*, 57 (April, 1784), 320—a review of *A Letter to her Grace the Duchess of Devonshire*, in which the duchess is reprimanded for "the impropriety of her conduct."

[55] See *The Life and Political Opinions of the late Sam House*, 2nd ed. (London, n.d.)

[56] There are two Larpent MSS of *The Election of the Managers* (LA 659 and 663). LA 659 contains Colman's application for the license, dated 18 May 1784. Several passages in the text are underlined or deleted, almost certainly by Larpent. LA 663 is an almost identical text. The deleted passages of LA 659 are included, but have again been deleted. This MS also has a prologue not in LA 659 and some additional songs at the end (to make up for the material lost because of the censorship?). *The Election of the Managers* was acted at the Little Theatre on 2 June 1784. Quotations given here are from LA 659.

[57] Calista is from Rowe's *The Fair Penitent;* Philly Nettletop is the *nom de guerre* of Lady Bab Lardoon in John Burgoyne's *The Maid of the Oaks;* Lady Temple, unidentified (in LA 663 Lady Teazle from *The School for Scandal* is substituted); Melpomene is Mrs. Siddons; Thalia is Mrs. Abington.

[58] Horace Walpole, *Horace Walpole's Correspondence with Mary and Agnes Berry and Barbara Cecilia Seton*, ed. W. S. Lewis and A. Dayle Wallace (New Haven and London, 1944), 2: 199 [*Yale Edition*, vol. 11]. See also Frances Gerard, *Some Celebrated Irish Beauties of the Last Century* (London, 1895), pp. 100-17.

[59] [Walley C. Oulton], *The History of the Theatres of London* (London, 1796), 2: 93.

[60] The one-act version of *The Irishman in Spain* was published in 1791 with a preface in which Stuart said he would publish the full text of *She Would Be a Duchess* "with an Address to the Marquis of *Salisbury*, and Dedicated to *the Gunnings*." It was also reported in *The Times* on 18 August 1791 that the original farce would be published, "with the additions and alterations of those great *literary* geniusses—General GUNNING and the Duke of ARGYLE," which suggests that Gunning's brother-in-law may have had a hand in the censorship (but neither he nor Gunning made any "additions" to the play). But Stuart did not in fact publish *She Would Be a Duchess*, and the farce which was intended to cause further discomfort and embarrassment to the Gunning family has remained in well-deserved obscurity since 1791 in the Larpent manuscripts.

[61] *Report from the Select Committee on Dramatic Literature: with the Minutes of Evidence*, House of Commons, 2 August 1832, p. 145, paras. 2585-87.

[62] *The Parliamentary History of England, from the Earliest Period to the Year 1803* (London, 1806-20), 32: 441.

[63] Ibid.

[64] In "The Completion of *The School for Scandal*" in *TLS*, 28 Dec. 1967, p. 1265, C. J.

L. Price discusses the affair in detail and also shows that Moses was not based on Hopkins, but probably on one Jacob Nathan Moses.

[65] See Richard Cross's diary, quoted in *The London Stage*, Part 4, 1:359. Smart's prologue is printed in the *London Magazine*, 22 (April, 1753), 191

[66] Walter Long (suitor to Elizabeth Linley before her elopement and marriage to R. B. Sheridan), for example, was ridiculed by Samuel Foote in *The Maid of Bath* (L.T.H., 26 June 1771), and Long's appeals to the Lord Chamberlain to suppress the play were ignored. See C. J. L. Price, "Hymen and Hirco: A Vision," *TLS*, 11 July 1958, p. 396.

[67] See Basil Williams, *The Whig Supremacy 1714-1760*, 2nd ed., rev. by C. H. Stuart (Oxford, 1962), pp. 58-67.

Chapter 6. Profaneness and Immorality a Century after Collier

[1] James J. Lynch, *Box, Pit, and Gallery: Stage and Society in Johnson's London* (Berkeley and Los Angeles, 1953), p. 271.

[2] For Garrick's managerial revisions of some of the old plays, see Harry William Pedicord, *The Theatrical Public in the Time of Garrick* (New York, 1954), chap. 4. Emmett L. Avery discusses similar revisions of Congreve's plays in chap. 7 of *Congreve's Plays on the Eighteenth-Century Stage* (New York, 1951). For the treatment of Jonson's plays see R. G. Noyes, *Ben Jonson on the English Stage, 1660-1776* (Cambridge, Mass., 1935), especially pp. 92-97, 143-48, 208-13, 258-65. Mary E. Knapp shows how the epilogues to plays reflected the new morality in the later years of the century in chap. 9 of *Prologues and Epilogues of the Eighteenth Century* (New Haven, 1961), and there is a good chapter on morality in Leo Hughes' *The Drama's Patrons. A Study of the Eighteenth-Century London Audience* (Austin and London, 1971), pp. 120-53.

[3] *The Complete Works of William Hazlitt*, ed. P. P. Howe (London and Toronto, 1930-34), 6: 162.

[4] *The Theatrical Public in the Time of Garrick*, passim.

[5] 31 (Oct., 1762), 595.

[6] *Memoirs of Richard Cumberland* (London, 1806), pp. 202-03.

[7] Ibid., p. 225.

[8] [Walley C. Oulton], *The History of the Theatres of London* (London, 1796), 1: 156. Oulton prints both epilogues, 1: 157-60.

[9] *The Reminiscences of Thomas Dibdin* (London, 1827), 2: 65.

[10] Stuart Curran, *Shelley's Cenci* (Princeton, 1970), p. 7. Harris at Covent Garden apparently "considered the theme of incest in *The Cenci* to be so objectionable that he would not even submit the part of Beatrice to Miss O'Neil for reading" (Arthur C. Hicks and R. Milton Clarke, *A Stage Version of Shelley's 'Cenci,'* Caldwell, Idaho, 1945, p. 15). Thomas Love Peacock doubted if *The Cenci* would have been licensed even if Harris had accepted it. He was surely right. (See Percy Bysshe Shelley, *The Letters of Percy Bysshe Shelley*, ed. Roger Ingpen, London and New York, 1909, 2: 718n.)

[11] Noel Perrin, *Dr. Bowdler's Legacy. A History of Expurgated Books in England and America* (London, 1970), p. 5.

[12] Helen Sard Hughes, *The Gentle Hertford, Her Life and Letters* (New York, 1940), p. 238.

[13] Ibid., p. 242.

[14] *The London Stage*, Part 3, 2: 1035.

[15] *The Gentle Hertford*, p. 451 n. 43.

[16] H. K. Banerji, *Henry Fielding* (Oxford, 1929, reprint 1962), p. 75.

[17] E.g. Millamour to Mrs. Useful in I. ii: "Thou art the First Minister of *Venus*, the first Plenipotentiary in Affairs of Love, and thy House is the noble Scene of the Congress of the two Sexes. Thou has united more Couples than the Alimony-Act has parted, and sent more to bed together, without a Licence, than any Parson of the *Fleet*." Or Heartfort to Millamour, I. vi: "What, is your Levee dispatch'd? I met antiquated Whores going out of your Door as thick as antiquated Courtiers from the Levee of a Statesman, and with as disconsolate Faces." According to Banerji, *Henry Fielding*, p. 75, "the licenser had been censured for being too remiss in the discharge of his duties," as far as *The Wedding Day* was concerned.

[18] The Earl of Rochester's *Poems on Several Occasions*, first published in 1680, was the subject of more than one prosecution in the seventeenth century on grounds of obscenity. (See Donald Thomas, *A Long Time Burning*, London, 1969, pp. 20, 23, 24*n*., 76.) John Cleland's *Memoirs of a Woman of Pleasure* has been pursued by the law continually since its publication in 1748-49. (See *A Long Time Burning*, passim.)

[19] The consequences of the behavior of someone like Lord Brilliant are interestingly illustrated in a brief, and censored, passage in James Cobb's and Thomas King's pantomime, *Hurly Burly; or, The Fairy of the Well* (D. L., 2 Jan. 1786). The Larpent MS (LA 715) includes a note from King to Larpent, in which he expresses the hope that "the alteration made in the enclosed Copy will do away [with] whatever may have been thought exceptionable." Two passages are marked for deletion. The second is an advertisement in a daily paper: "*Country Girl big with Child*. Wants a Place. A young Woman who has lived Servant of all Work—She wou'd not dislike living with a single Gentleman, and has no objection to Children. She can have an undeniable Character from her last Place."

[20] T. B. Shepherd, *Methodism and the Literature of the Eighteenth Century* (London, 1940), p. 198*n*.

[21] Above, p. 119.

[22] The 1761 (and other printed editions) of *The Register Office* contains a note at the end of the text: "As there is a *palpable Similarity* between the Characters of Mrs. COLE in the *Minor*, and Mrs. SNAREWELL in the foregoing Performance; it may not be unnecessary to declare, that the *Register-Office* was put into Mr. *Foote's* Hands in *August* 1758, on his Promise of playing it at one of the Patent-Theatres in the ensuing Season." Mrs. Cole and Mrs. Snarewell are both bawds who have been converted to Methodism, although in neither case does the new religion interfere with the old trade. It is quite possible that Foote, as Reed implies, stole his ideas for Mrs. Cole from Reed's Mrs. Snarewell. *The Minor* was first produced in Dublin on 28 Jan. 1760 and in London (at the Little Theatre) on 28 June 1760. It is worth pointing out, however, that Mrs. Cole and Mrs. Snarewell had a predecessor in Fielding's Mrs. Haycock, a procuress in *Miss Lucy in Town* (1742) who, after hearing an "excellent sermon on Kennington Common," repents heartily of her sins, but cannot give up her profession because she was "bred up in the way." B.D., 3: 198 cites a 1744 source for Mrs. Cole and Mrs. Snarewell.

206

[23] Don Quixote's mistress.

[24] *The London Stage*, Part 4, 1: clxxi.

[25] Oulton (*History of the Theatres of London*, 1: 12-13) shows that even after the censorship some members of the C. G. audience objected to "the *low* humour occasionally introduced."

[26] The subject of eighteenth-century pornography and contemporary attitudes towards it is well discussed by Donald Thomas in *A Long Time Burning*, particularly chapts. 5 and 7. Thomas also reprints examples of eighteenth-century pornography, including *An Essay on Woman* and selections from *Harris's List . . .* (pp. 375-78 and 381-84). Both of these works were, in fact, subjects of government prosecutions, but others like them continued to circulate freely. A further useful selection of the century's pornography can be found in the anthology, *Venus Unmasked*, compiled by Leonard de Vries and Peter Fryer (London, 1967).

[27] Thus there were many complaints about the licensing of Moncrieff's *Tom and Jerry; or, Life in London* (LA 2262; Adelphi, 26 Nov. 1821), a burletta depicting London's fashionable vices (drinking, gambling, whoring, etc.) A correspondent in *John Bull* for 16 Dec. 1821 argued that "it is the duty of HIS MAJESTY'S Lord Chamberlain to interpose his authority to check an exhibition of scenes which are unknown and unthought of by decent or well regulated people," and the Lord Chamberlain received letters (now kept with the licensing manuscript) expressing surprise that he had licensed such an "obnoxious" and "poisonous and disgusting" play.

[28] Murray Roston, *Biblical Drama in England from the Middle Ages to the Present Day* (London, 1968), p. 180.

[29] Ibid., p. 189.

[30] William Blackstone, *Commentaries on the Laws of England*, 10th ed. (London, 1787), 4: 59: "all profane scoffing at the holy scripture, or exposing it to contempt and ridicule . . . . are offences punishable at common law by fine and imprisonment, or other infamous corporal punishment."

[31] Ibid., 4: 60.

[32] P.R.O. L.C. 7/9, f. 124v.

[33] *Monthly Review*, 28 (Feb., 1763), 167.

[34] Jeremy F. Bagster-Collins, *George Colman the Younger*, *1762-1836* (Morningside Heights, New York, 1964), p. 290.

[35] *Four Discourses on Subjects Relating to the Amusement of the Stage* (Cambridge, 1809), p. 83.

[36] Rowland Hill, *A Warning to Professors; Containing Aphoristic Observations on the Nature and Tendency of Public Amusements* (London, 1833), pp. 20-21n. (First published in 1805.)

[37] British Library, Add. MS 27,833, ff. 73-74.

[38] George Colman the Younger, *John Bull; or, The Englishman's Fireside*, LA 1371 (C.G., 5 March 1803).

[39] Huntington Library MS 16677. I am indebted to Mr. Hal Dendurent for bringing Arnold's letter to my attention.

[40] See above, p. 45.

[41] *Theatrical Inquisitor*, 1 (1812), 75.

[42] David Mayer III, *Harlequin in His Element. The English Pantomine, 1806-1836* (Cambridge, Mass., 1969), p. 244.

Chapter 7. Stage Censorship and Society, 1737-1824

[1] Miguel de Cervantes, *The History of the Ingenious Gentleman Don Quixote of La Mancha*, trans. P. A. Motteux (Edinburgh, 1910), 2: 382-83.

[2] *Report from the Select Committee on Dramatic Literature: with the Minutes of Evidence*, House of Commons, 2 August 1832, p. 82. para. 1312.

[3] Ibid., p. 86, para. 1405.

[4] Ibid., p. 160, para. 2871.

[5] Ibid., p. 30, para. 361.

[6] Ibid., p. 33, paras. 395-98.

[7] Ibid., p. 207, paras. 3726-27.

[8] Ibid., p. 208, para. 3736. Place also argued this position in a conversation with the then Examiner of Plays, George Colman, in July 1833. The conversation is reported in Place's "Notes for a History of the Play Houses and other Places of Public Amusements," British Library Add. MS 27,833, ff. 117-18.

[9] Francis Ludlow Holt, *The Law of Libel* (London, 1816), pp. 56-57.

[10] Few details of the parliamentary debates on the Licensing Bill have been recorded. It is said to have been vigorously opposed in both Houses. In the Commons William Pulteney "did roast" Walpole "most violently" and "spared not Sr Robt nor Sr Wm Yonge urging that this restraint upon the Writers for the Stage, was a certain preamble to the taking away the Liberty of the Press in general . . . " (*Reports on the Manuscripts of the Earl of Eglinton, Sir J. Stirling Maxwell, Bart., C. S. H. Drummond Moray, Esq., C. F. Weston Underwood, Esq., and G. Wingfield Digby, Esq.*, London, 1885, p. 267, *Historical Manuscripts Commission*, no. 10).

[11] *The Parliamentary History of England, from the Earliest Period to the Year 1803* (London, 1806-20), 1: 335.

[12] *Areopagitica: A Speech of Mr. John Milton, for the Liberty of Unlicens'd Printing, to the Parliament of England* (London, 1738), p. vi.

[13] Samuel Johnson, *The Works of Samuel Johnson* (Oxford, 1825), 5: 335.

[14] Ibid., 5: 342.

[15] Ibid., 5: 337.

[16] Henry Fielding, *Miscellaneous Writings*, ed. William Ernest Henley (New York, 1903, reprint 1967), 2: 92. See G. Levine, "Henry Fielding's 'Defense' of the Stage Licensing Act," *English Language Notes*, 2 (1965), 193-96.

[17] Alexander Pope, *The Dunciad* [1742 text], ed. James Sutherland (London, 1943), p. 345, lines 41-44 (Twickenham ed., vol. 5). Other allusions in Pope to the Licensing Act or the licensing of plays are in the *Epilogue to the Satires. Written in 1738. Dialogue I*, lines 41-42, and the *Epilogue to the Satires. Written in 1738. Dialogue II*, lines 1-2 (Alexander

Pope, *Imitations of Horace, with An Epistle to Dr. Arbuthnot and The Epilogue to the Satires,* ed. John Butt, 2nd ed., London and New Haven, 1961, pp. 301-13, Twickenham ed., vol. 4).

[18] See Jonathan Swift, *A Project for the Advancement of Religion, and the Reformation of Manners* (1709) in *Bickerstaff Papers and Pamphlets on the Church,* ed. Herbert Davis (Oxford, 1939), p. 56.

[19] The duke of Grafton, the Lord Chamberlain, foolishly gave permission for a company of French actors to take over the Little Theatre in the Haymarket for the 1738-39 season. The Licensing Act had closed the theater to English actors and when the Frenchmen appeared on 9 Oct. 1738 the packed audience rioted until the actors left the theater. Benjamin Victor, who was present, gives a full account of the riot in *The History of the Theatres of London and Dublin, from the Year 1730 to the Present Time* (Dublin, 1761), 1:47-53.

[20] Hildebrand Jacob, *The Nest of Plays,* C. G., 25 Jan. 1738 [three one-act comedies: *The Prodigal Reform'd, The Happy Constancy,* and *The Tryal of Conjugal Love*]. On the title page of the printed text (1738), it is described, correctly, as "the first PLAY licenced by the LORD CHAMBERLAIN, since the late ACT concerning the STAGE."

[21] James Miller, *The Coffee-House,* D. L., 26 Jan. 1738.

[22] Quoted, like the London *Evening Post* comment, in *The London Stage,* Part 3, 2:699.

[23] See the preface to *The Coffee-House.*

[24] *The London Stage,* Part 3, 2:703.

[25] Other new plays of this period, including George Lillo's *Marina* (C. G., 1 Aug. 1738) and Henry Carey's *Margery* (C. G., 9 Dec. 1738) met with no opposition of this kind.

[26] Colley Cibber, *An Apology for the Life of Mr. Colley Cibber,* ed. R. W. Lowe (London, 1889), 1:278n.

[27] The *Morning Chronicle,* 28 Aug. 1775.

[28] See, for example, issues of 6, 8, 9, 10, 11, 13, 15, 24 June, and 6, 7, 9, 16 July. An earlier essay against political drama, from the *Daily Gazetteer* of 7 May 1737, is reprinted in *Essays on the Theatre from Eighteenth-Century Periodicals,* ed. John Loftis (Los Angeles, 1960), pp. 54-57 [The Augustan Reprint Society, nos. 85-86].

[29] See, for example, the *Craftsman* of 28 May, 4, 18, 25 June, and 2 July.

[30] Torbuck's account of these events is in a preface, "The Bookseller to the Reader," in the published text of *Sancho at Court* (1742).

[31] See above, p. 55.

[32] George Bernard Shaw, *Shaw on Theatre,* ed. E. J. West (New York, 1958), p. 73.

[33] J. T. Kirkman, *Memoirs of the Life of Charles Macklin* (London, 1799), 2:278.

[34] Frederick Reynolds, *The Life and Times of Frederick Reynolds* (London, 1826), 2:181, 237. See also Reynolds' preface to *Begone Dull Care* (1808) where he argues that playwrights before the Licensing Act "were not checked in their satirical and original flights, by Act of Parliament—and if they had thought of dramatizing a *baby general,* or a *foppish clergyman,* they had no LICENSER to prevent them. *They* likewise were allowed the free use of that easy and inexhaustible source of creating mirth, called '*double entendre.*'"

[35] The *London Review of English and Foreign Literature,* 9 (March, 1779), 173.

[36] The *Monthly Mirror,* 1 (Dec., 1795), 41.

[37] Ibid., 1:184-85.

[38] Larpent MS diary, 13 Feb. 1796.

[39] The *Monthly Mirror*, 2 (Sept., 1796), 302-03.

[40] Ibid., 2:432.

[41] There is a convenient list of eighteenth-century pamphlets in Frederick T. Wood, "The Attack on the Stage in the XVIII Century," *Notes and Queries*, 173 (1937), 218-22.

[42] Marvin Carlson, *The Theatre of the French Revolution* (Ithaca, New York, 1966), p. 3.

[43] Preface to *Killing No Murder* (1809), p. v.

[44] The *European Magazine*, 20 (Aug., 1791), 142.

[45] William Blackstone, *Commentaries on the Laws of England*, 10th ed. (London, 1787), 4:151-52.

[46] See above, p. 189 n.94.

[47] Quoted in Emmett L. Avery, *Congreve's Plays on the Eighteenth-Century Stage* (New York, 1951), p. 116.

[48] The *Gentleman's Magazine*, 48 (Feb., 1778), 57.

[49] 2nd ed. (Leeds, 1786), p. 5.

[50] *The New British Theatre: A Selection of Original Dramas, not yet acted; Some of which have been offered for Representation, but not accepted: with Critical Remarks by the Editor* [John Galt] (London, 1814-15), 2:xiii.

[51] James Plumptre, *Four Discourses on Subjects relating to the Amusement of the Stage* (Cambridge, 1809), p. 259.

[52] James Plumptre, *A Letter to the Most Noble the Marquis of Hertford ... on the Subject of a Dramatic Institution* (Cambridge, 1820), p. 6. There is an urgent appeal for strict censorship in the anonymous *Observations on the Effect of Theatrical Representations, with Respect to Religion and Morals* (Bath, 1804), pp. 28-29.

[53] Horace Walpole, *Horace Walpole's Correspondence with George Montagu*, ed. W. S. Lewis and Ralph S. Brown, Jr. (New Haven and London, 1941), 1:48 [*The Yale Edition of Horace Walpole's Correspondence*, ed. W. S. Lewis, New Haven and London, 1937-, vol. 9].

[54] "Of the Stage," *An Enquiry into the Present State of Polite Learning in Europe* in *Collected Works of Oliver Goldsmith*, ed. Arthur Friedman (Oxford, 1966), 1:323.

[55] *St. James's Chronicle*, 3-5 Dec. 1795.

[56] See above, p. 101.

[57] *Report from the Select Committee*, p. 218, paras. 3932, 3934.

[58] Ibid., p. 145, para. 2588.

[59] *The Obscenity Laws, A Report by the Working Party set up by a Conference convened by the Chairman of the Arts Council of Great Britain* (London, 1969), p. 35.

[60] Jean Jacques Rousseau, *Oeuvres Complètes de J. J. Rousseau*, ed. P. R. Auguis (Paris, 1824-25), 2:26, 33.

[61] Colley Cibber, *An Apology for the Life of Mr. Colley Cibber*, 2nd ed. (London, 1740), p. 296.

[62] Thomas Holcroft, *Seduction* (London, 1787), preface.

[63] In the prelude to *The German Hotel* (1790).

[64] John Hawkesworth, *Amphitryon; or, The Two Sosias*, altered from Dryden, preface (Bell's edition, 1797, vol. 21).

[65] See, for example, the *True Briton*, 31 Jan. 1793.

[66] *A Complete History of the English Stage*, 5: 377-78.

[67] Margaret S. Carhart, *The Life and Work of Joanna Baillie* (New Haven, 1923), p. 100.

[68] *Observations on the Importance and Use of Theatres: their present Regulation, and possible Improvements* (London, 1759), pp. 8-9.

[69] See Donald Thomas, *A Long Time Burning, The History of Literary Censorship in England* (London, 1969), chaps. 3 and 5-8.

[70] *Report from the Select Committee*, p. 36, para. 442.

[71] James Sutherland, *English Satire* (Cambridge, 1958), p. 133.

[72] *Apology*, p. 239.

[73] Ibid.

[74] Harry William Pedicord, *The Theatrical Public in the Time of Garrick* (New York, 1954), pp. 51-63.

[75] See Tobias Smollett, *The Expedition of Humphry Clinker*, ed. Lewis M. Knapp (London, 1966), pp. 37, 115.

[76] Quoted in Mary Knapp, *Prologues and Epilogues of the Eighteenth Century* (New Haven, 1961), p. 154. Miss Knapp describes the eighteenth-century theater as "a savage place" (p. 153).

[77] James Boaden, *Memoirs of the Life of John Philip Kemble* (London, 1825), 2: 259-60.

[78] Carlson, *Theatre of the French Revolution*, passim.

Index

213

Index

Index